EMPLOYMENT 'MIRACL

CHANGING WELFARE STATES

Processes of socio-economic change (individualising society and globalising economics and politics) cause large problems for modern welfare states. Welfare states, organised on the level of nation-states and built on one or the other form of national solidarity, are increasingly confronted with, for instance, fiscal problems, difficulties to control costs, and the unintended use of welfare programs. Such problems – generally
speaking – raise the issue of sustainability because they tend to undermine the legitimacy of the programs of the welfare state and in the end induce the necessity of
change, be it the complete abolishment of programs, retrenchment of programs, or attempts to preserve programs by modernising them.

This series of studies on welfare states focuses on the changing institutions and programs of modern welfare states. These changes are the product of external pressures
on welfare states, for example because of the economic and political consequences of
globalisation or individualisation, or result from the internal, political or institutional
dynamics of welfare arrangements.

By studying the development of welfare state arrangements in different countries, in
different institutional contexts, or by comparing developments between countries or
different types of welfare states, this series hopes to enlarge the body of knowledge on
the functioning and development of welfare states and its programs.

EDITORS OF THE SERIES

Gösta Esping-Andersen, University of Pompeu Fabra, Barcelona, Spain
Anton Hemerijck, the Netherlands Scientific Council for Government Policy (Weten-
    schappelijke Raad voor het Regeringsbeleid (WRR))
Kees van Kersbergen, Free University Amsterdam, the Netherlands
Jelle Visser, University of Amsterdam, the Netherlands
Romke van der Veen, Erasmus University, Rotterdam, the Netherlands

PREVIOUSLY PUBLISHED

Jelle Visser and Anton Hemerijck, *A Dutch Miracle. Job Growth, Welfare Reform and
    Corporatism in the Netherlands*, 1997 (ISBN 90 5356 271 0)
Christoffer Green-Pedersen, *The Politics of Justification. Party Competition and Wel-
    fare-State Retrenchment in Denmark and the Netherlands from 1982 to 1998*, 2002
    (ISBN 90 5356 590 6)
Jan Høgelund, *In Search of Effective Disability Policy. Comparing the Developments
    and Outcomes of the Dutch and Danish Disability Policies*, 2003 (ISBN 90 5356
    644 9)
Maurizio Ferrara and Elisabetta Gualmini, *Rescued by Europe? Social and Labour
    Market Reforms from Maastricht to Berlusconi*, 2004 (ISBN 90 5356 651 1
Martin Schludi, *The Reform of Bismarckian Pension Systems. A Comparison of Pen-
    sion Politics in Austria, France, Germany, Italy and Sweden*, 2005 (ISBN 90 5356
    740 2)

Employment 'Miracles'

A Critical Comparison of the Dutch, Scandinavian, Swiss, Australian and Irish Cases versus Germany and the US

Uwe Becker | Herman Schwartz (eds.)

AMSTERDAM UNIVERSITY PRESS

The publication of this book is made possible with a grant of the GAK-Foundation (Stichting Instituut GAK, Hilversum).

Cover illustration: Vincent van Gogh, Afternoon Siesta

Cover design: Jaak Crasborn BNO, Valkenburg a/d Geul
Lay-out: Adriaan de Jonge, Amsterdam

ISBN 90 5356 755 0
NUR 754

Contents

Preface

The very positive economic and particularly employment development that took place in the decade up to 2001 (or even longer) in Denmark, Ireland, the Netherlands, Australia and, since the second half of the 1990s, Finland and Sweden has been at the centre of much recent discussion in comparative political economy. Because this development contrasts markedly with near stagnation in France, Germany and Italy, it has been characterised in terms of 'miracles' and 'models'. The Netherlands and Denmark attracted the most attention because their strong employment growth and employment stabilisation at very high levels, respectively, occurred in the framework of welfare systems that are still comparatively generous and that clearly differ from the USA and the UK. In the latter two countries, high employment and low unemployment went together with levels of inequality and poverty not (yet?) acceptable in the northwest of the European continent. It is no surprise, therefore, that politicians, journalists and scientists in other countries where employment has stagnated or even declined started discussing whether they could learn something from Denmark and the Netherlands.

To a large degree, the tenor of this discussion exalted the miracle economies, focussing on successful wage restraint agreements between capital and labour that was hidden under labels like new social pacts and competitive corporatism. Critical accounts were relatively rare. This situation is the context for our book, which critically scrutinises the dominant view by asking whether these small countries can figure as models for other countries. Thus, we ask how important conscious policies and agreements really have been in the miracles, and the degree to which positive developments in the small economies have been facilitated by favourable conditions and accidental, 'lucky' circumstances. We find that conscious policies played a much smaller role than most analyses suggest. All our countries benefited from the very smallness of their economies. They also benefited from lucky changes in their external environment, like sharply rising selective American investment (Ireland), the accelerating demand for commodities by Asian countries (Australia) and particularly the way that global disinflation triggered a wealth effect and rising private consumption through the house price increase in Australia, Denmark, Ireland and the Netherlands (much as happened in the late 1990s and the early 2000s in the USA, the UK and Sweden). Finally, we also consider the degree to which these miracles are durable. What happened when the bubble burst in the early 2000s? Would the model status of the small economies survive the bursting of the bubble?

The initial step on the way to this book was the organisation of two meetings. One was a workshop that discussed the most publicized model economies of Denmark, the Netherlands and the USA at the Annual Conference of the American Political Science Association in 2001. The second conference, at the University of Amsterdam in early 2002, considered a broader set of countries including Switzerland, because of its remarkable and very special trajectory, and as the contrast case, Germany. This so-called 'expert meeting' was sponsored by the Dutch foundation of scientific research (NWO; grants 490-01-318 and 460-01-110P), and the papers presented there formed the first draft of this book. For critical comments on these drafts as well as for constructive suggestions, we thank Tjitske Akkerman, Karen Anderson, Brian Burgoon, Robert H. Cox, Lei Delsen, Michael Krätke, Ilona Ostner, Henk Overbeek, Erik Seils, Geoffrey Underhill and Mara Yerkes. After this meeting, the authors and the editors worked around their other obligations for quite a while to discuss and re-discuss these and subsequent drafts to bring them into their current form. Finally, we have to mention that we are heavily indebted to the editorial assistance of Natascha van der Zwan.

Uwe Becker and Herman Schwartz

Amsterdam and Charlottesville, March 2005

1   Introduction: Miracles, Mirages and Markets

Herman Schwartz and Uwe Becker

Introduction

Europe entered the 1990s with high unemployment but high expectations. Unemployment, which had nearly doubled to 10 percent in the European Union (EU) in 1978-88, was abating, falling back to 8.1 percent by 1991. Maastricht, the Single European Act and currency union promised to create a true continental market and help reduce unemployment further. And while most economies were sliding into recession at the beginning of the 1990s, the usual business cycle could not but help revive employment and growth over the coming decade.

Indeed, during the 1990s European economies revived unevenly, the euro was launched despite the EMS crises of the early 1990s, and the EU Commission and Court of Justice hastened economic integration. Yet in most countries something went terribly wrong with employment during this decade. In its early years, recession rolled around the continent, driving total unemployment up to post-war highs. Germany, France and Italy, alongside Spain, Finland and Sweden, were hit particularly hard with unemployment levels not seen since the 1930s, and these three large countries, containing more than half of the EU's population, also experienced shallow recoveries. Overall, unemployment did not begin falling until the late 1990s, with total EU unemployment back at its 1990 level of just over 8 percent by 2002. But by 2003 European unemployment started to rise again with the large continental countries again in the worst position.

In contrast, some of the smaller European countries performed remarkably well in the 1990s and early 2000s (cf. Tables 1.1 and 1.2). These so-called miracle economies made substantial progress towards restoring the "magic squares" of the 1950s/1960s. The Keynesian magic square combined full employment, low inflation, external balance and fast growth. In Europe, Ireland, Denmark, the Netherlands as well as Austria (not covered here) all enjoyed rising employment, current account and fiscal balance, and low inflation during the 1980s/1990s upswing. In the second half of the

Table 1.1 Basic employment data for the small 'model countries' in comparative perspective

	Employment Rates																				Standardized Unemployment Rates				
	Overall (15-64 yrs)					Part-time share*			Full-time equivalents		Age 15-24			Age 55-64			Women (15-64yrs)								
	1983	1990	2001	2002	2003	1990	2002	2003	1990	1999	1990	2002	2003	1990	2002	2003	1983	1990	2002	2003	1983	1990	2001	2002	2003
Australia	62.5	67.9	68.7	69.2	69.3	22.6	27.5	27.9	57	56	61.1	59.6	59.9	41.8	48.2	50.1	51.9	57.0	62.1	62.2	9.9	6.7	6.8	6.4	6.1
Austria	62.9	65.5	67.8	68.2	68.2		13.5	13.6	62	64	54.9	51.7	50.7		28.1	28.9		49.7	61.1	61.2			3.6	4.3	4.4
Belgium	54.6	54.4	59.7	59.7	59.3	13.5	17.2	17.7	51	53	30.4	28.5	27.1	21.4	25.8	28.1	44.5	40.8	51.1	51.4	12.1	6.6	6.7	7.3	8.1
Canada		70.3	70.9	71.5	72.1	17.1	18.7	18.8	63	63	67.1	57.3	57.8	46.3	50.4	53.0		62.7	66.8	67.7		8.1	7.2	7.7	7.6
Denmark	71.7	75.4	75.9	76.4	75.1	19.2	16.2	15.8	71	70	65.0	64.0	59.4	53.6	57.3	60.7	72.8	70.6	72.6	70.5		7.2	4.4	4.6	5.6
Finland	73.2	74.1	67.7	67.7	67.4	7.6	11.0	11.3			52.2	39.4	38.5	42.8	47.8	49.9		71.5	66.1	65.7		3.2	9.1	9.1	9.0
France	60.8	59.9	62	62.2	61.9	12.2	13.7	12.9	56	56	29.5		24.1	35.6		39.3	55.6	50.3	55.8	56.0	8.3	8.7	8.5	8.8	9.4
Germany		62.2	64.1	65.3	64.6	13.4	18.8	19.6	59	59	56.4	44.8	42.4	36.8	38.6	39.0	52.5	51.2	58.8	58.7	7.7	4.8	7.8	8.6	9.3
Ireland	53.9	52.1	65	65		10.0	18.1	18.1	49	56	41.4	45.3	45.8	38.6	48.0	49.3	37.8	36.6	55.2	55.4	14	13.4	3.9	4.4	4.6
Italy	54.5	52.6	54.9	55.6	56.2	8.9	11.9	12.0			29.8	26.7	26.0	21.9	28.9	30.3	40.1	36.2	42.0	42.7	8.8	8.9	9.5	9.0	8.6
Netherlands	52.1	61.8	74.1	74.5	73.6	28.2	33.9	34.5	51	58	54.5	70.5	68.4	29.7	42.0	44.9	40.2	47.5	65.9	65.8	12.0	5.9	2.5	2.7	3.8
Norway	73.9	73	77.9	77.5	75.9	21.8	20.6	21.0			53.4	56.9	55.3	62.9	68.4	68.8		67.2	73.9	72.9		5.7	3.6	3.9	4.5
Sweden	78.5	83.1+	75.3	74.9	74.3	14.5	13.8	14.1	72	66	66.0	46.5	45.0	69.4	68.3	69.0	78.3	81.0	73.4	72.8	3.5	1.7	4.9	4.9	5.6
Switzerland	73.8	78.2	79.1	78.9	77.8	22.1	24.7	25.1			68.3	65.3	63.2	63.1	64.8	65.6		66.4	71.6	70.6			2.6	3.2	4.1
UK	64.3	72.5	72.8	72.7	72.9	20.1	23.0	23.3	62	61	70.1	61.0	59.8	49.2	53.3	55.5	62.5	62.8	66.3	66.4	12.4	6.9	5.0	5.1	5.0
USA	66.2	72.2	73.1	71.9	71.2	13.1	13.1	13.2	65	67	59.8	55.7	53.9	54.0	59.5	59.9	63.5	64.0	66.1	65.7	9.5	5.6	4.7	5.8	6.0

+ Significant statistical break thereafter, lowering rates.

* The part-time shares of most European countries in 1990 included all jobs from 1 to 35 hours a week; thereafter the definition of part-time work became 1 to 30 hours.

Sources: OECD 1995, Statistical Annex; OECD 2003a:175 and Statistical Annex; OECD 2004, Statistical Annex

Table 1.2   Economic basic data: GDP growth, labour productivity, labour costs and export shares; annual changes in percent

	Annual GDP growth		Productivity (GDP/hour)		Real wages		Real unit labour costs		Export shares	
	80-90	90-00	80-90	90-02	91-95	96-00	91-95	96-00	1983	1994
Australia	3.2	3.5	1.3	2.2					1.1	1.1
Austria	2.3	2.3			2.0	0.7	-0.1	-1.0	0.9	1.0
Belgium	2.1	2.1	2.1	1.7	1.8	0.5	0.2	-0.6	2.9	3.3
Canada	2.8	2.8	0.9	1.5					4.4	4.0
Denmark	1.9	2.2	1.7	1.8	0.6	1.3	-1.1	-0.1	0.9	1.0
Finland	3.1	2.2	2.8	2.7	0.1	0.8	-2.1	-1.1	0.7	0.7
France	2.4	1.8	2.9	2.0	0.5	1.1	-0.6	-0.3	5.1	5.7
Germany	2.2	1.6	2.0	2.5	2.0	0.0	-0.1	-0.4	9.6	10.4
Ireland	3.6	7.3	3.8	4.7	1.8	1.8	-1.3	-2.7	0.5	0.7
Italy	2.2	1.6	2.1	1.7	-0.5	0.1	-1.7	-1.1	4.1	4.6
Japan	4.1	1.3	3.5	2.4	0.9	0.4	0.3	-0.4	8.4	9.0
Netherlands	2.2	2.9	1.9	1.2	0.9	0.9	0.0	-0.2	3.9	3.6
Sweden	2.2	1.7	1.2	2.0	0.0	3.2	-0.2	0.9	1.5	1.5
Switzerland	2.1	0.9	1.0	0.4					1.5	1.7
UK	2.7	2.3	1.9	2.2	0.8	2.4	-1.1	0.5	5.5	5.2
USA	3.2	3.2	1.2	1.6	0.7	2.0	-0.4	0.1	12.1	12.4

Sources: OECD 2002a: 32f; OECD 2004a; European Commisson 2003: 113ff; Scharpf and Schmidt 2000: 371 (export shares).

decade they were joined by Finland and Sweden as they astonishingly recovered from their crises. Britain also performed relatively well. Outside Europe, the same was true for the USA and Canada, and Australia entered the miracle league. While none of these has all the elements of the 1950s/1960s magic square, they all scored better on the relevant indicators than they each did in the early to mid-1980s. Some saw unemployment rates fall to levels not seen since the 1960s. And all did better than France, Germany and Italy – though even they had a few years of considerable GDP growth in 1998-2001. The miracles attracted considerable academic and journalistic attention because their success did not visibly rest on the wholesale assaults on unions and welfare state that characterized Thatcher's Britain or Reagan's America. Academic pilgrims to the miracle economies sought policy solutions to Europe's unemployment and growth problems. Many of these analysts credited traditional corporatist policy responses to macro-economic imbalances for the miracles' successes. In this understanding of the employment miracles, wage restraint permitted enhanced international competitiveness and thus created growth in output and employment. Thus, for example, the Wassenaar Agreement around wage restraint in the Netherlands was seen as restoring Dutch competitiveness in world markets and igniting a decade of stable growth. The analyses also tended to have an analytical bias in favour of country-specific policy initiatives, and to assume that policymakers made rational responses to the problems confronting them. This put much causal weight on visible policy choices that were then assessed as either effective or ineffective in setting things right. The possibility that many policy choices might have been irrelevant and that economies benefited from changes in the larger global economic environment was lost on these analyses.

Did analysts ask the right questions, look at the right evidence, and get the right answers about the causes and effects of the miracles? This book questions this, which is why it tries to apply normal social science to an analysis of the miracle economies. The authors approach the miracles by asking three empirical questions so that they can then return to and answer the causal question about the origins of the miracles. First, empirically, we want to know just how miraculous these macroeconomic miracles were. Did they really represent a substantial deviation from prior trends? Many of these countries did face substantial economic problems at the start of the 1980s. But over a longer-term perspective that encompasses several sets of ten-year business cycles, the miracles could perhaps represent a return to trend, rather than a deviation from a (worsening) trend. Similarly, because the "miracle" economies were partially defined by reference to some other set of non-miracle economies, it could simply have been that both sets of countries just changed places with their reference group.

The second empirical issue concerns the economic measures used to define the miracles. Here simple empirical issues have been obscured rather than highlighted by the miracle discourse. The "numbers" that comprise the magic square are all proxy measures for more important underlying changes in the economy. Good inflation and growth numbers, for example, are proxies for profitability and productivity. Similarly, use of standardized unemployment rates as a proxy for how many people are working could hide considerable broad unemployment disguised in disability schemes, early retirement, part-time work, and withdrawal from the labour market. Thus, we tried to avoid using only standardized unemployment measures as the metric for success, preferring instead to look at employment levels, and in some cases even at total working hours for the average employee.

The third empirical issue is whether the fruits of and costs involved in cre-

Table 1.3   Basic social data: Income inequality, poverty rates (defined as income lower than 50 percent median) and net unemployment replacement rates (incl. housing assistance)

	Year	Gini-coeffi-cient	Percentile ratio 90/10	Poverty rate	Replacement rates 1999*
Australia	1994	0.311	4.33	14.3	46.0
Austria	1997	0.266	3.37	8.0	64.0
Belgium	1997	0.250	3.19	8.0	63.5
Canada	2000	0.302	3.95	11.4	65.5
Denmark	1997	0.257	3.15	9.2	63.5
Finland	2000	0.247	2.9	5.4	64.5
France	1994	0.288	3.54	8.0	71.0
Germany	2000	0.252	3.18	8.3	65.5
Ireland	1996	0.325	4.33	12.3	42.5
Italy	2000	0.333	4.47	12.7	46.5
Netherlands	1994	0.253	3.15	8.1	75.5
Sweden	2000	0.252	2.96	6.5	72.5
Switzerland	1992	0.307	3.62	9.3	76.5
UK	1999	0.345	4.58	12.5	32.0
USA	2000	0.368	5.45	17.0	57.5

* Average of two family types at Average Production Worker (APW) level, first six months of unemployment. Average of a) fully insured single APW and b) fully insured couple with single-earner APW and two children. After 6 months (U.S.) or 1 year (most other countries) the rates become lower, in the U.S. dramatically lower.
Source: LIS 2002; Alan and Scruggs 2004 (for the replacement rates)

ating the miracles were evenly distributed. Was rising employment accompanied by substantial hidden costs like rising inequality, poverty or social exclusion? The figures in Table 1.3 answer this question negatively, and it is just this combination of employment growth and generous social security that renders the "miracles" the topic of a model discussion. A related empirical issue is the degree to which rising employment in the miracle economies reflected changing gender relations and an increase in female labour market participation. It appears that all "employment" miracles involved a dual "feminisation" of the work force: rising female employment but also the increase of the number of, often low-paid, part-time and flexible jobs – though there are differences here between three of the four Scandinavian countries (the labour market of which "feminised" earlier) where part-time work decreased (Denmark and Sweden) or remained low (Finland) in the 1990s and the other small miracle countries.

Luck, pluck, and stuck in the employment miracles

All of these issues point to the importance of actors and factors that are usually excluded from the "neo-corporatist" causal versions of the miracle stories. Most causal stories about the miracles come out of the corporatist concertation literature. Although Andrew Shonfield articulated parts of the core argument as early as 1965, three seminal contributions brought this literature to full fruition by the late 1970s and early 1980s. First David Cameron's (1978) empirical argument linked trade exposure to the size of government. Second, a set of essays edited by Peter Lange (1982) and Peter Gourevitch (1984) showed the positive contributions of unions and the divergent consequences of differing union structures in negotiations over macro-economic policy outcomes. Third, Peter Katzenstein's (1984, 1985) twin books on democratic corporatism argued for the importance of a shared sense of social purpose. In essence, all three argued for the presence of a political exchange in which unions gave up current wages and security in a given job for social benefits and security in employment. This political exchange, they said, produced wage restraint, superior inflation and employment outcomes, and thus international competitiveness. While this line of argument bifurcated in the 1990s into a "Central bank independence" stream and a "Collective bargaining" stream, it lately has reconsolidated as a stream looking at the interaction of unions and central banks, much as in Scharpf's 1987 work, *Crisis and Choice in European Social Democracy*.

Thus, from the perspective of these arguments, the late 1990s boom in Europe is a function of prior pacts restraining wages, which is why analysts hunted for evidence of pacting in the "model" economies. But the rate of growth of gross fixed capital formation in the European Union 15 barely changed from the decade of the 1980s to the decade of the 1990s, suggesting some problems with this argument. If this causal orientation towards bargains between social partners is incorrect, then there is a large problem transferring "lessons" from the miracle economies – the lessons have been mis-learned and will be misapplied. Many of the chapters here thus present evidence that the underlying reflation mechanism in these economies was not wage restraint but rather the historically specific combination of housing market booms driven by disinflation, unusually exuberant American import demand that inflated profit margins for firms turning strong dollars into weak euros, and shifts in the composition of employment, but not the total number of hours worked, that made more income available for consumption.

Use of the corporatist concertation argument also reflects a causal bias towards an inward, domestic-centred view. This is consistent with Fritz Scharpf's dichotomisation of policy research into interaction-oriented research (which asks: why do governments *respond* to problems) and problem-oriented research (which asks: why do these problems *exist* for the government). Both views obscure the relationship between 'internal' policy choices and the external environment. Thus, many policy studies assume that agents are capable of assessing their environment, making bounded policy choices, and thereby remedying the problems that sent them in a search for policy choices in the first place.

Despite acknowledging the structural constraints imposed variously by path dependence, institutional legacies, or norms (either as logics of appropriateness or more profoundly as identities), most policy studies are imbued with the notion that this strategic behaviour by actors allows them to attain their preferred objectives, which usually are to change local structures either at the margin or more profoundly in order to bring them into greater conformity with their environment. Most policy studies "prove" this assertion by looking at relatively bounded periods of time in which a given policy change is followed closely by an improvement (or decline, if they wish to lament a policy change) in the conditions that actors are addressing. This mentality colours both optimistic and pessimistic views of the viability of the welfare state in an era of increasing "globalisation", or more specifically an era of increased trade and capital flows. Take, for example, Martin Rhodes' analyses (1998, 2001) of Spanish, Dutch and Italian growth, which he attributes to "competitive corporatism", or Niamh Hardiman's (2001) efforts to apply this to an analysis of the Irish miracle, or the similar analysis presented in Hassel and Ebbinghaus (2000) with respect to European pensions reform. All of them argue that firms and workers are deliberately "pacting" to share the costs of adjustment to world markets. In these analyses, firms, workers, and politicians share an apparently correct assessment of the challenges posed by world markets, the kinds of changes needed to bring local economies into conformity, and the will to make those changes.

Here we wish to suggest that this sort of behaviour, which we will label "pluck", is relatively absent from most of the miracle economies. Instead, these economies are mostly characterised by "luck" and "stuck". Positive outcomes – e.g. GDP growth and increased levels of employment – can occur if the external environment changes in ways that make what were dysfunctional and unchanged institutional structures and policies more functional in the context of the new environment. Dynamics that are endogenous to a given but dysfunctional institutional structure can generate or prevent changes that accidentally make institutional structures more functional in the context of a changed environment. In this situation actors make no positive response to changes in their external environment, continue to unconsciously replicate existing policy routines, and yet nonetheless benefit from an exogenous change or changes that make those policy routines look better. This is luck. During the 1990s, disinflation and falling interest rates due to the balancing of the us federal budget created a major, positive, external stimulus for countries that luckily enough possessed housing markets capable of transforming falling interest rates into new purchasing power and rising employment.

What about stuck? Stuck arguments would suggest that local institutions evolve incrementally according to logics of appropriateness held by actors in those institutions, and that the institutional outcomes were either better than prior configurations or at least less dysfunctional than those into which the competition stumbled. In a stuck situation, the actors' conscious policy responses to a changed environment or a challenge are conditioned by embedded notions about the social purpose of their activity and what could be attained given the existing institutional landscape. In that sense they are not perfectly free choices, but rather conditioned by accidental or incidental qualities of those organisations. Because the external environment (the world market) surrounding any given set of production and public sector institutions is also not characterized by optimal organisations, local organisations merely have to be less dysfunctional than their global competitors in order to look "good". Note that stuck arguments are thus not arguments for convergence toward any optimal organisational form, nor do they offer much guidance about policy transferability. As Alchian and others have argued, markets are like ecologies. Firms display a multitude of strategies – expressed as organisational structures – that can be well or ill suited to their environments. Most analysts understand this to mean that competition will extinguish unsuitable organisational structures. But while competitive pressures force firms to adapt their strategies (organisational structures) to the environment, they do not necessarily enforce conformity or predominantly tend to extinguish non-conforming firms. During the 1990s the revival of corporatist routines, we argue, created a major, negative, internal limit on the expansion of local purchasing power and the subsequent expansion of employment.

Pluck can be distinguished from stuck by the degree to which the actors' behaviour deviates from national logics of appropriateness and constitutes new (or substantially reconstitutes old) institutions based on a strategic appreciation of and response to problems created by a misfit between local institutions and the environment. This admittedly sets a very high standard for intentional behaviour in order to avoid the post hoc, propter hoc arguments that characterise many policy analyses. The typical policy analysis has a binary view of actor behaviour. The only two choices are passivity and action, with action understood as a positive choice for a "new" policy. In this view, any time a positive choice for a "new" policy is followed by a good outcome, actors are credited for their strategic behaviour and for the instrumental appropriateness of their policies. But it is precisely because local routines can give rise to "new" but arguably *bad* policy choices that happen to be rewarded by the environment simply because other localities are making even *worse* policy choices (for whatever reason), that it is important to make the distinction between "stuck" and "pluck".

Distinguishing luck, stuck, and pluck requires us to consider how the external environment changed or did not change during the 1980s and 1990s, before turning to the usual summary of the chapters which introductions necessarily contain. We will also say a bit about the strategy of comparison the book uses in order to be able to make arguments about the degree to which the policy lessons from the miracle economies are transferable.

Globalisation and the miracles

All the miracle economies confronted a changing external economic environment in the 1980s and 1990s. This change can be summed up in two words: globalisation and Europeanisation. But both words need to be unpacked if they are not to obscure specific dynamics. Unpacking them shows that globalisation and Europeanisation tended to have the same effects. Both increased trade and capital flows, both tended to pull more married women into the economy, and both put pressure on governments to make their public sectors more cost efficient. In addition, Europeanisation committed governments to fiscal balance and improved employment. At least at a rhetorical level, it provided support for moving in the sort of direction taken by the miracle economies. Nonetheless, the failure of all EU nations to move in that direction suggests that like globalisation, Europeanisation led to diverging, not converging, outcomes. For this reason we will conflate Europeanisation and globalisation in the discussion below.

What role did globalisation play in the employment and economic miracles described in this book? Generally speaking, globalisation has been characterised as a pernicious force. A host of arguments suggests that globalisation constrains governments' use of macro-economic policy to ameliorate unemployment, forces cutbacks in the welfare state, and is causing a shift in the distribution of GDP away from labour and towards capital. These arguments also suggest that globalisation promotes the homogenisation of national models. But this simplistic vision is clearly wrong for three reasons.

First, at the most general level, globalisation is about the emergence or re-emergence of markets in economic and social spheres that states had closed to markets after the Great Depression. But markets tend to generate differentiation, because markets produce winners and losers. Consequently, globalisation as an economic phenomenon cannot be a force for homogenisation or convergence (Berger and Dore 1996). Even if political actors swayed by common ideas try to force all economies into one mould, market-based competition will differentiate those economies on the basis of factors politicians cannot control. In turn, globalisation does not uniformly lead to an erosion of all welfare states or to rising unemployment everywhere. Economic winners will enjoy more or better employment, and have more resources to deploy on their welfare states. This means that political responses to perceived economic problems matter, because they can affect a country's position in the world markets.

Were our miracles then the outcome of good policy, understood as brilliant strategic responses to changes in the world economy? This seems doubtful for two reasons. First, all of the small economies studied in this volume possess substantial market power in the world economy. Even when they export relatively undifferentiated commodities, they often supply a hugely disproportionate share of world exports for those commodities. Australia and the Netherlands, for example, supply 40 percent and 32 percent of world exports of animal hair and of fresh flowers and vegetables, respectively (Intracen website). Bad policy could lead to some erosion of each country's market share, but it would take years of sustained bad policy to cause a total displacement of production into new suppliers.

Second, the simplistic globalisation argument is wrong because status quo local policies could combine with changes in the global economy that accidentally favoured local conditions to produce strong growth. This seems to be what happened in the Netherlands. There, local policies of wage restraint that were intended to boost competitiveness in world markets produced no increase in Dutch shares of world goods markets (Salverda, below). Indeed, Dutch wage restraint may have tended to depress local employment by dampening local consumption. Instead, falling global interest rates, the tax deductibility of mortgage interest, and mortgage refinancing generated classic Keynesian stimulus to the economy as homeowners steadily reduced their mortgage payments. Increases in gross fixed capital formation for non-residential purposes lagged capital formation in housing until the very end of the 1990s, suggesting that domestic, rather than export markets, led growth, and that domestic growth came from housing. So some of our economic and employment miracles could be seen not only as benefiting from globalisation but also perhaps being a consequence of globalisation, in this case the integration of financial markets that permitted rapid transmission of interest rate changes globally.

If globalisation is about the expansion of trade and capital flows as part of the re-emergence of markets, then globalisation will have quite complex effects on income and employment. Expanded trade access, for example, will have the effect of concentrating production in regions with existing production competence, permitting them to attain greater economies of scale. Although foreign direct investment (FDI) can shift the location of production, FDI tends either to disperse best practices models for production or to shift the production of labour-intensive, cost-sensitive production to low-wage labour-surplus areas. But both of these do not automatically reduce total employment, because both also lower the prices of the goods being produced. This generates substitution effects, as consumers shift consumption to other goods, creating employment in those other sectors.

Trade also creates more demand for transportation and financial services related to trade, and this too increases employment. So globalisation changes the geographic and sectoral distribution of employment rather than reducing global employment. This is especially clear when we look at the state-owned or -regulated services in the transportation, power and water generation and distribution, and retail and wholesale distribution sectors. The precise redistribution of gains within a society remains a political choice.

Finally, globalisation and the welfare state are not in direct conflict. Many of the processes encompassed in globalisation have causal roots in the prior existence of the welfare state, and simultaneously create political demand for expansion of state-sponsored social protection. States' efforts to create markets by privatising state-owned services did remove insulation from market pressures. But it also created new demands for access to education, for early retirement, and for services facilitating female labour market participation. Below we consider four specific pressures on our cases in more detail. While three of these are conventionally seen as being 'global' in origin, and one 'domestic', all in fact derive from the interaction of local welfare states with the expansion of global markets. The specific pressures are low-wage competition from Asia (and for our European cases, increasingly, Eastern Europe), expanded intra-OECD FDI, the marketisation of the service sector, and married women's uneven re-entry into labour markets.

The first specific global pressure on our cases came from the emergence of high-volume but low-wage production of manufactured goods in Asia. The post-war system of social protection essentially priced low skilled male labour out of manufacturing markets in the OECD. Unionisation and tight labour markets raised wages above the levels that prevailed in many Asian and Latin American economies characterised by overt repression of labour unions; welfare states raised the reservation wage. It is important not to overstate the wage gap, because productivity is much lower in most of Newly Industrialising Asia, making the relative gap in *unit costs* much smaller than the absolute wage gap. Nonetheless, even by 2000, manufacturing wage costs in the richest Asian economies only stood at about 40 percent of the US level, while wages in the poorest were less than 10 percent (US Bureau of Labor Statistics website). This provided a big incentive to relocate labour-intensive production involving little skilled labour away from OECD economies.

And indeed, labour-intensive industries characterised by batch production at individual workstations, like garment assembly, shoes, toys, luggage, and cheap household goods, all gradually did move offshore to Asia along with some other capital-intensive but medium-skill industries like ship-building and consumer electronics. In turn, the supply industries for these sectors also migrated to collocate with their sources of final demand. Thus, even some capital-intensive industries like fibre production and textiles weaving eventually relocated to Asia. From 1980 to 2000 industrialising Asia more than doubled its share of total world trade from roughly 8 percent to nearly 20 percent, reflecting even larger shares (circa 40 percent) of industries like woven clothing, or consumer electronics assembly (WTO website; Intracen website).

This shift put downward pressure on wages and employment at the bottom end of the labour market, because low- or no-skill men were unable to shift into other forms of employment. Adrian Wood argues that this sort of Southern competition alone accounts for a loss of at least 9 million OECD manufacturing jobs, equivalent to about two-thirds of Euroland's total unemployment in 1998 (Wood 1994:67). In almost every OECD economy, both the number of manufacturing jobs and the number of hours in manufacturing have fallen since 1990, and in many, employment has fallen by about 1 percent per year since 1979 (US Bureau of Labor Statistics website). But this pressure did not operate uniformly on our cases. First, our countries started with different volumes of labour-intensive manufacturing. Second, the response to the disappearance of labour-intensive manufacturing could take the form of lost jobs, falling wages, fewer hours of work, or substitution of capital for labour.

Low-wage competition generated two natural, market-based responses. First, falling prices for increasingly commoditised manufactures increased disposable income in the economy as a whole, shifting demand towards services and better quality manufactures in all of our cases. Second, this shift permitted firms that had been labour-intensive to respond to low-wage competition by moving upmarket and substituting capital for labour, although this did not happen uniformly in all our cases. While these shifts helped GDP to grow, they also potentially exacerbated the wage/employment problem at the bottom of the labour market. For example, from 1980 to 1993 employment in textiles, clothing and footwear (TCF) in the USA declined by 30 percent, in the Netherlands by 40 percent, and in Sweden by 65 percent. All told, European TCF employment contracted by 800,000 jobs (ILO website).

The second specific pressure on our cases came from capital flows among rich countries, rather than to low-wage ones. This kind of investment tended to generate good jobs at high pay. But it also necessarily involved a reduction in the total number of manufacturing jobs, because this investment almost always involved displacement of lower productivity firms in the host (recipient) economy. Successful multinational firms uniformly have higher productivity than firms in their host economy. In the six largest OECD economies, on an unweighted basis, the ratio between assets and employment for inwardly investing manufacturing firms at the beginning of the 1990s was 1.6 (versus a nominal economy-wide ratio of 1), suggesting higher capital intensity and lower than average direct employment from FDI (UNCTAD 1993, p. 5). Thus, when FDI occurred in existing sectors, it carried in more efficient production norms, causing job losses as domestic firms adapted to higher productivity levels or simply exited the market. The only case where FDI generated substantial numbers of new jobs was Ireland, where MNCs built completely new export complexes in electronics and chemicals.

The third pressure on employment in our countries came from the marketisation of the public sector and especially infrastructure and transportation services. Virtually all of these were publicly owned at the beginning of the 1980s, and virtually all had been commercialised or privatised by the end of the 1990s. Regulation of prices and profits in nominally privately owned utilities firms had the indirect effect of guaranteeing stable wages and employment for relatively unskilled workers. Pervasive public ownership in Europe often carried with it civil service status for these workers. Both guaranteed a degree of overstaffing. Deregulation of public utilities in the USA and the export of this model through the World Trade Organisation led to parallel deregulation and privatisation in Europe and elsewhere (Schwartz 2001a).

Although deregulation permitted new firms offering new services to enter markets, the net employment effect was a loss of jobs in most places. For example, the share of telecommunications employment in total employment in Sweden, the USA, Britain and Denmark fell by 30 to 50 percent in the 1990s (Héritier and Schmidt 2000, pp. 577-578). Again, however, there were winners and losers in this process. Some former public service providers aggressively expanded outside their former product and geographic markets, absorbing private sector rivals and shifting the location of employment. For example, the Dutch postal service KPN grew significantly by facilitating the flow of packages into Europe, between European countries, and, sometimes, even inside their neighbours as firms tried to avoid using less nimble and more expensive local posts.

The last pressure on employment levels came from a once-only re-integration of married women, especially married women with children, into formal labour markets. The reintegration of national markets through globalisation (here, increased FDI and trade) increased the returns from education in ways that favoured labour market re-entry by married women at the same time that they began to desire employment. Voluntarily or involuntarily, women surrendered the social protection afforded them by male breadwinner wages and exposed themselves directly to labour markets. From 1970 to 1996, the average rate of female labour market participation in the OECD rose 15 percentage points to 63 percent in a fairly linear increase.[1] There was of course substantial variation, with the Scandinavian and Anglo economies seeing 20 percentage point rises off already high rates of female labour market participation, while the continental economies saw roughly 10 percentage point increases off a lower base. Meanwhile, the average level of male labour force participation in the OECD fell from about 90 percent to 83 percent in 1970-96. Much of this was a withdrawal of older manufacturing workers choosing early retirement in the face of low wage competition or demands for greater skill levels or new skills.

Two things link female labour market re-entry to globalisation. First, the destruction of male breadwinner jobs in the bottom half of the income distribution through increased trade and increased inward FDI coincided with, and indeed enabled, a shift of employment away from manufacturing and towards services, especially in the smaller European economies. This shift largely benefited women. They were more willing to accept the higher emotional and social intensity, and the part-time and "flex-time" nature of much service sector employment.

The second factor relevant to the discussion of globalisation concerns the returns from education. On the demand side for jobs, women had to confront the fact that they could no longer depend on men as reliable wage earners or marriage partners, although again, this was less true in the continental economies. But it is also true that their own, increased rate of higher education not only permitted them access to a much broader range of jobs than before, but also at much better rates of pay than before. Competition with imports manufactured with low-wage labour and the increased salience of inward FDI in all OECD economies shifted the demand for skilled and credentialed labour upward. Women were well positioned to take advantage of this shift in demand. Women's rates of higher education had not only equalized with those of men in most OECD countries by the 1980s, but by the 1990s substantially exceeded those for men in many countries (Jönsson 1999, pp.4-5, but see also Daly 2000).

Finally, women's labour market entry was a self-sustaining process. Not only did one part of the welfare state – education – assist labour market entry, it also created demands for expansion of other public and publicly subsidised branches like child and elderly people care. It created demand for more private and public services, which women typically staffed. In this sense, globalisation – understood as the expansion of labour markets into part of the female population – created demand for an expansion of the formal welfare state, and indeed could not have occurred in the absence of the formal welfare state as a place for married women to (re-)enter labour markets and as a support for that (re-)entry.

A specific (corporatist) variety of capitalism?

One of the questions touched upon in the preceding section was whether globalisation had forced the small miracle economies to develop in a liberal direction. The answer has to be that despite some similarities with respect to deregulation of labour markets, welfare retrenchment and reorganisation, tax cuts, and an increasing reliance of firms on the stock market for access to new capital, they nonetheless have largely retained their specific character, and that two of them – Australia and Ireland – anyway already featured strong liberal traits before recent developments took shape. Moreover, it is not clear whether the changes that have taken place in the 1990s have been induced solely by increased global competition. The end of the rather leftist politico-ideological tide in the late 1970s/early 1980s, the breakdown of Soviet socialism a decade later, the stagnation of Japanese capitalism and the recent economic strength of liberal, American capitalism could also have been of causal importance here. And perhaps one has to add changing expectations of both firms and citizens of the variety and quality of services from the public sector as a base for the liberalisation of the public sector.

The explanation of political-economic changes is not the subject here, however. The question rather is whether the small miracle economies constitute a specific variety of capitalism and whether this gives them a competitive edge. These questions make sense because the discussion about varieties or types of capitalism has had a strong revival in recent years and because, apart from Australia and Ireland, the small countries discussed in this volume have a number of relevant features in common that render them similar in politico-economic terms. All of them are prominent corporatist political economies, where corporatism is understood both as an institutional structure for regular consultation on issues such as wages, investment and social security between organised capital and labour (as well as politicians in the tripartite variety of corporatism), and as the specific and more or less symmetric agreements and exchanges between the labour market parties located in that institutional framework. As the historical record shows, the institutional framework does not automatically generate these agreements. Because corporatism involves a form of macroeconomic regulation or coordination, it is not surprising that, as the data in Table 1.4 show, the European continental countries in our sample also have high coordination scores in the most prominent and roughest typology of capitalist varieties – that of Hall and Soskice (2001), which distinguishes between liberal market economies (LMES) and coordinated market economies (CMES). Australia and Ireland, by contrast, are located in the vicinity of the liberal pole where the USA, Britain and Canada are also found.

Ireland is worth a special note. Its liberal traits have recently been reinforced by a centralised 'competition state' (Boyle 2004), and it has also been mentioned as one of the examples where so-called new social pacts have brought about success (Hassel and Ebbinghaus 2000). Social policy and the interests of labour are not exchanged against those of capital, however, but subordinated to the needs of the economy. Perhaps this is a 'new corporatism', but it is quite different from the symmetrical and exchange-based corporatism discussed in this section.

With the exception of Finland, the continental 'miracle' countries also share an unbroken associational tradition from medieval guild structures to modern corporatist institutions (Crouch 1993, p. 299ff), and related to this continuity a past marked by a weak feudalism, the absence of absolutism or at least of absolutist repression, traditions of a relatively low level of polarisation between social classes and a relatively high level of social trust (al-

Table 1.4   Coordination and corporatism scores of the small 'model economies' in comparison (mid-1990s)

	Coordination Index according to Hall and Gingerich (scale 0 to 1)	Average* Corporatism Score (scale 1 to 5)
Australia	.36	1.7
Austria	1.00	5.0
Belgium	.74	2.8
Canada	.13	1.2
Denmark	.70	3.5
Finland	.72	3.3
France	.69	1.7
Germany	.95	3.5
Ireland	.29	2.0
Italy	.87	1.5
Netherlands	.66	4.0
Norway	.76	4.9
Portugal	.72	1.5
Spain	.57	1.3
Sweden	.69	4.7
Switzerland	.51	3.4
UK	.07	1.7
USA	0.00	1.2

* Of the coorporatism rankings of 13 different inquiries by different authors.
Sources: Hall and Gingerich 2001: 46; Siaroff 1999: 185

though for a long time combined with clear hierarchical distinctions and elitist paternalism), and a rather evolutionary process of democratisation (Katzenstein 1985). Finally, these countries share a socially anchored notion of the general interest, which is presumably what is at stake when unions and employers negotiate wage levels, working time, labour flexibility, etc. with an eye to their effects on economic growth, employment and inflation. Responsibility for the common good evolved as an affair of socio-political associations as well as of the state.

Would it make sense to construct a corporatist type of capitalism? Yes. This is because the number of countries with a high degree of corporatism is considerable – apart from the miracle countries, also Austria, Norway, Germany and, at a somewhat lower level, Belgium (and because there appear to exist different forms of politico-economic coordination). A brief look at Table 1.4 reveals that France, Italy and Spain as well as Portugal score relatively high in the coordination index, but low in the corporatism ranking. One has to wonder whether it is plausible to put together these forms of capitalist regulation under the heading of coordination, and possibly the picture becomes even more complicated when the peculiarities of eastern Asian and central and eastern European market economies are also taken into consideration. If one decides to construct a corporatist type (and possibly some other additional types), then the next question is the criteria that underpin the category.

The theories on the varieties of capitalism currently discussed do not explicitly reserve space for a separate corporatist type. Early empirical arguments about corporatism had already emerged in the 1920s (Hilferding 1924), were revived in the 1960s (Shonfield 1965 and Galbraith 1967), were formalized by Schmitter (1979), before then taking a turn into the welfare state literature through the notion of forms of 'welfare capitalism' (Esping-Andersen 1990). But Katzenstein's *Small States in World Markets* (1985) and Albert's *Capitalisme contre capitalisme* (1991) were the first to explicitly consider the interaction of corporatism and the contemporary form of globalisation and the different potentials for adjustment that inhere to different political economies. Albert, descriptively referring to corporatism without specifying a distinct corporatist capitalism, identifies two types that he judges to present alternative but viable models of adjustment to global capitalism: the 'Rhineland model,' encompassing Europe and Japan, and 'Anglo-Saxon capitalism'. Hutton (1995), who distinguished 'stakeholder' from 'shareholder capitalism', Dore (2000) and Hall and Soskice (2001) with their 'liberal' and 'coordinated' varieties of capitalism all present similar typologies and the argument that each type possesses different institutional advantages in international competition. Rhodes and van Apeldoorn (1997), who identify Anglo-Saxon, Germanic and Latin forms of capitalism, and Amable (2003; cf. Hollingsworth and Boyer 1997), who distinguishes among market-based Anglo-Saxon, social democratic, continental European, Mediterranean and Asian 'social systems of innovation and production', present non-dichotomous typologies.

If we accept a dichotomy between liberal and non-liberal types, then the question is whether or not the non-liberal type has to be sub-divided, and the basis for constructing consistent subordinate categories. A simple dichotomous typology is clearly an oversimplification of reality and obscures fundamental analytical differences, as Hall and Soskice (2001, p.33ff) note (cf. also the critical discussion in *European Comparative Politics* 1, no. 2, 2003). Corporatism *is a way of organising capitalism* that is not only different from a purely arms-length transaction, market-based economy, but also different from etatist economies that rely on political regulation, and from communitarian economies in which huge industrial-financial conglomerations crowd out independent businesses.

Although the key criterion for distinguishing among variations of capital-ism has to be the form that its organisation or regulation takes, it should be supplemented by other criteria. But the choice of these criteria is a function of what it is we want to know about these capitalisms. Is the object of in-quiry only how (macro-) economic processes are coordinated or also how economic and social goals are coordinated and balanced? Most typologies are descriptive and dodge this question of appropriate criteria. Hall and Sos-kice (2001, p.6) opt to look only at micro-economic processes and thus cen-tre their theory on the firm. They use divergences in relationships among firms, between firms and investors, between firms and employees, and the ways that skills formation occurs to distinguish types of capitalism. By con-trast, the 'regulation theorists' (Amable, Boyer, Hollingsworth) offer a very broad catalogue of criteria that also include the macro-relationship between capital and labour, the 'conceptions of fairness and justice' held by them, the norms, rules and 'receipts for action' prevailing in a society, and the structure of the state and its policies (Hollingsworth and Boyer 1997, p. 2).

It is not necessary here to discuss the question of the appropriate criteria in detail, but it is obvious that a typology containing corporatism has to be built on a broader set of criteria similar to that of 'regulation theory'. Euro-pean corporatism is a macro-politico-economic phenomenon, and it in-volves the relationships between capital and labour, state and economy as well as a normative set of interaction patterns. The same holds for the broadly understood liberal, etatist and communitarian varieties. And all of these varieties involve certain ways of relating social security and welfare to economic performance. It is here where a further distinction comes in be-tween social democratic, which stresses equality of condition, and conser-vative, which stresses care and harmony, as sub-forms of the corporatist, etatist and communitarian varieties of capitalism. These sub-forms depend on power relations and dominant 'conceptions of fairness and justice'. Putting together the whole picture, we have

1 a basic dichotomy between liberal and coordinated capitalism, where the latter
2 is divided into corporatist, etatist and communitarian varieties that can
3 be further divided into social democratic and conservative sub-types.

It is important to stress that we are talking about ideal types that should not be confused with real capitalist countries. Real cases only approximate ide-al types more or less, and typically are hybrids containing elements that might qualify them for other types, if viewed only in isolation. Because of the basic dichotomy of liberal and coordinated capitalism, it does not make sense to construct a liberal sub-variety of corporatist capitalism, but it is of course possible that corporatist and liberal elements come together in a country and constitute a specific hybrid. It is often said that Switzerland – with the lowest corporatism score of our continental countries – has a strong liberal component (Katzenstein 1985), and in some periods of Dutch capitalist development, liberalism has also played a prominent role, while etatism has joined corporatism in other periods. In Scandinavia, this combination has been important. And where Scandinavian corporatism is mainly social democratic, Dutch and Swiss corporatism has mainly been conservative. In fact, our continental model countries are nothing more than hybrid political economies with a strong corporatist component.

The next question we have to address is whether the corporatist model countries have a competitive edge because of their corporatism. Or in the words of Hall and Soskice: Do they have corporatist institutional advantages? Without doubt, they have the institutional possibility to negotiate economic, social and, if they intend to, environmental targets by adjusting wage growth, profits, taxes, social security benefits, regional development and environmental measures. This is advantageous at least for parts of a corporatist country's population because it reduces the risk of poverty and social exclusion and environmental damage by unfettered market forces. But is it also an advantage in international competition?

Katzenstein (1985) and Scharpf (1991 [1987]) and more recently a number of analysts of 'new social pacts' (e.g. Hassel and Ebbinghaus 2000; Pochet and Fajertag 2000) have argued that corporatism facilitates the improvement of competitiveness by making it possible to credibly exchange nationwide wage restraint for, among other things, social rights. Our model countries plus Austria and Portugal are typically presented as the main examples of social pacts, although allegedly non-corporatist Australia, Ireland and Italy have also been identified as countries with new social pacts. And it has been these countries, and particularly the Netherlands, that have been the focus of recent social pact discussions. Similarly, Martin Rhodes (1998, 2000) has labelled German arrangements 'competitive corporatism'. The core assumption in this discourse is the conviction that reducing wage costs is a key for improving competitiveness: 'Wage restraint is part of a supply side policy of employment and economic growth by restoring competitiveness and sound public finances' (Hassel and Ebbinghaus 2000, p.4). We have to see whether the contributions to this volume will support this view.

What about the quite different argument advanced in the variety of capitalism literature about coordinated market economies (CMEs)? This argues that CMEs are quality-sensitive while LMEs are rather cost-sensitive (Hall and Soskice 2001, p.37). The argument holds that in CMEs the capital-labour-state networks and their long-term orientation have brought about an education and training system that generates a higher skill level for the labour force than that found in LMEs. In turn, this results in a concentration on quality production, that renders cost (and wage) competition less urgent for CME countries. CMEs have 'comparative institutional advantages' in quality production.

It is probably true that CME companies are more oriented towards long-term perspectives than LME companies, because of their stronger inter-firm networks, their lesser reliance on the stock market for financing, and the stake (direct or indirect) unions and/or politicians have in their activities. It is not obvious, however, that this long-term orientation is causally linked to prevailing education and training systems in the countries under consideration. These countries possess quite different training systems, and the famous apprenticeship system that is said to be the basis for quality goods production in the car, machinery and tool industries of the German-speaking countries is not a general feature of all CMEs (cf. Estevez et al. 2001). Moreover, one can question the existence of a direct link between a certain training system and quality production. Is the hierarchical, typically Fordist production system that is said to prevail in LMEs (but also in France; cf. Boyer 2000, p.29) less able to produce quality than a skill-based system of flexible specialisation? A striking result of one of the very few comparative investigations of quality production (Aiginger 2000) is the unexpectedly high ranking of the USA and Britain – indeed, Britain is ranked just behind Germany. Another question is how good is the quality of so-called quality goods? Sometimes one wonders whether, for example, the construction, car repair or utilities branches in the USA are really producing inferior quality compared to their German, Swedish or Swiss equivalents. And what about those coordinated political economies that do not share in the quality image – such as Belgium, France and the Netherlands?

These questions do not suggest that CMEs in general and the corporatist variety in particular do not have specific comparative institutional advantages. They only imply that the matter is complex and that more research will have to be done. The picture becomes even more complicated when one takes into consideration that countries are not only hybrid in the sense of combining aspects of different varieties such as corporatist consultation and liberal employment protection, but that they also reveal the co-existence of different politico-economic constellations and production strategies. Branches with strong unions co-exist with branches with weak unions;

Table 1.5   Comparative advantages (merchandise) of main OECD countries in 2002

	Main industrial sectors revealing comparative advantages*; ranking based on share in total exports	Exports as %/GDP excl. and incl. services	
Australia	Minerals (36%; 3.19); fresh food (21%; 4.85); basic manufactures (10%; 1.35); processed food (8%; 2.02)	18.2 (2000)	22.9 (2000)
Austria	Non-electronic machinery (18%; 1.85); basic manufactures (13%; 1.71); transport equipment (12%; 1); miscellaneous manufactures (11%; 1.3); wood products (9%; 2.97)	35.6	52.1
Belgium	Chemicals (28%, 2.4); transport equipment (15%; 1.19); basic manufactures (8%; 1.14); processed food (6%; 1.43)	86.6	91.0
Denmark	Non-electronic machinery (14%; 1.45); chemicals (13%; 1.13); miscellaneous manufacturing (12%; 1.4); processed food (12%; 2.83); fresh food (11%; 2.68)	32.5	44.2
Finland	Wood products (26%; 8.32); IT and consumer electronics (19%; 1.86); non-electronic machinery (13%; 1.27); basic manufactures (9%; 1.28)	33.8	38.2
France	Transport equipment 21%; (1.67); chemicals (16%; 1.43); non-electronic machinery (11%; 1.12); basic manufactures (8%; 1.07); processed food (8%; 1.89)	21.7	27.3
Germany	Transport equipment (23%; 1.80); non-electronic machinery (17%; 1.71); chemicals (14%; 1.26); miscellaneous manufacturing (9%; 1.02); basic manufactures (9%; 1.18)	30.8	35.5
Ireland	Chemicals (41%; 3.56); IT and consumer electronics (22%; 2.11); electronic components (11%; 1.21); miscellaneous manufacturing (9%; 1.01); processed food (8%; 1.97)	75.6	94.7
Italy	Non-electronic machinery (19%; 1.93); miscellaneous manufacturing (12%; 1.38); basic manufactures (11%; 1.5); clothing (6%; 1.68); leather products (5%; 3.67); textiles (5%; 1.86)	20.9	27.0
Japan	Transport equipment (26%; 2.08); non-electronic machinery (16%; 1.64); electronic components (15%; 1.62); IT and consumer electronics (13%; 1.20); miscellaneous manufacturing (9%; 1.01); basic manufactures (7%; 1.01)	10.5	11.2
Netherlands**	Chemicals (18%; 1.59); IT and consumer electronics (16%; 1.49); processed food (12%; 2.82; miscellaneous manufacturing (11%; 1.02); fresh food (10%; 61.8	2.25)	52.7

Norway	Minerals (64%; 5.66); basic manufactures (8%; 1.06); fresh food (5%; 1.17)	31.2	41.8
Sweden	Non-electronic machinery (16%; 1.97); wood products (15%; 4.78); transport equipment (13%; 1.06); chemicals (12%; 1.05); basic manufactures (10%; 1.40); miscellaneous manufacturing (9%; 1.03)	33.8	43.3
Switzerland	Chemicals (33%; 2.87); miscellaneous manufacturing (21%; 2,46); non-electronic machinery (17%; 1,72); basic manufactures (8%; 1,11)	32.3	44.3
UK	Chemicals (15%; 1,32); non-electronic machinery (13%; 1.33); IT and consumer electronics (13%; 1.25); transport equipment (13%; 1.0); minerals (12%; 1.01); miscellaneous manufacturing (11%; 1.23)	18.0	25.8
USA***	Transport equipment (16%; 1.28); non-electronic machinery (14%; 1.46); chemicals (13%; 1.15); electronic components (12%; 1.32); miscellaneous manufacturing (11%; 1.32); fresh food (6%; 1.38)	6.7	9.7

* The first figures between brackets refer to the share of the sector in total exports (exclusive of services), the second show the ratio of exports to imports in the respective sectors; a value higher than 1 indicates a comparative advantage.
** Dutch comparative advantages in IT and consumer electronics are due to re-exports; cf. Kuster and Verbruggen 2001.
*** IT and consumer electronics divided, the US would have comparative advantages in IT.
Sources: ITC 2004; OECD 2003b; WKO 2003: 13; WTO 2003: 24; Nationmaster 2004

the industrial sector – which most studies on capitalist varieties concentrate on – co-exists with the quite differently organized service sector; both sectors exhibit considerable intra-sectoral diversity with both quality-oriented branches and Fordist branches. And multinational companies – at least the big ones – have their own 'regimes of border-crossing corporate governance' (Streeck 2001a, p.5).

In this sense the whole variety of capitalism literature is an institutionalist restatement of Ricardo's argument about comparative advantage: Liberal political economies are as good in the production of quality goods as coordinated political economies, but since they are even better in mass production and high technology, they tend to concentrate there. CMEs that are less competitive in mass production (large-scale) can concentrate therefore on quality production based on small-scale flexible specialisation that is particularly found in the machines, instruments and tools industry. *To some degree* this is supported by the data in Table 1.5. But even where this distinction between mass production and flexible specialisation-based quality production is appropriate, in a context where manufacturing is only good for a third or less of GDP, the latter will only be a relatively small part of the entire economy.

This means, coming to the final point to be made here, that the discussion about institutional complementarities has to be viewed in this light. What is complementary to a number of branches need not necessarily be complementary in other branches or the economy as a whole. Moreover, nobody knows exactly what is complementary and what not because the question of complementarities is a question of interpretation (Streeck 2002, p.4). A political economy as a whole is open for many changes as well as for policy confusion, and path dependence therefore should not be exaggerated. Perhaps it is mainly transformation costs, the inertia of action and power relations that keep political economies on 'path', but not the requirements of institutional complementarity.

What the chapters say

All 'miracle chapters', i.e. with the exception of those on the contrasting cases of Germany and the USA, examine the dimensions of the 'miracles', their social implications and their causes. Most attention was paid to the Netherlands in the international discussion, so this is the case we start with. Most analyses concluded that its economic success was brought about by conscious action. This is the basis for the claim that the Dutch model should serve as an international example. But Wiemer Salverda shows that this claim collapses in the face of detailed data as well as in comparison with the 1970s. Causal relationships worth mentioning between the pursued policy of wage restraint, exports and job growth cannot be detected. Salverda also shows that the success of the Dutch model should not be exaggerated. It was strongly limited to a few aspects of the labour market. While the total number of people employed increased dramatically, this largely occurred through a shift of working hours from the male core labour force to students, youth and married women who took on very short working hours in pursuit of "pin money". Meanwhile, despite a gentle rise after 1985, the total number of hours worked per capita remains below the level set in 1979. Similarly, with the exception of the late 1990s, Dutch GDP growth per capita was not higher than that of its five major competitors, the USA, Belgium, Germany, France and the UK, and relied much more on labour mobilisation than on increased productivity.

The Danish case was less spectacular, and Sweden only regained international attention in the late 1990s. As Christoffer Green-Pederson and Anders Lindbom argue, these countries traded places in the eyes of those looking for social democratic success stories. During the 1970s and 1980s, Sweden was a model country for foreign observers seeking ways to keep unemployment at golden age levels. However, as unemployment increased to 10 percent in Sweden during the early 1990s, the same observers portrayed this country as a failure. Denmark occupied Sweden's role as an economic miracle by bringing down its traditionally high unemployment to roughly 5 percent in the decade after 1993 and maintaining a high employment rate at the same time. According to Green-Pedersen and Lindbom, this success was the result of conscious labour market and welfare policies made possible by changes in the party composition of the government. The authors provide some support for the stylised picture of Denmark as a miracle economy, but they also say that Sweden should not be portrayed as a failure. For the very recent Swedish labour market performance might merit a 'miracle' description, too, compared with many of the big European countries. Despite labour market successes, both of these universal welfare states face significant macro-economic problems such as the huge size of the black labour market and the costs of public employment. Normal policy routines may not suffice to keep things on track.

The next Scandinavian country included here, Finland, was recently named the 'Nokia model' because of the prominent role this high-tech company played in this small (not even 5 million inhabitants) country's recovery from its severe crisis in the years after 1989 when unemployment hit the 20 percent mark. Today, this percentage is more than halved, and Finland has become a star performer in terms of technological achievement, education and economic growth. According to Jaakko Kiander, its very strong revival since the mid-1990s can neither be explained by liberal reforms of the labour market (that were barely in place) nor by fundamental changes in public policy. Rather, traditional monetary policy and pro-cyclical fiscal policy were of considerable importance. Conscious adjustment to increased global competition at the public as well as private level appears to be the second part of the story and resulted in a long-term orientation of the national innovation system and technological breakthroughs. In spite of the crisis in the early 1990s and industrial restructuring, Finnish political governance and corporatist institutions remained relatively stable. This does not support the view that the Finnish recession was caused by system weaknesses of the Nordic model.

Switzerland, our next country, presents a remarkable and very special case, although not for the reasons usually advanced. For decades, this country has had, together with Iceland and Norway, the highest employment rate in the world and, on average over these decades, also the lowest unemployment rate. In the 1990s, however, Swiss GDP and productivity growth were considerably below OECD averages. Moreover, the welfare system, regularly described as the most liberal one on the European continent, became more generous in those years when retrenchment politics prevailed elsewhere. And yet the country maintained its high employment and low, though somewhat increasing, unemployment levels. This is what might be considered a miracle according to François Merrien and Uwe Becker. The miraculous development was possible because slow productivity growth was accompanied by job destruction. Swiss exports and export market shares remained relatively stable. This is the second aspect of the miracle and appears to be due to the markets and market niches Switzerland is active in (except for bulk chemicals, particularly machine tools and instruments, pharmaceuticals and other fine chemicals) as well as to the strong image of the country as a supplier of quality goods and services. This suggests both that Switzerland was stuck, and that the usual corporatist logics do not provide much analytic traction there.

Ireland, the 'European tiger', is a case that barely fits the parameters of (symmetric) corporatism and that is often presented as benefiting from its special location in a more globalised economy. Mary Daly's chapter distances itself from this claim. She shows that the Irish story needs to be cast in terms of an interaction between policy, politics and economics as well as American investment that could qualify for a combination of pluck and luck; luck that was also accentuated by a strong house price bubble. Ireland's long-run growth strategy was underpinned by significant adaptation of political institutions and compromises among interest groups. She further argues that the attribution of 'success' to the Irish model may be premature. The last few years have shown that Ireland's particular dependence on exports by multinational firms made it particularly vulnerable to recession in the USA. At the same time, Ireland's economic success created social problems that now pose a challenge for both the sound management of public finances and the maintenance of the policy consensus that underlay fiscal balance in the first place. 'Success' has polarised society between winners and losers and enforced a series of economic/social trade-offs between social and economic goals.

As in Ireland, Australia's housing and equity market also contributed to GDP growth and rising employment – despite an occasionally unfavorable external economic environment. Herman Schwartz's paper compares the dynamics and substance of Australian policy responses to its prior poor export, employment, and fiscal performance to see whether remediation should be attributed to pluck, luck, or just being stuck. While luck, in the form of growing Asian demand for Australian mineral exports, certainly helped, the Australian case is one in which luck favored the prepared. A range of 'pluckish' policy choices in the 1980s made it possible for Australia to translate this external demand into rising employment and accelerated productivity growth rather than higher inflation, and also helped Australia overcome the potentially bad luck of the Asian financial crisis. At the same time, the Australian state expanded some forms of social protection without increasing its fiscal deficit or public debt. This suggests a range of transferable policy options for European economies currently facing problems similar to those Australia confronted in the 1980s.

The model case for all who want to liberalise the economy is the USA. It contrasts the European 'miracles' and Australia by its sheer size as well as by its degree of labour market flexibility and its really residual welfare system. American success permitted some to advocate the advantages of the LME model over the CME model. But Cathie Jo Martin's chapter on the success of the American economy throughout the 1990s calls into question the neat division of the world into LMEs and CMEs, as well as the lessons to be learned from the US case. Much of what made the 1990s an economically successful decade in the US has nothing to do with the kinds of policy prescriptions that might emerge from an LME model of economic and employment growth. Instead, Martin's analysis of the American model in the latter part of the 1990s shows that as in Ireland, success may be transitory, that success has created large distributional inequities, and that success may reflect circumstances outside of the American model. What the American model shows most strongly is how aggregate demand and employment continue to be closely tied together, and how the American housing and equity markets rapidly transformed disinflation into expanded demand. This contrasts with the larger European economies, where the structure of housing and equity markets, along with more monetarist central banks, impeded this transformation.

The final chapter discusses Germany as a case contrasting the development of the USA and the miracle economies that is regularly advised, just as France and Italy, to liberalise its political economy and to learn from the success stories. Becker suggests that the usual comparisons with the small model states and the USA miss important scalar differences, however. Regions within southern Germany that are as large as the small model economies have experienced "miracle"-like levels of employment and GDP growth even while Germany as a whole experienced low employment and GDP growth and continued high unemployment during the 1990s. According to the mainstream view, aggregate German stagnation reflects poor adjustment to globalisation, overly high non-wage labour costs, and too many economic rigidities. But Becker argues that Germany is no more rigid than Sweden or the Netherlands. Moreover, one still cannot seriously discuss the German political economy without taking into consideration the bad luck caused by the continuous, large costs of German unification. In contrast, the model economies have partly benefited from luck. All this means that one has to be careful in comparing small to big countries and that too much stress on rigidity versus flexibility is misleading.

Note

1 Separate data for married women only are not available. So the figures here and below understate the shift in married women's labour market behaviour.

2 The Dutch Model: Magic in a Flat Landscape?

Wiemer Salverda[1]

Introduction

Of all the 'models' discussed in this volume, the Dutch one is the most famous one – possibly because the Netherlands is not as small as Ireland and Denmark, because it came from far behind, and because it managed to combine spectacular employment growth with competitiveness and the maintenance of a generous, though somewhat retrenched, welfare system. The Netherlands has witnessed a rapid decline in the unemployment rate that brought it to one of the lowest levels of all OECD countries. At the same time, the country's job growth was about the highest in the OECD area (see Chart 2.1); within one and a half decades it had mutated from a country with an employment rate of just over 50 percent to a high employment economy. These developments were regarded as something of a miracle, particularly because previously, between 1975 and the early 1980s, the country was known for the 'Dutch disease'.[2] Feelings of admiration are aroused by these outcomes because the Netherlands is also thought to have brought this result about by conscious action, and can therefore serve as an example for other countries that do not want to take the liberal, American route. And because corporatism is supposed to have played a crucial role in the Dutch development, the country also serves as a model case in discussions on 'competitive corporatism' and 'new social pacts'. The model image appears to have survived even though Dutch performance lost much of its lustre in the economic downturn after 2002, as the Netherlands fell from the top range to the bottom end of GDP performance among EU member states.

In the early 1990s, despite several years of employment growth, nobody thought about characterising the Netherlands as a model. A rather critical view on the economy prevailed in the Netherlands, where newspapers described corporatism as eroding (*de Volkskrant*, December 24, 1991; *NRC Handelsblad*, November 20, 1992). A few years later, scholars of industrial relations still described Dutch corporatism as 'weak' (Van Ruysseveldt and Visser 1996; cf. Hemerijck 1995, p.186). At that time, it was hard to imag-

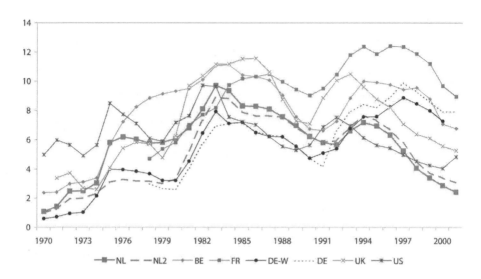

Chart 2.1   Standardised unemployment rates.
Source: OECD n.d.

ine that the corporatist *Foundation of Labour* should receive in 1997 the prestigious Carl Bertelsmann Award 'for innovative concepts and exemplary proposals for the solution of central socio-political problems'. Between 1995 and 1997 the perception of Dutch corporatism and the Dutch economy completely changed. In the mid-1990s the disparity between employment growth in the Netherlands and employment losses in some of the neighbouring countries and Sweden became obvious. This was discovered earlier abroad than in the Netherlands itself, and in 1996 and early 1997 many foreign newspapers and magazines – e.g. *Le Nouvel Observateur, Business Week, The Economist, Le Monde, Die Zeit, Wirtschaftswoche* – started to praise the Dutch economy, wrote about an employment 'miracle' and characterized Dutch corporatism as a model.

In the Netherlands these positive voices did not remain unnoticed. A landmark was Visser and Hemerijck's *A Dutch Miracle*, published in late 1997. They identified a corporatist consensus of unions and employers on wage restraint as the basis of employment growth and described the unions' attitude toward wages as a result of social learning: After the 'immobile corporatism' of the 1970s, the unions 'convinced themselves that improving the profitability of Dutch industry was a *sine qua non* for whatever strategy of recovery and job growth' (1997, p.81; originally, the learning argument was presented by Hemerijck and Van Kersbergen 1997) and that wage moderation would trigger a causal chain of higher exports, higher profits, higher investment and higher employment. According to Visser and Hemerijck, this learning found its first expression in the now famous Wassenaar Agreement of November 1982 that the authors interpreted as an agreement on exchanging wage restraint for jobs. In this interpretation '*Wassenaar* has become to Dutch industrial relations of the past 15 years what *Saltsjösbaden* (1938) was for Swedish labour relations in the 1950s and 1960s' (p. 81).

In the international discipline of comparative political economy, the book of Visser and Hemerijck fell on fertile soil. Its main messages were repeated (particularly in Scharpf 2000), and the 'Dutch model' gained a prominent place in the discussion on the 'third way' of which it became considered 'a proof' (Rhodes 1998) or even the 'Mecca' where Anglo-Saxon growth and employment rates did not involve the 'social trauma known from the US and Britain' (Levy 1999, p.243). It was also named 'the most advanced example of "competitive corporatism"' (Rhodes 2001, p.184), and the Wassenaar Agreement was presented as the exemplary case in the discussion on 'new social pacts' (Levy 1999; Hassel and Ebbinghaus 2000; Pochet and Fajertag 2000; Rhodes 2001) that identified wage pacts in traditionally corporatist countries such as Austria, Denmark and Switzerland, but also in Finland, Ireland, Italy and Portugal as the basis of GDP and employment growth. Among labour economists, Nickell and Van Ours (2000) thought favourably about the Dutch miracle linking to unemployment not employment (because of high disability levels), and explained the Dutch experience from broad institutional change especially regarding wage bargaining and unemployment benefits.

In the meantime, this discussion has faded away, and the critical voices on the Dutch politico-economic development have gained some more influence. The main points of the critical views have been that:

- the picture drawn of the Dutch development, particularly by non-Dutch authors, tends to be too idyllic because it largely ignores the huge unemployment hidden in the disability scheme (Van Oorschot and Boos 2000),
- the influence of Wassenaar should not be overestimated because drastic wage restraint started already in 1979 (SCP 2000, p.290; Delsen 2000, Salverda 2000),
- power relations have been at least as important as consensus for agreements such as that of Wassenaar (Becker 2001a),
- wage moderation by agreement is perhaps less important than supposed, while wage moderation by labour market pressures has been more important (Hartog 1999, Delsen 2000),
- increased profitability did not bring about higher investment (Kool et al. 1998),

- export growth was rather modest (Salverda 1999) and can barely be considered a basis for employment growth in a comparative perspective; exports of domestically produced goods even declined (decreasing from about 75 percent in the mid-1980s to 60 percent in the mid-1990s) (Kusters and Verbruggen 2001).
- wage differentiation and what could be called 'mortgage Keynesianism' on the basis of the spectacularly rising house prices have been strong forces of economic and employment growth (Becker 2001b) and that
- long-term wage restraint might have taken away the necessary incentives for productivity growth (SCP 2000; Kleinknecht and Naastepad 2002; in the decade to 2002 Dutch productivity growth was only half the EU average).

I will not extensively discuss whether the protagonists or the critics of the consensus and wage restraint-based miracle are right, and I will not describe the recent development of the Dutch welfare system (see for this Van der Veen and Trommel 1999). Rather, I will investigate whether the claims of success can be upheld against detailed evidence of the Dutch labour market and social policy in a long-term and comparative perspective. Do the figures justify talking about a miracle? To answer this question I will, in sections 2, 3 and 4, consider performance in each of three fields: the labour market, the economy and the social sphere, respectively. Sub-questions to be answered are: what happened to employment and unemployment, what happened to the economy (that is, where did the jobs come from?) and, finally, to whom did the jobs and incomes go? I conclude that the success of the Dutch model is strongly limited to a few aspects of the labour market. In the final section I will explore to what extent the performance relates to policies or even a 'model', focusing on the evolution of wages, and how this limited success may fit Herman Schwartz's framework of 'luck, pluck or stuck'.

Labour market performance

The view that Dutch unemployment has now reached a very low level is based on the ILO's standardised unemployment rate as published by the OECD. Since 1999 the Netherlands has had a lower unemployment rate than any of the other countries shown including the USA. The present Dutch level is also clearly below that of the second half of the 1970s. However, a few observations are worth noting (cf. Salverda 2005). First, by comparison there appears to be a relatively large incidence of 'grey' unemployment in the

Netherlands surrounding the official unemployment that fits the precise criteria of availability and intensity of job search.[3] Apparently, the precise ILO criteria are capturing idle labour supply differently in different countries. This may already close a significant part of the international unemployment gap. In addition, the OECD statistic on discouraged workers[4], which has been available since 1992, provides a level for the Netherlands that is well above that of the neighbouring countries (Belgium, France, Germany, UK) and the USA and has also remained largely unchanged throughout the 1990s in spite of the strong decline in the official Dutch unemployment rate. Consequently, there is reason to doubt whether the standardised rate adequately captures the level and the change in unemployment.

A second observation relates to the fact that the unemployment rate is calculated using the labour force as the denominator. A rapid growth of employment – although of great importance in itself – can mislead one to think that an economy is serving job demands better than before. However, with rapid job growth a decline in the unemployment *rate* may even go together with an increasing burden of unemployment. The unemployment-to- population ratio (UPOP) offers some insights here. It does not change international relativities, but it slightly increases the recent Dutch levels in comparison to earlier years, bringing the unemployment peak of the 1990s closer to that of the 1980s and the recent low levels closer to those of the late 1970s. Nevertheless, the fact still stands that the unemployment ratio fell considerably during the second half of the 1990s, more than during the 1980s from a peak that was at roughly the same level.

More important in relation to the economic process is to enquire into the nature of the employment that serves as the main fraction of the denominator of the unemployment rate. The SUR is based on head-count figures of employment and unemployment and implicitly assumes that these are of equal significance across countries. I will consider this issue in the remainder of this section. The ILO unemployment rate takes each and every job into account for its denominator no matter how small the number of hours put into work. For the Netherlands, and equally for various other European countries, this is a problematic approach both chronologically and internationally. An increasing divergence has been developing between hours worked and head-count employment as is indicated by the falling average annual hours worked per person according to OECD data. Nowhere was the decline as strong as in the Netherlands (- 26 percent). The decline was similar in the Continental countries but less in the UK (- 12 percent); in the USA the hours/persons ratio was virtually stable (- 4 percent). Two factors contributed to the European declines: shortening of the full-time working week

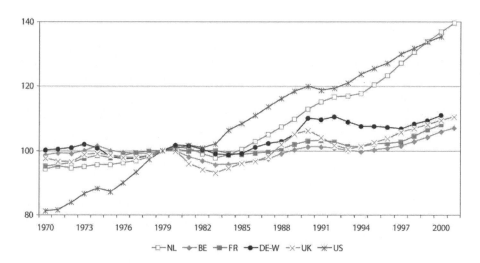

Chart 2.2 Employment (persons) growth, 1970-2001 (1979 = 100).
Source: OECD n.d., CBS 1996a

and the increasing incidence of part-time jobs. The Netherlands has witnessed an impressive increase in the number of part-time jobs, making it the world champion of part-time employment with a share of about 40 percent of all employed persons. At the same time the number of full-time jobs remained roughly stable. On balance, all employment growth was in part-time positions. The implication is that labour market performance in terms of hours worked, which is important for both the worker (income) and the employer (output) and directly relates to the economic process, can deviate very considerably from head-count employment. Also, as a labour market process, the unemployed may be looking for more substantive jobs than are actually available.

It is important for any comparison, be it over time or international, to consider this on a per capita basis as Dutch population growth was substantial and considerably exceeding that of the other four European countries of Chart 2.1 (33 versus 9 percent, 1970-2001). It should be noted that US growth was still higher at 39 percent. Chart 2.2 presents the results of combining hours worked, jobs and population.[5] Contrary to Chart 2.1, it brings Dutch employment growth much closer to European levels than to the American. The USA still registered a non-trivial growth, while for the Netherlands the employment-hours-to-population ratio did not even fully return to the level of 1979 let alone that of the early 1970s. It implies that the employment rate of the 1990s is lower compared with these earlier years. Dutch employment growth was also no longer a miracle compared either to the UK or, during most of the 1980s, to the other European countries. The superior Dutch employment performance compared with other European countries appears to be a relatively recent phenomenon limited to the second half of the 1990s – after the first foreign praise of the polder model began.

Concerning Dutch employment, it is important to note the rapid increase in the share of (contractually) flexible jobs. Their number doubled in absolute terms, and the incidence grew to 11 percent of all jobs in 2001. Both numbers and growth were strongly concentrated among youth (cf Salverda 2004b).

Finally, where did the jobs come from, from a sectoral point of view? As in many other countries the levels and shares of agriculture, manufacturing and other types of goods production fell drastically. In terms of hours per capita, the size of the goods sector was halved between 1970 and early 2000s – most of it had already happened before 1985. Service-sector jobs, by contrast, have grown substantially – private services more strongly than public.[6] Growth in terms of hours lagged substantially behind jobs, and in terms of hours worked per capita, it did not even fully make up for the goods sector's decline as total hours-employment per capita fell by 11 percent. Over time, goods and private services seemed to move together, albeit with a level difference; public services went in the opposite direction.

Summarising, Dutch labour market performance turns out to be disappointing if measured in terms of hours per capita, apparently driven by part-time and very small jobs in services with a very strong redistribution between women and youth. Public employment played a minor role.

Economic performance

The very measure of performance used in mainstream economics is GDP per capita. I will make do with that here though it should be clear from the start that the concept is seriously flawed, being unable to capture important welfare effects such as those of increasing leisure time – which may be an important element of Dutch (and European) accomplishments.

Chart 2.3 shows how GDP evolved in different countries on a per capita basis and how the Netherlands performed compared to other countries. Evidently, there were no miracles here – again. Over the three decades as a whole, Dutch economic growth was simply average, but it clearly lagged behind the other countries for a long time. Between 1975 and 1987 it fell from 5 percent above average to 10 below. Until the end of the period, it recovered

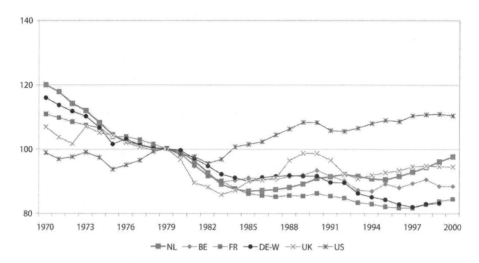

Chart 2.3 Employment-hours-to-population 15-64 growth, 1970-2001 (1979 = 100).
Source: OECD 2002b, 2003c and see Chart 2.2 for population data

only half of the lost ground. Actually, annual Dutch GDP performance relative to the other countries was better between 1988 and 1991 than in recent years, after 1994. Among the European countries the Belgian economy always performed better than the Dutch. The Netherlands did better only relative to France in the early 1990s and to Germany since then.

If measured against the total number of persons in employment, Dutch productivity growth (+ 54 percent since 1970) trailed far behind that of the other countries, including the USA, particularly since 1979.[7] The gap in GDP per person in work widened by some 20 percentage points. This is a troubling observation given the apparent competitiveness of the Dutch economy in terms of unit-labour-costs and export-price and the high ranking of its entrepreneurial climate that is found in many surveys. However, here in particular, the economic relevance of the hours approach to employment becomes clear. If, by contrast, GDP productivity is measured on the basis of hours worked (Chart 2.4), the Netherlands exactly matched the international average, roughly equal to the UK, better than the USA, and lagging behind the other continental European countries. Not totally surprising, Belgium performed best.

If we look at economic performance in more detail, we find a strong growth of exports and imports while investments and private consumption grew at lower rates much closer to GDP. However, if we again consider this from an internationally comparative point of view, we find amazingly little relation to exports, in spite of the fact that these are often considered the

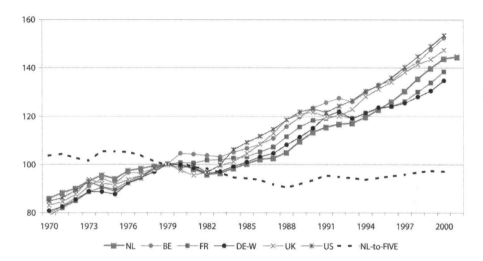

Chart 2.4   GDP growth per capita 15-64, volumes (1979 = 100).
Source: OECD 2002b, 2003c, OECD n.d., CBS 1996a, CBS n.d.

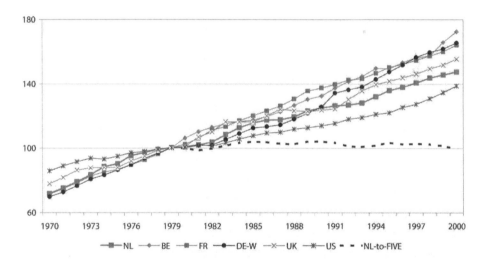

Chart 2.5   Volume of GDP per hour worked, 1970-2001 (1979 = 100).
Source: OECD 2002b, 2003c. Weighting with population, see Chart 2.2

stronghold of the Dutch economy (Chart 2.5). Other countries managed to increase the volumes of their exports per capita better. This particularly applies to the 1990s when the Dutch economy as a whole showed superior growth. Notably, the growth of Dutch imports per capita fell substantially behind. The very substantial current-account surplus that the Netherlands has maintained since the early 1980s seems to relate more to sluggish imports behaviour than to thriving exports.

Summarising, we can say there was nothing outstanding about the Dutch economic performance over the period as a whole. The performance bears out the relevance of the hours approach to the labour market. What remains is an undisputed miracle of jobs distribution, which apparently went well together with the average economic performance. It rests on the Dutch economy's exceptionally rapid growth of part-time employment. This can be valued as a means to enhance labour market participation. The optimistic lesson is that a country does not have to refrain from changing its labour market set-up because of economic constraints. The important question is who benefited from the jobs growth and the concomitant incomes, particularly while average income growth followed the international pattern.

Social outcomes

It is important to consider the composition of employment-hours worked not only at the aggregate level, as was done in Section 1. The extreme growth of part-time jobs must also bear on the structure of employment and labour supply. On balance, virtually all of jobs growth has gone to women. Their numbers in employment rose by almost 150 percent while the number of men in work grew by less than a quarter.[8] However, in terms of hours worked, female employment grew at only half the pace of their jobs while men registered no change, on balance. Finally, in terms of hours worked per capita, men lost one-quarter while women gained one-third. Though but a far cry from 150 percent, the female growth was impressive indeed. It is illuminating, however, to consider the age dimension also (see Chart 2.6). Paradoxically, since about the mid-1980s, when hours data by age first became available on a systematic basis,[9] adult men aged 25 to 64 appear to have more or less retained their position in employment hours, with a share slightly below 60 percent. Adult women and youth (ages 15-24) have divided the rest amongst them. They traded places – quantitatively speaking – and the male decline is concentrated among youth. Behind this is, first, a strong demographic decline in the young population which was unprecedented in the post-war period and more substantial than in many other countries: minus 25 percent since 1987. Second, the participation of youth in education grew significantly – as in the other countries. Finally, the gap

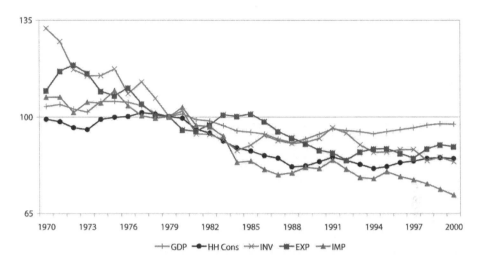

Chart 2.6 NL Aggregates relative to all five countries, volumes (1979 = 100)

Per capita 15-64, current population weights.

HH Cons = Household Consumption, INV = Investment, EXP = Exports, IMP = Imports

Source: CBS 1980ff.

between head-count and hours-count employment is most extreme for Dutch youth. Since 1987, the average adult working week remained stable at some 33 hours per week, while the youth average declined from 31 hours to less than 25. Among youth, there was an absolute decrease in full-time jobs, while at the same time the incidence of jobs with very few hours expanded to around one-third of total head-count youth employment. Together, this can explain the fact that the employment-to-population ratio of Dutch youth is the highest of the OECD area for the head count: 70 percent in 2001.[10] The very small jobs allow a substantial overlap between education and the labour market compared with the other countries.

Female employment grew primarily in private services, doubling the numbers over the 1980s and 1990s. Female public sector employment also grew but less so, and its share among women declined. However, it grew more than for men, and as a consequence women now make up the majority of the public sector work force. Absolute female numbers in goods production were low but stable, and the share dwindled (CBS 1996a). The wage distribution of female employment improved somewhat. The low-wage share among women fell, and the middle range grew (Salverda 2004a, Table 6). Female jobs growth started from an extremely low level of participation in the 1970s and together with the strong fall in the youth population, this makes the Dutch labour market outcomes a rather special case that does not seem readily transferable to other countries.

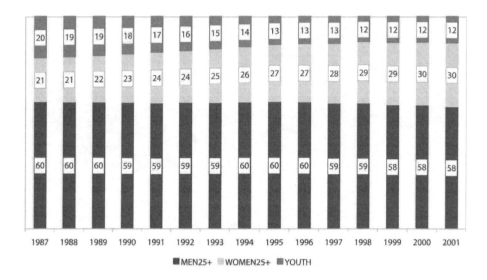

Chart 2.7   Employment-hours (%) by age and gender, all jobs, NL, 1987-2001.
Source: CBS 1980ff; cf. CBS 1996b

Households

So far, we have considered jobs in relation to the persons occupying them. For the social effects it is important to situate this in the households these individuals are part of. From 1977 to the end of the century we find an increase in the number of households in work by 1 million. Although impressive, this seems rather modest in comparison with the 2.5 million increase in the number of employed individuals. Apparently, most of the additional jobs went to households that already had a person employed. The number of two-earner households increased by 1.5 million while at the same time the number of one-earner households was more than halved, falling by one million. As a consequence of this, women in couples have completely bridged the gap in employment participation between them and singles[11] (Chart 2.7).

Complementary to the growth of two-earner households, the number of workless households doubled in size in the early 1980s and started to fall from this higher level only very gradually after 1994. Therefore, it is no surprise that the unemployment of vulnerable groups continued to be high. Youth, minorities and low-skilled persons still had unemployment rates up to four times higher than prime-age men. From an industry point of view, employment grew most in private (+ 120 percent) and public services (+ 96 percent) and fell in goods production. The picture is substantially different, however, for employment hours per capita: +30, +9 and -51 percent, respectively.

Incomes

So far, so good for the question of where the jobs went. Besides employment, income is the other important vector of social effects. Incomes are strongly related to activities in the labour market, and household income inequality increased substantially by Dutch standards. Household incomes fell across the board with the unemployment crisis of the 1980s, but households with an income from labour market activity managed to repair this damage after 1985, two-earner households in particular. Households on benefit, however, never recovered. Unsurprisingly, income inequality rose, particularly between 1985 and 1990 in the lower half of the distribution. Poverty rates felt little effect of the increase in employment over most of the 1990s. See Table 2.1.

Table 2.1   Households' real incomes, Netherlands

Real average disposable incomes x 1000 guilders (1995 value)

	All	Inactive		Active			
		All	Benefit	All	2-earner	1 earner	others
1977	47.5	34.1	36.9	53.1	60.4	53.3	40.6
1985	41.1	33.4	28.3	48.1	55.5	49.1	33.8
1997	46.5	33.6	28.3	53.9	69.2	58.1	27.4

Inequality: ratio of incomes

	1977	1981	1985	1990	1994	2000
D9:D1	2.66	2.67	2.70	3.16	3.21	3.17
D9:D5	1.74	1.74	1.76	1.79	1.78	1.75
D5:D1	1.53	1.53	1.54	1.77	1.80	1.81

Poverty rate (share in relevant population; %)

	1990	1994	2000
Low	15	16	12
Minimum	11	11	9

Source: CBS 1999a, pp. 22 and 115, 1999b, 1999c.

Policies, the model and the results

What kind of policies did the Dutch pursue to obtain these results? Are the policies part of a model, and do they relate to the above outcomes? Various policies have been very actively pursued. Five types can be distinguished:

- extensive and prolonged moderation of gross wages;
- substantial lowering of public expenditure and restructuring social security aimed at supporting wage moderation;
- permanent pegging of the Dutch guilder to the Deutsche Mark;
- flexibilisation of labour, including the growth of part-time work and of flexible labour contracts;
- policies directly aimed at lowering unemployment through job creation and specific wage subsidies were pursued.

The first three types go back to the period of the Wassenaar Agreement on wage moderation of 1982. The growth of part-time labour was a feature throughout and may have been stimulated by the general reduction of the working week, which was the other part of the deal concluded in Wassenaar. Finally, the stimulation of public job growth was politically boosted especially during the 1990s. I focus here on the first policy, wage moderation, which is the most important and also best characterises the Netherlands, and leave aside the other policies.

Wages

In the above discussion of social outcomes, I left wages out because I want to consider them here as an instrument for bringing about results, as an input for economic performance. Naturally, they are an output as well and the main contribution to incomes at that. Chart 2.8 shows the development of the Dutch real average hourly wage over time. During the 1970s it increased steeply. Immediately after 1979, however, wages fell against consumer prices, and it took until 1987 before they returned to the earlier level. The increase that happened since then has been slow, bringing about an increase in purchasing power of no more than 13 percent up to the end of the period. Note that this is on an hourly basis.

Because of shrinking hours per person, the increase in real incomes was less. If deflated by GDP prices – which may be closer to the perception of wages as a cost from the point of view of enterprise – the dip of the early 1980s was short-lived, and the subsequent increase was slightly more sub-

Chart 2.8   Employed women by household situation, 1981-2001. % of respective population
Source: CBS n.d.; OECD 2002b, 2003c; hours worked see Chart 2.2.

stantial (25 percent). In any case the rate of increase in real wages was significantly lower after 1979 than before. However, if we compare wages (GDP deflated) to hourly productivity, which amounts to wage costs per unit of production, the break is even clearer. During the 1970s earnings and productivity seemed to balance each other. Between 1979 and 1985, however, wages lagged substantially behind the productivity increase. This was followed by a ten-year period of fluctuations with a slow downward tendency that finally settled in 1995 at a stable level, 15 percent below that of the end of the 1970s.

Policies and model

Chart 2.8 also shows the average wage rate concluded in collective agreements between employers and unions. These rates provide the basis for individual pay in most cases, and average real earnings can deviate positively because of composition change and additional pay on top of the wage scales. In the absence of an increase of negotiated wages rates, individual earnings can still rise, e.g. if annual increments are paid because people age.

The rates indicate that, generally speaking, wage moderation was consciously doctored. It is the type of policy that comes closest to what could be termed the Dutch model in the sense of institutions.[12] During the post-war recovery until the early 1960s, wage developments were controlled by the government, any increase depended on its permission. This was based on a widespread consensus which was institutionalised in various platforms of negotiation between employers, employees and the government, particularly the Labour Foundation and the Social and Economic Council at the national level. In spite of the changing formal involvement of the national level with wage formation, the institutional structure as such was alive and kicking throughout the post-war period, with an occasional setback as at this moment of economic recession. During the 1990s the tradition grew even stronger that the national employer and employee confederations would meet twice annually with the government to exchange views on wages, taxes and social security. Although they do not formally negotiate, the meetings may nevertheless change the behaviour of each of the three parties involved. So formally, wage formation is free and decentralised – with the exception of the statutory minimum wage, the level of which is determined by law – but effectively, national-level recommendations may bear heavily on decentralised outcomes.

Finally liberated through labour market pressures, the earlier phase of moderation of the 1950s came to an end in the early 1960s. Wage earnings increased rapidly after 1963, but as we have seen, during the 1970s the increase was generally in line with productivity. After the strong rise in unemployment of 1980, however, moderation made an abrupt comeback, and again now, like a reflex, the first response to the current economic difficulties is to restrain wages.

The strong and prolonged wage restraint of the 1980s and 1990s is usually related to the so-called Wassenaar Agreement which was concluded under government pressure by unions and employers at the end of 1982. However, as we could see in Chart 2.8, earnings as well as wage rates started to decline in real terms already in 1980. Wage rates continued to fall after 1982 when real earnings were already increasing, albeit very slowly.

The significance of the Agreement lies elsewhere. First, at the national level, it seems that the target was not real wages as such but their relation to productivity. Although productivity already put wages at a distance before the Wassenaar Agreement, most of the divergence occurred after 1982, and the gap was never closed again. Second, the average is hiding an important sectoral difference. Not private sector wages were hit most but those of the public sector (see Chart 2.9). This is a paradox because the country's export dependency was the main argument for pursuing policies of restraint, and exports are the responsibility of the private sector. Up to 1985 public sector pay lost 15 percent of its purchasing power, and it returned to its previous

Chart 2.9   Average hourly wage in the Netherlands (1979 = 100).
Source: CBS 1996a, pp. 72 and 86, CBS n.d.

level only in the mid-1990s. By contrast, in the private sector gross earnings returned to their previous level already in 1983. Public servants' pay was nominally lowered and frozen for a long time – a unique experience in the OECD area. Apparently, also in corporatism, some are more equal than others. This approach has served to drastically cut public expenditure aimed at decreasing the gap between gross and net wages.[13] Consequently, net private sector wages have suffered less in terms of purchasing power than would otherwise have been the case, but this does not necessarily mean that net wages developed more favourably than gross because at the same time social contributions grew, e.g. for unemployment insurance.

The move against public-sector wages was complemented by the lowering and freezing of the statutory minimum wage, which plays a pivotal role in determining social security benefits. Notably, the average[14] of the elaborate Dutch system of age-related minimum wages saw its purchasing power erode as much as the American minimum wage (-28 percent, 1979-2000). In addition, we note that there was a strong age effect, as youth wage rates, minimum wages, earnings and incomes lagged very considerably behind their adult equivalents.

In the early 1990s the institutional machinery responded even more quickly to rising unemployment than in the early 1980s, again stimulated by the government. Employer and employee confederations concluded two agreements, "Breathing Space" in 1983 and "New Course" in 1994. These had immediate effects on the wage increases negotiated for new collective agreements. Almost within a year average negotiated wage increases fell from 4.5 to 0.5 percent. Although the effect on aggregate wage rates was small – and this time the public sector was treated equally – productivity leaped again ahead of earnings, thus widening the gap, which before (1989–1993) had tended to decline. This brought wages even further down relative to productivity than before (1993-1997) (Chart 2.8).

Effects

The Netherlands is often seen as the country most strongly geared to wage moderation. Chart 2.10 bears this out unequivocally: the Netherlands had the lowest level of real-wage-to-productivity during virtually all of the thirty-year period, falling to about 55 percent at the end of the period. Nonetheless, it should be noticed that similar declines occurred in the other Continental countries, but not in the UK or the USA. On balance, Germany, France and Belgium appear to have practised wage restraint in relation to (GDP) prices and productivity at a speed that is comparable to the Netherlands (see Table 2.2) but with a difference in level and timing. Apparently, the Dutch model has been copied elsewhere, plausibly under the influence of European unification – after all Maastricht is a Dutch town....

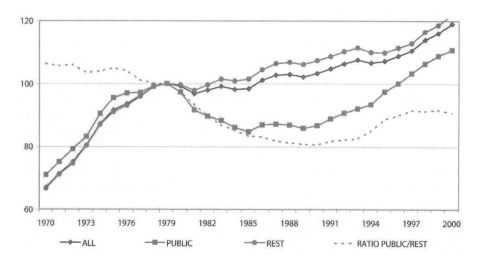

Chart 2.10 Average real hourly earnings, public sector vs rest (1979 = 100).
Source: OECD 2002b, 2003c; for compensation of employees see Chart 2.4.

Table 2.2   Real hourly wages and hourly productivity, 1979-2000

	Netherlands	Belgium	Germany (W)	France	UK	USA
Real wage	+25	+38	+48	+35	+49	+33
Productivity	+47	+57	+65	+60	+55	+39
Wage/ productivity	-15	-12	-10	-15	-4	-4

Source: see Chart 2.10

At the same time this shows that different combinations of wage increase, price increase and productivity growth can generate similar outcomes. There is more than one road leading to Rome. The Dutch restraint of the purchasing power of wages was extreme with no more than a 25 percent increase over the last two decades, but this was matched by a smaller increase in productivity, whereas in Germany, Belgium and France the two matched at a higher level. Naturally, wages and productivity are also linked through capital-labour substitution. Wage moderation may have delayed capital-labour substitution and therefore productivity growth, as suggested by the OECD (2002c, 49). For this reason the Dutch low-wage policy may ultimately turn out to be a dead-end street.

Finally, the low-wage road may also instigate a lack of demand in the national economy.[15] Private incomes feeding consumer demand depend strongly on labour incomes. It is telling that the Dutch employment success of the late 1990s had little to do with wage moderation or exports – the flagships of the model. On the contrary, the last six years were the first period since the end of the 1970s that real wage growth matched productivity growth, partly because productivity growth slowed down but mainly because real wages grew more rapidly. In addition, exports did not perform noticeably better in a comparative perspective. Paradoxically, these are the years that the Dutch economy appeared to do better. Together with the gains from capital income and soaring housing prices,[16] wage incomes have contributed to the importance of private consumption as a driving factor behind economic growth over these years (see Chart 2.7). In this context, the wage restraint may also have contributed to the immense growth of two-earner households; a second income is a feasible way to escape from the income effects of wage restraint at the household level.[17]

These outcomes oppose the Continental to the Anglo-Saxon countries where the gap between productivity and wages was much smaller, and private consumption played a much more prominent role. Apparently, there

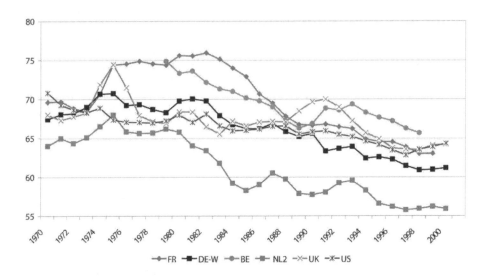

Chart 2.11 Hourly wage to GDP-productivity, % (aug2002).
Source: OECD n.d.

was more flexibility in the European economies when it came to the wages-productivity trade-off. Here we may be nearing the core of the transatlantic employment differences. It is telling that in the face of the present economic difficulties, the Continental countries – in contrast to the USA and UK – immediately seem to resort to public-sector budget cuts and wage restraint. The European Union is as much a closed economy as the USA, but amazingly little attention is paid to the self-contained part of the European economy, while the US government stimulated spending on various occasions. In a sense, the Netherlands is only the most extreme case of the European way.

Conclusion: luck, pluck or stuck?

Summarising, we can say that the Dutch political economy was extremely successful in generating more jobs. At the same time, however, in an international context its economic performance was mediocre, its productivity lagged, and consistent with this, its labour market success in terms of hours worked per capita was not particularly outstanding. Over the period 1970-2000 as a whole, hours per capita fell by 20 percent; over the shorter period since 1979, long years of jobs growth after 1985 did not entirely make up for the rapid loss of the early 1980s. This hours approach also threw a different light on the gender aspect of employment and incomes. The structure of employment moved much less quickly away from the old breadwinner model than it may seem in a head count.

Adult men roughly maintained their share in employment hours, while adult women and youth traded places. In addition, when the Dutch relative performance finally improved at the end of the 1990s, this was not related to the essentials of the Dutch model and its policies as commonly perceived, i.e. wage moderation and exports. On the contrary, strong domestic consumption growth, composed of wage growth instead of moderation, the wealth effect (Gramlich 2002) stemming from rising house prices (by 60 percent between 1996 and 2000; Sutton 2002) and the related increase in tax-favoured mortgages for consumption purposes (Becker 2001b) played a prominent role. Could it be argued that the Dutch performance relative to others could only be disappointing because it had already attained such a high level of productivity or exports? If true, this argument also suggests that the Dutch model cannot be indefinitely successful and will ultimately run out of steam. Indeed, the fact that the Dutch economy is at the low end of the European performance range during the present economic conjuncture does not really help to advertise the case.

To a certain extent this hinders applying the "luck, pluck or stuck" approach as it is difficult to apply when there is little variation. With this focus, one may also tend to overlook the costs attached to the success and the coherence of an economy where certain parts may flourish exactly because others decline. Finally, in a more detailed consideration of the Dutch evolution, "luck" seems to apply primarily to the demographic aspects of the national situation favouring success: low levels of female employment participation at the start and strong declines of the youth population later, but it may also have some relevance to the consumption growth – and stock and housing wealth behind it – in recent years. Regarding pluck and stuck, it is important to realise that the basic institutions of Dutch wage formation (Labour Foundation and Socio-Economic Council) have remained virtually unchanged since their inception after the war in spite of the many changes made at a more detailed level e.g. in the system of social security. The institutions were there for better or for worse and not unequivocally for one or the other.

Consequently, stuck applies to the institutions and basically also to the economic performance in a comparative perspective. However, the institutions' stickiness does not apply at all to the labour market revolution, in spite of the fact that the specific institutions seem more directly related to the labour market than to the economy. Would the framework of models and policies offer an alternative? In the debate about the diverging cross-national (particularly cross-Atlantic) developments in labour market performance of the 1980s and 1990s, the concept of a 'model' often appears to be the preferred vehicle for understanding, at the expense of 'policies'. The undercurrent seems to be that the institutions of the American labour market allow more flexibility to the individual actors, especially enterprise, to react to unexpected developments – the 'external shocks'. Over the period, many countries have started doubting and doctoring their models, and several country models have temporarily enjoyed international popularity during part of the period as the leading example – German, Swedish, Danish, Dutch, New Zealand's, you name it.

It is not clear-cut how the model concept relates to institutions, policies and outcomes. Certainly, models basically comprise institutions, in the sense of formal and informal rules of behaviour, but it would to be too simple to stop there. Naturally, institutions may allow, hinder or stimulate certain types of individual behaviour, but in each country both individual behaviour and institutions are also influenced by policies. In addition, models may generate particular policies automatically, e.g. wage moderation in the Dutch case, or they may do without it – not needing them because the corresponding behaviour is already there, e.g. flexible labour contracting – or they can have difficulty adopting specific kinds of policy because they conflict with its institutions. If there is no a priori relation between models and policies – as strongly suggested by the clear change of policies in the Netherlands between the 1960s, 1970s and 1980s with an unchanged model – both have to be treated separately concerning their effects, and it has to be acknowledged that good models can be thwarted by bad policies and vice versa. In addition, policies and models may serve different aims and have different scopes. All this rests on the assumption that outcomes relate to this, be it policies or a model, and to some extent that successes of the past provide some guarantee for the future. Behind it all is a belief that models and/or policies can be introduced at will and that there is sufficient room for success, in other words that the success of a (national) model is self-propelled and does not depend on the fact that the outside world is different. What if there were room for only one successful model at a time and if copying it were well nigh impossible or even detrimental to the success of the specific model? A national model may be using its international environment for its own success and leave little or no room for its successful adoption and application by other countries at the same time. In other words, would the Europeans be able to adopt the American model without causing any negative effects on that model's success in the USA? Models and policies cannot be fully studied in isolation. Finally, the concept of a model may imply more coherence than is warranted and undervalue conflicts of interest, but even in the world of models there may be no free lunch.

It is way beyond the scope of this contribution to systematically unravel the workings of the Dutch model, Dutch policies and Dutch performance. Hopefully, it will suffice to list a number of observations from the above argument that seem to call into question the mutual relationships within this three-fold complex and the flattering Dutch outcomes.

First, important and perhaps even essential ingredients of the Dutch success of job creation were the very low employment participation rate of women at the outset and the large demographic decline of youth towards the end. Evidently, these circumstances cannot be recreated at will, thus thwarting a role in repeating a similar success in the future (cf. Keese 2000, p.59).

Second, the fact that the Wassenaar Agreement actually came at the end of real wage moderation instead of starting it seems to point to ingrained individual behaviour affecting the aggregate level. The same may apply to the recent shrinking of the economy. Individual parsimony in consumer spending in favour of savings may precede analogous types of government behaviour at the national level. Perhaps the people in Europe value savings more than Americans as they are more aware of uncertainties and more strongly focused on the long term.

Also, neither the growth of part-time jobs nor that of contractually flexible jobs in the Netherlands was initiated by the institutions. Naturally, the institutions may have accommodated to developments that go on independently, without causing them.

Finally, the Dutch seemed to have achieved the best of all worlds: employment growth without increasing inequality, and even the luxury of doing it part-time! Richard Freeman (1998) sung its praise. But this is only if one overlooks the drawbacks of what is basically a second-earner model: the large amount of 'grey' unemployment, the persistent labour market vulnerability of certain groups such as the low-skilled and minorities, the strong decline in social security entitlements and incomes and the concomitant rise in income inequality, household worklessness and enduring poverty. It has partly used the public sector to bail out the economy and recently began to be confronted with the diminished attraction of public sector employment in the labour market.

In conclusion, one can say that the working of the dominant set of institutions and policies in the Netherlands is primarily adaptive and not initiating, making itself small in a big nasty world.

Notes

1 I am very grateful to Uwe Becker for his extensive comments and suggestions.

2 This notion referred to the large reserves of natural gas that purportedly led to an overvalued currency, damaging manufacturing exports and thus raising unemployment and the public deficit.

3 The European Labour Force Survey enquires into the number of people 'desiring work', that is persons who would like to work and are available but did not actively look for it during the last four weeks. In the Netherlands, their number well exceeds the official unemployment level while it is only half of that in the rest of the EU.

4 Labour market statistics portal at www.oecd.org

5 Dutch employment figures consistent with the dotted line of Chart 1 were used.

6 Part of the service-sector growth concerns outsourcing from goods production to temporary agency work.

7 This is rightly seen by some as a measure outdated in the era of part-time work (hours worked should be the denominator), but it is still popular, cf. e.g. Netherlands Bank, Annual Report 2001, p. 87.

8 Estimation based on combining two series of labour accounts (1969-1996 and the more comprehensive 1995-2001) from Dutch Statistics.

9 Rough estimation based on class means for four classes of jobs: <12 hours, 12-19, 20-35 and 35-or-more hours per week.

10 OECD 2002d, Table C. Hours-count figures seem to be well above Belgian and French but below British and German (estimated from OECD x).

11 It is an interesting and important question to what extent women expanded their labour market participation to compensate for stagnating or falling male income, but the answer is outside the scope of this contribution.

12 Cf. Hartog, 1999, 76, for the view of wage moderation as a post-war tradition.

13 The specific wage restraint has given the Netherlands the smallest public sector of the OECD area and led to important problems of quality with the public provisions and attraction of labour supply.

14 Youth minimum wages, up to the age of 22, are much lower. They were lowered on separate occasions, and 1979 employment weights were used to determine the evolution of the average minimum wage.

15 Cf. European Commission, *The EU Economy: 2002 Review*, p. 67-68 for a similar argument pertaining to the present downturn.

16 IMF, 1999, 53, was an early attempt to pay attention to rising prices of housing.

17 This shift in household incomes may have contributed to the housing prices which soared more than anywhere else. Further study of the housing market would be needed to determine the extent to which this is a 'bubble'. The holy cow of Dutch income taxation is deductibility of mortgage interest payments – this was even improved for two-earner households recently.

3   Employment and Unemployment in Denmark and Sweden: Success or Failure for the Universal Welfare Model?

Christoffer Green-Pedersen and Anders Lindbom

Introduction

During the 1970s and 1980s, Sweden became a model country for foreign observers. At times when unemployment in many other countries reached a level of more than 10 percent, Sweden kept its unemployment at golden age levels. In the beginning of the 1990s, the Swedish model collapsed. Unemployment sky-rocketed to almost 10 percent, and foreign observers lost some of their interest in the Swedish model. Denmark has experienced a reverse development. In the 1980s, the country was plagued by high unemployment. However in the 1990s, Denmark became a new model country as unemployment decreased to around 5 percent. Today, a discussion of the Danish "miracle" is taking place (Schwartz 2001 b and c, Green-Pedersen 2001 and 2003, Hemerijck and Schludi 2000, and Becker 2001c).

This chapter provides a closer look at this stereotypical picture of the two countries. The focus of the chapter is on the development of unemployment and employment in the two countries. The miracle discussion also refers to other economic indicators such as public finances, growth, and inflation, but employment and unemployment have tended to attract the most attention (cf. Scharpf 2000). We aim to do two things. First, to provide a more detailed look at the development of unemployment and employment in the two countries. Upon a closer look, how positive or negative were the developments in the 1980s and the 1990s actually? And do they match the stereotypical picture sketched above? Second, we provide an overview of socio-economic, especially labour market policy in the two countries. This includes both the historical content of these policies and the adjustment made to them in the 1990s. The aim of this second part is to search for possible explanations for the development of employment and unemployment. Explaining the actual development of unemployment and employment is difficult, but we provide some tentative conclusions.

A further reason for paying attention to the developments in the two countries is that they are both examples of a "social democratic" type of political economy (Scharpf and Schmidt 2000 and Huber and Stephens 2001a). This refers to a political economy with 1) a generous and "decommodifying" welfare state offering transfers and services based on citizenship, 2) a labour market with high levels of both public and female employment, 3) centralized wage-bargaining. In times of alleged challenges such as increased international economic integration and technological changes, the future of this model has been debated. For instance, Iversen (2000) has argued that a number of structural preconditions for the social democratic model have disappeared and that the countries need to shift to a "commodifying" social and labour market policy. Scharpf (2000), on the other hand, provides a much more positive evaluation of the social democratic model. At the very least, the Danish experience in the 1990s shows that the model is quite viable in an internationalised economy. In the conclusion, the implications for this debate on the future of the social democratic model will be discussed alongside possible lessons for other countries.

Employment and unemployment: what happened?

As a starting point, it is worth looking in detail at the development of unemployment and employment in the two countries. In the following, we shall examine a number of indicators starting in the 1980s, wherever the data are available.

Denmark

Unemployment rates are, of course, an important indicator, and the "miracle" description of Denmark in the 1990s definitely refers to the decline in unemployment. Table 3.1 shows both the standardised OECD unemployment rate and the nationally defined unemployment rate.[1] The latter indicator reports a somewhat higher level of unemployment than the former throughout the period. However, both figures show a strong decline in unemployment after 1993: from 10.1 percent in 1993 to 4.3 percent in 2001 according to standardised unemployment rates, and from 12.4 percent in 1993 to 5 percent in 2001 according to the nationally defined unemployment rate. Going back in time, the period from 1980 to 1993 has generally been one of high unemployment, but both indicators show a significant drop in unemployment in the mid-1980s, and according to the standardised figures, unemployment in 1985 and 1986 was only slightly above the 2001 level.

However, not all that glitters is gold, and the official unemployment rates can be misleading as a considerable hidden unemployment exist, involving people of working age receiving other cash benefits than unemployment benefits. Table 3.1, therefore, also presents figures for broad unemployment measured as the number of people aged 18 to 66 receiving cash benefits[2] as percentage of the broad labour force, that is employed people and people aged 18-66 receiving cash benefits (cf. OECD 1998a). In 2000, broad unemployment was 23.1 percent, so hidden unemployment is clearly there. However, the decline in unemployment after 1993 is real as broad unemployment has declined from 26.8 percent in 1994 to 23.1 percent in 2000. Yet, arguments about moving the unemployed into other schemes seem valid with regard to the period from 1993 to 1994 when broad unemployment increased from 24.8 percent to 26.8 percent while standardised unemployment decreased from 10.1 percent to 8.2 percent.

A different angle on labour market performance is to look at employment. Table 3.1 presents figures on employment level. Also from this angle, the development in the late 1990s has been quite positive. The overall employment level has increased from 71.8 percent in 1994 to 75.8 percent in 2001.[3] Table 3.1 also shows that the job growth in the late part of the 1990s started in both the public and the private sectors, but since 1998 it has, in absolute terms, mainly taken place in the private sector. Yet, whereas the private sector witnessed falling employment during the recession from 1988 to 1994, public sector employment remained unchanged, implying that the public share of total employment increased, and the private share of total employment remains lower today than it was in 1988.[4]

The question then is how to evaluate the development in Denmark in the 1990s. First of all, the miracle discourse is right in so far as the development after 1995 has been positive on all accounts. Unemployment and broad unemployment have both declined significantly, and employment has gone up. If one compares the economic upturn in the later part of the 1990s with the mid-1980s, the picture is more mixed. Unemployment has declined further in the 1990s than in the mid-1980s, especially according to the national definition of unemployment, but broad unemployment is higher today than it was in the mid-1980s and employment lower. However, the starting point for the upturn in the late 1990s was worse than the starting point for the upturn in the 1980s. Both unemployment and broad unemployment were higher in the beginning of the 1990s than they were in the beginning of the 1980s, and employment was slightly lower. Thus, from that perspective the development in the late 1990s looks more "miraculous" than the upturn in the mid-1980s.

Table 3.1   Employment and unemployment indicators for Denmark

Year	Standardised unemployment (%)	Unemployment (national definition)	Public sector employment (in thousands)	Private sector employment (in thousands)	Broad unemployment	Employment rate
1980	-	7	-	-	-	74.2
1981	-	9.2	-	-	-	74.5
1982	8.4	9.8	-	-	-	73.1
1983	9	10.5	-	-	-	73.4
1984	8.5	10.1	-	-	20,7	73
1985	7.1	9.1	-	-	20	74.4
1986	5.4	7.9	-	-	19.1	76.3
1987	5.4	7.9	-	-	19.7	77.1
1988	6	8.7	768	1876	20.7	77.5
1989	7.3	9.5	772	1849	21.6	76
1990	7.7	9.7	772	1834	21.7	75.2
1991	8.4	10.6	770	1821	22.7	74.3
1992	9.2	11.3	768	1800	23.6	73.4
1993	10.1	12.4	771	1759	24.8	72.7
1994	8.2	12.3	770	1750	26.8	71.8
1995	7.2	10.4	770	1769	26.4	72.5
1996	6.8	8.9	781	1792	25.9	73
1997	5.6	7.9	795	1812	25.2	73.4
1998	5.2	6.6	808	1834	24.4	74.1
1999	5.2	5.7	812	1854	23.5	75.2
2000	4.7	5.4	813	1874	23.1	75.6
2001	4.3	5.0	827	1892	-	75.8

Sources:
Standardised unemployment: OECD, Economic Outlook, various years
Unemployment: Statistisk tiårsoversigt
Public/private sector employment: Statistisk tiårsoversigt (National Accounts Statistics)
Employment: Statistisk tiårsoversigt (Labour Market Statistics)
Broad unemployment: Statistisk tiårsoversigt, own calculations

Sweden

Table 3.2 shows indicators on unemployment/employment parallel to the Danish ones for Sweden. No matter which indicator is chosen, the overall picture is one of very low unemployment in the late 1980s. Between 1991 and 1993, unemployment rises dramatically, and then the situation stabilises between 1994 and 1997. In the late 1990s the situation improves radically.[5]

Swedish unemployment rose much faster in the early 1990s than in Denmark, but from a lower starting point. Danish unemployment also started sinking earlier than in Sweden, but towards the end of the decade, it was sinking more rapidly in Sweden. In year 2001 standardised unemployment in Denmark was 4.3 percent, whereas it was 5.1 percent in Sweden. The picture is the same if we look at employment levels instead. Compared with Denmark, broad unemployment was very low in Sweden in 1990, only 15 percent, which probably reflects that Sweden had not experienced a severe economic crisis. When that happened in the beginning of the 1990s, the share of people who depend on public transfers for their support increased rapidly, and broad unemployment peaked at 25.2 percent in 1994. This category, however, started to decline earlier than unemployment. There has been a steady decrease in this value since 1994, and in the year 2000, it was 20.7 percent, which is lower than the Danish figure.

The number of employed in the private sector declined more quickly than the number of employed in the public sector when the crisis hit Sweden in the early 1990s. But from 1993 onwards, employment in the private sector has increased whereas it has remained relatively constant in the public sector. The share of the private sector of total employment has therefore significantly increased in comparison with 1990. Private employment in the year 2001 is actually higher than it was before the economic crisis of the early 1990s.

Another aspect of the Swedish data is that figures for employment, although very high in international comparison, probably give too positive a picture. Unlike many other countries, early retirement – or as it is sometimes called 'work-shedding' – has not been used extensively to handle the problem of older, less productive labour. However, the problem has spilled over to other public programmes, in particular sickness benefits. Figures on absence from work, which are presented in Table 3.2, are thus important for comparisons within Sweden over time. The swings in the level of absence have affected the labour market, increasing the demand for labour when absence was high and decreasing demand when absence was low. As absence has been high when the business cycle has peaked and low when it has reached the bottom, it has increased the swings in unemployment and employment. In reality, therefore, the swings in how well the labour market has been functioning are smaller than the data on unemployment and employment suggest. Whereas the difference between the highest level of employment (83.1 percent 1990) and the lowest level (70.7 percent 1997) is 12.4 percentage units, the difference is only 7.5 units when taking absence into consideration. The point is that the Swedish labour market neither functioned as well around 1990 as e.g. employment data suggest, nor performed as badly around 1997 as data suggest. As employment levels have risen

Table 3.2 Employment and unemployment indicators for Sweden

Year	Standard-ised unemploy-ment (%)	Unemploy-ment (national definition)	Public sector employ-ment (in thousands)	Private sector employ-ment (in thousands)	Sickness absence (% of popula-tion more than 1 week)	Broad unemploy-ment	Employ-ment rate
	A	B	D	E	F	G	C
1980	2	2	-	-	-	-	81
1981	2.5	2.5	-	-	-	-	81
1982	3.2	3.2	-	-	-	-	81.2
1983	3.5	3.5	-	-	-	-	81.3
1984	3.1	3.1	-	-	-	-	81.4
1985	2.8	2.8	-	-	-	-	82
1986	2.7	2.5	-	-	-	-	81.3
1987	1.9	2.1	-	-	-	-	81.7
1988	1.6	1.7	1633	2338	14.8	-	82.3
1989	1.4	1.5	1632	2393	15.1	-	82.3
1990	1.7	1.6	1652	2419	15.2	15.0	83.1
1991	3.1	3.0	1641	2351	14.4	16.5	81.0
1992	5.6	5.2	1593	2199	13.2	21.2	77.3
1993	9.1	8.2	1499	2034	11.9	24.4	72.6
1994	9.4	8.0	1392	2097	10.9	25.2	71.5
1995	8.8	7.7	1368	2170	10.8	23.8	72.2
1996	9.6	8.1	1338	2189	10.5	23.6	71.6
1997	9.9	8.0	1294	2203	10.3	22.7	70.7
1998	8.3	6.5	1308	2246	11.0	21.4	71.5
1999	7.2	5.6	1323	2310	11.0	21.3	72.9
2000	5.9	4.7	1321	2406	11.8	20.7	74.2
2001	5.1	4.0	1301	2508	12.5	-	75.3

Sources: (A) OECD, Economic Outlook, 69, 1998b
(B+C) Statistisk Årsbok 2000 (table 238) 1988-1998, 99-2000 AKU 2000, årsmedeltal
(D+E) Statistisk Årsbok 2000 (table 248) 1988-1998, 99-2000 from Margareta Henkel (SCB)
(F) AKU, various years, table 1a
(G) unemployed (www.ams.se/rdfs.asp?L=35); early retirement
(http://www.rfv.se/stat/socfakt/sjukh/forti.htm); sickness (www.rfv.se/stat/arsstat/ sjukh/sj-pag.htm); social assistance
(http://finans.regeringen.se/propositionermm/propositioner/bp02/pdf/bilaga3.pdf diagram 2.2); population 16-64 (AKU, various years).

again (75.3 percent in 2001), unfortunately the sickness absence has again started to rise. There is probably a direct link between the development of the two programmes. Most people get higher benefits being "sick" than being "unemployed" due to the low maximum benefit in the unemployment benefit scheme. At least as important is that the tightened rules for long-term unemployed have had spill-over effects, i.e. people have moved to sickness benefits instead.

CHRISTOFFER GREEN-PEDERSEN | ANDERS LINDBOM

Altogether, the actual Swedish development differs from the stylised picture presented in the introduction. Sweden was a success story in the 1980s and a failure in the first half of the 1990s, but Sweden has recovered quite well in the second half of the 1990s. Employment is still lower, and both unemployment and broad unemployment are higher than in 1990, but all figures have improved significantly since 1994.

Denmark and Sweden in international comparison

The "miracle" description of Denmark is very much based on the comparative perspective. Denmark has performed better than most other advanced welfare states in terms of employment and unemployment. Together with countries such as the Netherlands and Australia, Denmark thus constitutes a "model" country (e.g. Hemerijck and Schludi 2000, Schwartz 2001c, and Becker 2001c). However, the evaluation of Denmark depends on the country to which it is compared. As argued by Goul Andersen and Jensen (2002), there are quite a number of success stories in Europe. Not only Denmark and the Netherlands, but also Portugal, Austria, Switzerland, Norway, Ireland, and the UK have unemployment rates at the US level. Some of these countries are "special" economies like Norway and Switzerland, and Austria has experienced decreasing levels of employment during the last 20 years (Scharpf and Schmidt 2000: 342), but it is clear that it is mainly in comparison with the big European economies such as Germany, France, and Italy that the Danish development looks "miraculous". The big European economies have persistent high unemployment and have experienced declining employment.

The evaluation of the Swedish development also depends very much on the basis for comparison. Sweden has not reached its level of employment and unemployment of the 1980s, but on both accounts, Sweden in the 1980s was a unique success story. The Swedish values on employment and unemployment of the 1980s are, for instance, significantly better than the Danish ones in the 1990s. If one compares Sweden and Denmark in the year 2001, unemployment is only slightly lower and employment only slightly higher in Denmark than in Sweden, and Sweden actually has lower broad unemployment. The Swedish record in the late 1990s is also considerably better than that of all the big European countries. In summary, the actual development of unemployment and employment does not really justify the assertion that there is a Danish employment miracle and a Swedish failure when looking at the most recent data. Denmark has performed well in the later part of the 1990s, but so has Sweden. It is only compared to Sweden in 1980s that Sweden today can be considered a failure.

Unemployment and employment policies

In the above sections, the developments of unemployment and employment in Sweden and Denmark were discussed. The question then is how to explain these developments. In particular, the question is how to explain the positive development in Denmark after 1993 and also in Sweden during the last few years. It is here that lessons for other countries may be found.

Denmark

In the following, a short review of Danish unemployment policies is provided. As will become clear, there have been a number of measures directed against unemployment. However, the question is whether or not these measures in fact produced the positive development in the late 1990s. That will be discussed in the following section.

The Danish labour market policy has traditionally been passive in nature. Active labour market policies were never very well developed, as was the case in Sweden. Instead, Denmark combined liberal rules concerning hiring and firing workers with a generous unemployment benefit scheme, especially for low–income workers. Unemployment benefits were also characterised by easy access and after 1978, unending benefits (Björklund 2000).

Denmark experienced rising unemployment from the mid-1970s, but this did not lead to a change in labour market policy. Unemployment was to be combated through wage moderation and expansive fiscal policy, a strategy which failed on almost all accounts (Nannestad and Green-Pedersen, forthcoming). Especially, wage moderation proved impossible. The trade unions were radicalised around a demand for economic democracy based on central wage-earner funds and could not agree with the employer organisations on wage moderation. The government intervened three times in collective bargaining, but even that did not secure wage moderation (Due et al. 1993). The only new measure to combat unemployment was the introduction of an early retirement scheme (*Efterløn*) allowing workers aged 60 to 67 to withdraw from the labour market.

When the economic crisis was at its worst in 1982, a new Conservative-Liberal government took office, which changed macro-economic policy. The Danish currency was pegged to the German mark, the public deficit was brought under control through cuts and tax increases, and inflation fought through the abolishment of automatic indexation of wages and cash benefits. The main aim of these new measures was to fight inflation and the current account deficit. A reduction of unemployment was to come through the general improvement of the economy. This was actually what happened. The pegging of the Danish currency to the German mark brought interest rates down, and the abolition of indexation mechanisms limited wage increases, which again brought down inflation. The social partners reacted with moderate wage increases in 1983, but in the round of collective wage bargaining in 1985, they could not agree, and after a general strike, the government legislated wage moderation.

The results of the new policies came quicker than expected as the Danish economy entered an economic upturn in 1984 (Nannestad and Green-Pedersen forthcoming, Green-Pedersen 2003). As can be seen from Table 3.1, the upturn led to falling unemployment and increasing employment. Ten years before the "miracle", Denmark experienced a somewhat parallel development. However, a rising current account deficit led the government to institute measures to curb private consumption. This, together with a badly timed tax reform, killed the economic upturn. At the same time, the collective bargaining in 1987 implied huge wage increases that damaged foreign competitiveness. Denmark moved into a recession lasting until 1994.

The 1987 wage increases were interpreted as a sign that the level of unemployment reached in 1986 and 1987, 7.9 percent according to the national definition, was the level of structural unemployment, i.e. an unemployment level below this would lead to inflation (Andersen et al. 1999). This interpretation is debatable (Goul Andersen 1995). The wage increases in 1987 were initiated by the government, which allowed huge wage increases in the public sector just before an election (Nannestad and Green-Pedersen forthcoming). Real or not, the interpretation of the unemployment as mainly structural led to a change in the debate about unemployment as measures to combat structural unemployment were placed on the political agenda (Torfing 1999). However, new measures were limited before 1993. A few steps in the direction of active labour market policy were taken, but withdrawing people from the labour market continued under the Conservative-Liberal governments. The failure of the wage-bargaining system in the 1970s and several times in the 1980s also led to a "centralised decentralisation" of the Danish wage-bargaining system. Industrial-level associations of trade union and employers' organisations took over wage bargaining within limits set by the general organisations. This system delivered wage moderation at the end of the 1980s and beginning of the 1990s (Due et al. 1993).

In 1993, a new Social Democratic government took over. The Conservative-Liberal government had reduced inflation to around 2 percent and achieved a large current account surplus. The main economic problem for the new government was, therefore, unemployment. The debate about "structural unemployment" now materialised into a much stronger focus on active labour market policy (Torfing 1999). However, the new government also continued the strategy of withdrawing people from the labour market as three leave-schemes, educational, parental, and sabbatical leave, were made much more attractive and the early-retirement scheme for the 55-59 year olds (*Overgangsydelse*) introduced a couple of years before was extended to the 50-54 year olds (Loftager and Madsen 1997). Finally, the government "kick started" the Danish economy through a tax reform with expansive effects. These measures did result in falling unemployment rates, but also criticism that the unemployed had just moved into other schemes, an interpretation supported by the large increase in broad unemployment from 1993 to 1994.

The activation line has been continued and in several ways also intensified during the 1990s. Today, activation is compulsory for all unemployed persons after 1 year of unemployment, whether they receive unemployment benefits or social assistance, and young people are activated even earlier. However, the strategy of withdrawing people from the labour market has been changed. In 1995, the unemployment scheme was tightened significantly, and both the sabbatical leave and the early retirement scheme for the 50-59 year olds (*Overgangsydelse*) were closed for entrance. This new line has been continued by further tightening of the unemployment scheme and a significant retrenchment of the early retirement scheme for the 60-67 year olds (*Efterløn*) in 1998. In a more indirect way, the government also achieved a significant reduction in new cases of disability pensions (Green-Pedersen 2002). Increasing the supply of labour thus became a main objective for the government, which ruled until the very recent election, and is a policy likely to be continued by the new Conservative-Liberal government. After the "centralised decentralisation", the Danish collective bargaining system continued to deliver wage moderation during the 1990s (Schwartz 2001b, Andersen et al. 1999). However, the economic success in the late 1990s did put the system under pressure. In the round of collective agreements in 1998, the compromise reached was voted down by members of the trade unions, resulting in a general strike. This strike ended with a law which was more generous that the previous compromise.[6] In other words, the "no" from the trade union members had paid off, and this could be seen as a threat to the system of collective bargaining. However, the following round of negotiation in 2000 resulted in moderate wage increases without much trouble (Madsen et al. 2001).

Sweden

For a long time, the leading economic theory of the Swedish labour movement was the so-called Rehn-Meidner model. It called for an active labour market policy, a restrictive finance policy and a solidaric wage policy. The role of labour market policies was to fight the unemployment that resulted from the restrictive finance policy that kept the general level of demand in the economy down and the solidaric wage policy that kept wages high for workers in low-productive firms and sectors and therefore necessitated economic restructuring. Labour market policy helped to move workers from firms and sectors that could not handle the economic pressure to expansive firms, sectors, and regions of the country.

The main characteristic of Swedish labour market programs is and has been that active programs be more important than passive. In 1988 for example, the expenditure on active policies was twice the level of passive support, whereas in Denmark costs for activation were only a quarter of the expenditure for income supports (Torfing 1999, p. 13). The goal of labour market programs has been to make people participate in the labour market. This implied relatively strict demands on the unemployed. Demands in terms of geographic and professional mobility were made, and unemployed persons who did not comply risked losing their support (Furåker 1976, p. 111 f.). Large resources were also used to organise courses to re-qualify people to the ever-changing demands of the labour market.

The Swedish labour market seemed to work incredibly well in international comparison during the 1970s and 1980s. Unemployment was around 2 percent, whereas it approached 10 percent in many other countries within the OECD. This was often seen as an effect of active labour market programs (Rothstein 1996, p. 75). The Swedish model was, however, experiencing problems already in the 1970s and 1980s. The social partners did not manage to accomplish wage restraint, with declining international competitiveness as a result. This forced governments of different colours to use devaluations in order to restore competitiveness. In 1982 the social democrats made a devaluation of 16 percent, but by the late 1980s its benefits had been eaten up by insufficient wage restraint and low productivity growth. In the 1980s Sweden oscillated between centralised and decentralised forms of wage bargaining, but the general tendency was one of decentralisation. In the absence of peak-level control, unit labour costs rose much faster than in the rest of the OECD (Iversen 1999, pp.8, 190). The government, however, shares the responsibility for this. It deregulated the credit markets in 1985 when there were still generous tax deductions for consumer interest payments, and this fuelled an already overheated economy, making wage re-straint impossible (Stephens 1996).

Around 1990, open unemployment was about 1.5 percent, and the economy grew about 2.5 percent per year. The state budget was showing a surplus. But there were warning signs: inflation was around 7 percent, and wages rose by almost 10 percent. The trade deficit was around 2 percent of GNP. Inflation and wage raises had damaged Sweden's international competitiveness. Nevertheless, the shift in economic fortunes was both swifter and more dramatic than anyone had imagined. By the end of 1993, open unemployment had risen to almost 9 percent, and the economy had showed negative economic growth of about 2 percent for three years. The state budget showed a huge deficit (about 17 percent of GNP), and state debt was growing rapidly (Prop. 2000/01:100, appendix 5).

Unlike earlier crises, no attempts were made to accommodate cost and demand shocks this time. Instead, governments of both colours inadvertently made policies that had strong pro-cyclical effects. As the economy entered recession in 1990, a tax reform reduced the tax rate on capital income, producing a substantial rise in real after-tax interest rates. As a result, households increased savings and diminished consumption at a point in time when the economy was already in recession (Stephens 1996). Moreover, both the bourgeois government (1991-94) and the social democratic opposition invested a lot of their credibility in keeping a fixed exchange rate. After turmoil on the financial markets, however, they had to let the Swedish krona float in 1992, and it lost approximately 30 percent of its value.

Yet, again the development took a surprising turn. Around the year 2000, Sweden had had six years of economic growth averaging 3 percent a year. Unemployment and inflation had decreased, the state budget showed a surplus, and the debt had decreased for a number of years. There was also a trade surplus of more than 2 percent of GNP (Prop. 2000/01:100, appendix 5). The depreciation of the currency had with time restored competitiveness for the Swedish industry. The arrival of mass unemployment in Sweden did not lead to a major shift in the measures to combat unemployment. Active unemployment programmes were expanded dramatically, and at one point 5.3 percent of the labour force was in such programmes. Sweden also experienced some welfare state retrenchment, but the fundamental characteristics of its welfare model survived (Lindbom 2001). Unlike Denmark, Sweden has in practice – although not formally – still unending unemployment benefits. The strategy of the Swedish governments has been to try to re-establish wage moderation, public sector surpluses and then to let the economic upturn restore a low level of unemployment. Wage moderation failed in the mid-1990s when the export industry experienced dramatically rising profits due to the depreciated currency, but subsequent rounds in 1997-98 and 2001 have been calm and the increases moderate. There has been a renewed acceptance that the wage settlement in the manufacturing sector serves as a norm for the rest of the labour market. Employers and unions in the industrial sector agreed to set up a private mediation institute, which works as a voluntary substitute for incomes policy free of state intervention. A similar public institute was set up a couple of years later (Elvander 2002).

Policies and outcome – Is there a link?

The question remaining is which role did different political initiatives to combat unemployment and increase employment actually play. Establishing the link between policies and outcomes is not easy, but some tentative conclusions seem possible. The following starts with Denmark, focusing on the explanations for the "miracle" in the 1990s, and then goes on to the Swedish development.

With regard to the Danish miracle, it is evident that the economic upturn in the 1990s by itself has been an important factor. The fact that Denmark experienced a parallel development in the 1980s shows that a significant part of unemployment in Denmark in the early 1990s was not structural but simply due to the economic recession.[7] In other words, one important element behind the Danish "miracle" in the late 1990s was that the social democratic-led government was very successful in first "kick-starting" the economy after gaining power in 1993 and then bringing it to a soft landing around 1998 when an overheated economy was threatening (cf. OECD 2002e). This was where economic policy failed in the 1980s (Nannestad and Green-Pedersen forthcoming), and the more successful management in the 1990s can be explained by developments within Danish party politics (Green-Pedersen 2003).

A very important aspect of government influence on the business cycle is via regulation of the housing market. Part of the reason why the economy went into recession from 1988 to 1994 was that the tax reform in 1987 significantly reduced the tax deductibility of interest payments on mortgages. The upturn in the mid-1980s had caused rapidly rising housing prices, but the tax reform led to falling housing prices, and many homeowners became technically bankrupt as the market value of their houses was lower than their mortgage debt. When the government "kick-started" the economy in 1993, a very important element was thus directed towards the housing market. Government changes to the rules concerning refinancing of mortgages implied that homeowners could benefit from falling interest rates by refinancing their mortgages. At the same time, the maximum maturity was extended from 20 to 30 years. This meant a considerable boost to private consumption. The soft landing of the economy in 1998 was also achieved by reducing the tax deductibility of interest payments on mortgages. Compared to the late 1980s, the reduction in 1998 was more moderate. At the same time, new types of mortgages with flexible interest rates have become widespread, allowing many homeowners to benefit from very low short-term interest rates in recent years, so a meltdown of the housing market like that in the late 1980s has been avoided. In a country with extensive homeownership such as Denmark, rules concerning mortgages, interest rates and housing prices play a very important role in private consumption and, through this, also in employment. Thus, in both the 1980s and 1990s housing prices and employment have followed each other closely (cf. OECD 1999a, chap 4).

In Denmark unemployment has declined further in the 1990s, especially if measured by the national definition and from a higher level than in the mid-1980s. Denmark has not followed the more radical suggestions of the OECD (e.g. 1994) such as lowering minimum wages, but it has followed other suggestions to reduce structural unemployment. This includes retrenchments and tightening of unemployment benefits and other cash benefits and the introduction of active labour market policies. The OECD itself (2000a, 66-86), but also others (Andersen et al. 1999, pp.8-17 and Torfing 1999), have attributed the decline in unemployment to these structural reforms, therefore.

Yet, the argumentation is only based on correlation evidence: unemployment declined after the introduction of active labour market policies and other measures. The question is not an either/or, but rather how much effect the reforms have had compared with the general economic upturn. Different evaluations of active labour market measures such as job training, educational offers, and subsidised employment all show quite limited effects (Larsen forthcoming and Westergaard-Nielsen 2001), and Rosholm (2001) even finds that they lead to a smaller search effort and thus fewer people finding jobs. Other elements of labour market policies in the 1990s such as retrenchments of unemployment benefits may have been more effective. One can, for instance, point to the fact that youth unemployment declined sharply after the early and forced activation of people below 25 in both the unemployment benefit scheme and social assistance (Björklund 2000). However, in comparative perspective, Danish unemployment benefits are still quite generous (Finansministeriet 1998).

Altogether, there are strong indications that the economic upturn played quite a large role. According to this interpretation, unemployment declined further in the 1990s than in the mid-1980s simply because the economic upturn was governed much better by the government. The new wage-bargaining system has probably also been helpful in avoiding a repetition of the 1987 wage feast, which, however, was just as much politically initiated as a result of the old wage-bargaining system. The effects of structural reforms cannot, of course, be neglected. In relation to, for instance, broad unemployment, the closing of several of the schemes introduced in the beginning of the 1990s which allowed people to withdraw from the labour market has been important. However, there is reason to be sceptical about the very simple interpretations connecting the structural reforms, especially the introduction of active labour market policies, with declining unemployment.

The development of the Swedish labour market has, of course, been greatly affected by the varying fortunes of Swedish industry. Also in this case, it is hard to evaluate the importance of active labour market programmes. As mentioned above, it is tempting to attribute the very low Swedish unemployment in the 1970s and 1980s to the active labour market policies, but again this is merely a correlation argument. What is clear is that these policies faced a totally new challenge during the 1990s: mass unemployment. This made the policies more focused on quantity than quality in order to stop people from being permanently excluded from the labour force, but meant that policies became much less effective as measures to make the unemployed attractive on the labour market. The proportion of people who had found work 6 months after participating in active labour market programmes declined from 74 percent in 1989 to 25 percent in 1993 when it was at its lowest (Prop. 1999/2000:98, p. 15). The effectiveness can, of course, be expected to be lower when there is no real demand for labour. However, it is likely that the active labour market policy helped to make the dramatic increase in employment in 1998-2000 possible by stopping people from getting permanently excluded from the labour market. An indicator of this is that the number of long-term unemployed has declined dramatically. Thus, the Swedish experience indicates that active labour market policies are no miracle cure against unemployment. They cannot stop huge swings in the business cycle from affecting employment. But on the margin they can affect the structural level of unemployment and help the labour force to adapt to changing economic circumstances.

In Denmark the shift from Keynesian policies towards moneratist policies occurred earlier, was more gradual and better timed than in Sweden where the change came abruptly in the early 1990s. Therefore, although the

Swedish tax reform came only a few years later and in spite of it per se having the same consequences as in Denmark (lowering the value of deductions for mortgage costs), it occurred in a different economic environment. The unexpected German reunion made international interest rates soar, and the value of the Swedish crown lacked credibility in the eyes of the booming international financial markets, making Swedish interest rates even higher than international ones. For multiple reasons, therefore, the Swedish economy experienced an economic shock as real interest rates rose dramatically, causing the real estate market to plunge, leading to a crisis in the banking sector and an even more restrictive credit market. Domestic demand fell as a result, and this occurred on top of an international economic recession. Partly because of bad luck, the transitional problems of going from a high-inflationary economy to a low-inflationary one were, therefore, much bigger in Sweden than in Denmark in the 1990s. But today, the economic structures are highly similar, and it is not surprising that the levels of unemployment and employment are converging, too.

It deserves mentioning, however, that Denmark and Sweden have different economic structures in some respects (Benner and Vad 2000). Sweden has a relatively large industrial sector with some large corporations, for a small country. It has furthermore been exporting raw materials, in recent years particularly wooden products. In comparison with Denmark, Sweden has also been relatively dependent on sensitive export markets and a few companies. Finland is a country with a similar economic structure, and it was also particularly affected by the international economic downturn in the early 1990s, even more so than Sweden due to the simultaneous collapse of its trade with the Russian Federation (cf. Stephens 1996). The point is that it is likely that certain characteristics of the Swedish economy made it more vulnerable than other countries to the international economic downturn. Macro-economic policies do not alone determine the shifting economic fortunes of different countries.

Conclusions

This chapter has discussed whether the stylised picture of Denmark as a miracle and Sweden as a failure in terms of labour market performance in the 1990s is in fact true when examining the most recent data closely. The Danish performance was indeed positive. Whether it constitutes a miracle depends on one's definition of a miracle, but compared with the big European countries, the Danish performance does look quite impressive. When including the most recent years, the Swedish performance did not match the "failure" picture. In the year 2001, the Swedish labour market performance was only marginally worse than the Danish one, and it is only if one compares Sweden with its success in the 1980s that one can describe Sweden as a failure. A comparison with many of the big European countries could lead to a "miracle" description as well. If one adds to this that income distribution in the two countries is still among the most equal in the world (Fritzell 2001), it is tempting to speak of a miraculous universal welfare model.

However, the world is not so simple, of course. Both Denmark and Sweden have significant problems qualifying the miracle picture. For one thing, even though they have low unemployment, broad unemployment figures indicate that they share with many other European countries the problem of a considerable part of the workforce being on cash benefits, and even though broad unemployment has declined in recent years, it is still higher in both countries than it was before the economic crisis in the early 1990s. If one adds to this that the high tax levels lead to an extensive black economy, that the labour market is highly gender-segmented with women dominating the public service sector, and that unemployment rates for immigrants in Scandinavia are higher that in many other European countries, it is obvious that wonderland does not exist. Yet, the developments in both Denmark and Sweden are positive enough to warrant the question of what might other countries learn from them?

However, simple lessons to learn from the success of the two Scandinavian countries are difficult to find. For instance, both countries today invest heavily in active labour market policies, but it is difficult to document that it is having a strong effect. For instance, it could not prevent Sweden from experiencing mass unemployment in the early 1990s. At best, it seems that such policies make the labour force well prepared for economic upturns and to prolong upturns by avoiding situations where there is an acute shortage of certain types of labour at the same time as there is a high level of general unemployment.

One important factor behind the employment levels in Scandinavia is undoubtedly the service welfare state with its many public sector jobs (cf. Scharpf 2000). However, introducing such as system in other countries would require significant tax increases, for which few countries seem prepared. In searching for policy lessons from the Danish performance in the late 1990s, Scharpf (op. cit) also points to the high level of tax financing of the Danish welfare state and limited protection against being fired combined with generous unemployment benefits. However, Sweden has more financing through social contribution and more extensive protection against being fired, so the Swedish comeback in recent years makes it less obvious that these features are the key to the Danish success.

The – perhaps somewhat disappointing – conclusion seems to be that simple lessons from success stories are hard to find. As argued by Goul Andersen and Jensen (2002), if one looks at the small European countries, there seem to be quite a number of paths towards positive labour market performance, and they seem to have few things in common. In a way, this conclusion fits the idea of "varieties of capitalism" which has become quite influential within political economy (cf. Hall and Soskice 2001). Welfare states, labour market structures and more general economic structures fit together, and it is difficult to import just one element. At the general level, there is the distinction between liberal and organised market economies, with most European countries belonging to the latter group. However, within the organised market economies, there are considerable differences between, say, the German and Danish political economy (cf. Huber and Stephens 2001a). Therefore, simply importing some elements of the Scandinavian political economies will probably not solve the problems of, for instance, Germany.

With regard to the Danish case, Schwartz (2001b) has argued that it needs to be understood as a combination of luck, i.e. fortunate changes in the environment, pluck, i.e. strategic adaptation to the environment, and stuck, i.e. endogenous changes which happen to be advantageous. Looking at both Denmark and Sweden, it is evident that the overall macro-economic policy is a key factor in explaining the development of both employment and unemployment. Thus, the stable macro-economic policy that has been pursued in Denmark after 1993 is a key factor in explaining the "miracle", just as the fumbling policies in the 1970s were an important reason for the economic crisis. In the Swedish case, the meltdown of the Swedish economy in the early 1990s was much more the result of a failed macro-economic policy that an indication that a Scandinavian type of welfare state was no longer possible in a global economy (Huber and Stephens 1998). Once Sweden got its macro-economic policy back on track, the economy recovered quite quickly at the end of the 1990s. Whether this should be characterized as pluck or stuck is a matter of interpretation. As Sweden experienced in the early 1990s, the punishment from capital markets for a failed macro-economic policy is severe, so there are good strategic reasons for a sound macro-economic policy.[8] However, if one looks at Denmark and Sweden in the 1950s and 1960s, the macro-economic policies resemble the ones around today, including, for instance, budgetary surpluses, so one could also interpret this as stuck, i.e. a return to old practices. The shift towards active labour market policies in Denmark looks very much like "pluck", whereas the Swedish continuation of such policies is a case of "stuck". Yet, as argued above, the importance of supply-side measures seems less clear.

As described in the introduction, the viability of a social democratic type of political economy has been debated intensively in the light of a changing economic environment. When looking at the recent developments in Sweden and Denmark, the optimistic evaluation of, for instance, Scharpf (2000) seems to gain the most support. Even in a changed economic environment, both Denmark and Sweden have a much better labour market performance than most European countries. The optimism on behalf of "the Social Democratic model" expressed by Huber and Stephens some years ago (1998), which was partly based on the argument that bad economic management played an important role in the Swedish case, thus seems confirmed.

Others such as Iversen have argued that reforms of the Scandinavian welfare states in the direction of decentralised wage-bargaining, non-accommodating monetary policy and a less decommodifying welfare state were necessary. The two first changes have taken place in both Denmark and Sweden,[9] but even though some welfare-state retrenchments have taken place, their welfare states have preserved their fundamental characteristics (Lindbom 2001, Green-Pedersen 2002). Rather than lowering wages for unskilled labour to allow a private service sector to expand, the two countries have chosen to try to upgrade the skills and thereby the productivity of the unemployed.

The Scandinavian model is, however, not without future problems. For instance, it is an open question whether the more decentralised wage-bargaining systems can continue to secure wage moderation when unemployment is low, and the labour force is shrinking for demographic reasons. A further problem is, of course, the high levels of taxation necessary to fund the welfare state. It requires a willingness of Scandinavian citizens to accept such high levels of taxation and has negative side-effects such as an extensive black economy and diminished incentives to work. Finally, as mentioned before, Denmark and Sweden also have an extensive hidden unemployment problem, which has only been somewhat reduced by the economic upturn in the late 1990s. In other words, each recession seems to make this problem worse, and in the Scandinavian model where large tax payments are necessary for the service welfare state, paying cash benefits to large groups is problematic. The task for Scandinavian governments is, therefore, to use the macro-economic policy to avoid economic meltdowns as Sweden experienced in the early 1990s.

Notes

1 The standardized unemployment rate is comparable with that of other countries. It is based on the ILO definition of wanting, seeking and being available for a job, and the figures are derived from surveys. The national defined unemployment rate is based on the people having registered as unemployed at the national employment service (Andersen 2002). For most countries these figures are quite similar, but in Denmark the standardized unemployment rate underestimates unemployment (op.cit.).

2 People receiving student allowance and maternity benefits are not included.

3 The figures are not adjusted for part-time work, implying that the figures underestimate the increase in employment as part-time work decreased significantly in Denmark in the 1990s (Andersen 2002).

4 The figures on public and private sector employment are based on the national account. This is a data set which best allows separation of public and private employment. Unfortunately, comparable data are not available before 1988. The figures on total employment are drawn from the register-based labor market statistics, which goes further back in time, but is more difficult to break down into public and private employment. The two sources deviate slightly in the numbers for total employment.

5 Unlike Denmark where the nationally defined unemployment rate was somewhat higher than the standardised unemployment rate throughout the period, the situation in Sweden after 1993 is the opposite. The standardised unemployment rate is higher than the nationally defined unemployment rate. The reason is that nationally defined unemployment does not include people in the active labour market programmes that are so characteristic of Swedish labour market policies. This means that Swedish national data are not very useful for international comparisons, as they systematically underestimate real unemployment.

6 The government was under pressure as the strike went on just before the referendum on the Treaty of Amsterdam. Legislating wage increases at the same level as the compromise might result in No votes at the referendum as No votes could be seen as a vote against the government.

7 The Danish system with limit protection of workers against being fired but generous unemployment benefits can be expected to result in more fluctuation in unemployment. It is easy to fire people in bad times, but that also makes it more attractive to hire them in good times.

8 As argued by Mosley (2000), financial markets pay close attention to variables such as public deficits and inflation, but when governments have control of such basic macro-economic indicators, financial markets do not punish governments for having, for instance, a high level of taxation.

9 However, the degree of decentralisation of wage bargaining in Denmark is debated (see Wallerstein and Golden 2000).

4   The Evolution of the Finnish Model in the 1990s: From Depression to High-Tech Boom

Jaakko Kiander

Introduction

Finland has recently been much admired due to economic success. Finland has been in the news because of high rankings in competitiveness, technology, education and economic growth.[1] The success has largely been embodied in the growth of the Nokia group and ICT sector. Yet the economic boom and the success of the Finnish high tech industries are a relatively new phenomenon, starting from the mid-1990s. In fact, the years of good economic performance were preceded by an exceptionally deep recession in the beginning of the 1990s. At that time, the Finnish GDP shrank by 10 percent in 1991-93, and employment decreased by 20 percent. As a consequence, the unemployment rate rose from 3 to 17 percent between 1990 and 1994.

However, the economic crisis and the rise of unemployment turned out not to be permanent. Instead, the Finnish economy started a strong recovery, and unemployment fell during the latter half of the 1990s by 7 percentage points. Economic growth was fast, too, averaging 4 percent in 1994-2000. In 2001-03 the unemployment rate stabilised at the 9 percent level, mainly due to the recession of the European economy. The employment rate, however, was clearly higher than the European average, and the Finnish GDP per capita exceeded the EU average. It is also worth noticing that although the cyclical downturn increased unemployment throughout Europe in 2002-03, that did not happen in Finland.

This chapter discusses the roots of the crisis of the Finnish economy, and the factors which helped it to recover and to create the technology-driven growth of the last decade. Finland was by no means the only country experiencing a significant drop in unemployment and a revival in employment towards the end of the 1990s. Recent experience shows that numerous countries have been able to reduce their unemployment rates significantly, and more than anyone relying on earlier estimates of high structural unemployment would have predicted. These countries include Sweden, Denmark, Ireland, the Netherlands and Spain. In these countries employment has improved more than anyone relying on earlier estimates of high structural unemployment would have predicted. It is also noteworthy that this improvement took place without any deep labour market reforms – or at least it is hard to find evidence of such path-breaking institutional changes.[2]

How has that been possible in the case of Finland? The most obvious answer is rapid economic growth. After all, some kind of rebound in growth rates should not have even been surprising given the very deep and deflationary recession of the early 1990s.

Many commentators and analysts have been inclined to see the high unemployment and related underemployment as evidence of structural weaknesses typical to European welfare states – arising from the disincentives inherent in the European social model and overly regulated labour markets. It has been claimed repeatedly by e.g. the OECD and many others that the high unemployment of many European countries is structural by its nature and hence requires a certain set of reforms in order to be cured. Perhaps the most magisterial and exhaustive presentation of this evidence was provided by the 1994 OECD Jobs Study. Since then, the OECD has repeatedly emphasised the importance of incentive-improving structural reforms in its economic analysis as a necessary precondition of sustained improvement in employment. The set of proposed reforms usually includes cuts in taxes and benefits and labour market deregulation. It is commonplace that such proposals include only supply-side measures and exclude all references to the need for aggregate demand stimulus.

In light of the Finnish experience, such a uniform view of sclerotic European economies and rigid labour markets does not entirely fit the facts. The main conclusion of this chapter is that the institutional reforms (or the absence of them) seem to have played only a minor role in the emergence of unemployment and in the subsequent employment revival in Finland in the 1990s. In addition to the breakthrough of ICT technologies, more traditional macroeconomic factors like changes in monetary policy and exchange rate and pro-cyclical fiscal policy may have been of great importance. It is likely, too, that the fact that employment has not fully recovered, notwithstanding the rapid economic growth, can be largely explained by using the same macroeconomic factors. The surge in productivity and the rapid upgrading of the industrial structure which took place in the 1990s were changes that are harder to explain by traditional macroeconomics. They can be viewed as a result of a more complex process where long-term development of the national innovation system, technological breakthroughs and industrial change induced by 'creative destruction' were important components.

Despite economic shocks and industrial restructuring, Finnish political governance and corporatist institutions remained relatively stable. Like before political decision-making in the beginning of the new century was still largely based on national consensus building. The structures of the welfare state survived the fiscal crisis though the welfare state was forced to go through numerous small and incremental changes, which reduced many entitlements. The central labour market institutions – strong trade unions with high unionisation rate, and centralized incomes policy – remained almost intact.

The background of the Finnish miracle: the economic crisis of the 1990s

Eurosclerosis avoided in the 1980s

In the 1980s Finland was known among experts[3] as a small and relatively rich EFTA country with advanced welfare systems and corporatist labour market institutions. At that time, EFTA was a free-trade association of half-a-dozen small non-EEC European countries.[4] That group seemed to be immune to the rise of unemployment and related economic and social problems experienced elsewhere in Western Europe (or EEC countries) at the same time.

In the 1980s the unemployment rates in Finland and in other EFTA countries were among the lowest in the OECD, and the employment rates were the highest – the small countries seemed to be immune to the economic problems of the larger European countries (Katzenstein 1985). In the 1970s and 1980s unemployment rates rose almost continuously in the member countries of the EEC, while unemployment in the Nordic EFTA countries fluctuated between 2 and 6 percent without any serious upward trend. Finland together with the other EFTA countries were able to escape the perils of recession and mass unemployment plaguing most other European countries.[5]

Finally, that situation changed. After a long period of rapid economic growth[6] and almost full employment, the Finnish economy entered an unexpected and exceptionally deep economic recession in the beginning of the 1990s. To some extent, the same happened also in the USA and in the Western European countries, but in Finland the crisis was much more severe than elsewhere. In the case of Finland, one may even talk about a 'depression', because the crisis resembled very much the Great Depression of the 1930s.

Table 4.1   Summary of the cycles of the Finnish economy in 1978-2000

Period	Economic cycle	Labour market	Economic policy
1978-1985	Period of balanced growth with declining inflation rate	High employment	Regulation of financial markets, public sector growth
1986-1989	Period of unbalanced rapid growth	Full employment with wage inflation	Financial market deregulation
1990-1993	Years of economic crisis	Mass unemployment	Collapse of exchange rate regime
1994-2000	Period of export-oriented rapid growth and structural change with stable prices	Rising employment with wage moderation	Fiscal consolidation, tax reforms, EU and EMU membership
2001-2004	Cyclical downturn in export markets, strong domestic economy	Stable employment, slowly decreasing unemployment with continued wage moderation	Fiscal expansion through tax cuts and increased infrastructure investment

Financial market deregulation and the creation of a bubble economy

The Finnish economic crisis of 1990-93 was preceded by a debt-financed boom in the latter half of the 1980s (the different periods of economic growth are summarised in Table 4.1). That, of course, was not exceptional. Most OECD economies boomed in 1987-89, and some of them experienced speculative bubbles with rising asset prices. Well-known examples are the Japanese economic 'miracle' in the 1980s and the house price bubble in the UK, both of which were followed by recessions.[7]

In Finland and Sweden the bubble of the 1980s was caused by a credit expansion initiated by financial market deregulation. Before the liberalisation, the banking sector and credit markets were tightly regulated in Finland, and most households faced liquidity constraints – i.e., they were not allowed to borrow as much they would have liked. When these constraints were lifted in 1986 – as a part of an international wave of deregulation – household debt started to climb up quickly. Loans were used to finance purchases of houses and durable goods. Debt service was not expected to cause problems, because the real after-tax interest rates of households were expected to remain low due to the modest level of nominal interest rates, relatively rapid earnings growth and tax deductions. The indebtedness of the corporate sector increased rapidly, too. At that time, corporate taxation favoured debt finance, and firms – especially in construction and service sectors – were eager to invest. As a result, private sector debt and asset prices doubled within a short period (1986-1989). The bubble was good to the real economy. It helped to speed up economic growth, and to achieve full employment. The Finnish employment rate was record high at 74 percent in 1989-90.

The boom ended in 1990 when international interest rates started to increase. Domestic interest rates in Finland were linked to German interest rates through exchange rate targeting. The central banks of all Nordic countries had a policy to maintain their exchange rates almost fixed vis-à-vis other European currencies, which were linked to the Deutschmark.[8] As a consequence, the Nordic interest rates could not be lower than those in Germany. Additionally, any uncertainty about the sustainability of the fixed exchange rate policy would cause an additional rise in interest rates. Such worries started to increase in 1989. Due to inflation, both Finland and Sweden were losing their competitiveness, which reduced export growth. At the same time, a booming domestic economy raised the demand for imports. As a result, the current account deficit widened. In the Finnish case a special problem was caused by the disintegration of the Soviet Union, which reduced Finnish exports to that country.[9]

The recession: exchange rate targeting, interest rate shock and debt deflation

The crisis was closely related to the policy regime of exchange rate targeting. The attempt to maintain fixed parity with the Deutschmark finally turned out to be unsustainable. However, before that, the Bank of Finland (and the Swedish Riksbank) tried to defend the exchange rate by raising the domestic interest rates. This led to a three-year period (1989-92) of very high real interest rates. In an economy where households and firms had accumulated large debts, this interest rate shock was disastrous. As can be seen from Figure 4.1,[10] the interest rate shock was huge. Within two years the real short-term interest rate went up from 2 to 12 percent

With higher than expected interest rates, the debt-financed boom came to an end. The economic growth stopped in 1990, and in 1991 the economies of Finland and Sweden begun to shrink. The boom was followed by a bust – a three-year period of high interest rates, falling output and collapsing asset prices, debt deflation[11], financial and banking crisis and currency crisis.[12] High interest rates in a debt-ridden economy effectively constrained private

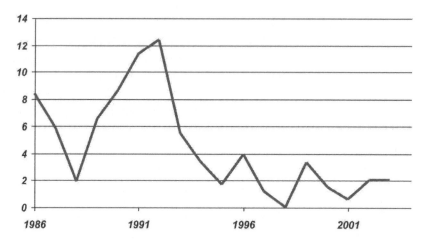

Figure 4.1 Real start-term interest rate

demand. Firms and households which had a few years earlier accumulated lots of debt now faced liquidity constraints and were forced to sell their assets. That fuelled further falls in asset prices. Within four years the Helsinki stock market index fell almost 70 percent, and house prices decreased by half. Falling asset prices caused negative equity and balance-sheet problems to indebted households, firms and their creditors. Solvency problems reduced consumption and investment; consequently, output and employment fell in both Finland and Sweden for three consecutive years (1991-93), and unemployment soared. In Finland the crisis was twice as great as in Sweden whether measured by output losses or unemployment; in Finland GDP shrank by 10 percent, and employment by 20 percent.

It is tempting to argue that the basic factor behind the recession was a monetary shock: a sharp rise of interest rates in 1989-90 bankrupted many debt-ridden firms and forced households to cut their spending, which caused a deflationary spiral and a recession. In that respect, the crises of Finland and Sweden can be seen as unintended consequences of changing economic policy regimes in Western Europe (i.e. financial market deregulation and strong commitment to a fixed exchange rate) and policy-makers' surprising determination to fight inflation, notwithstanding the fact that inflation was not a very serious problem at that time.

The explanation of the Finnish and Swedish recessions seems to be a macroeconomic policy failure, and a necessary pre-condition for the severity of the recessions of Sweden and Finland was the huge build-up of private sector debt after the financial market deregulation (cf. King 1994 for details). The monetary and exchange rate policies were not used in the 1990s to stabilise the economy – unlike in earlier crises in the 1970s and 1980s. Instead, things were made worse by the stubborn (but at that time fashionable) policy of exchange rate targeting which prevented the needed currency depreciation and which forced the central banks to maintain high interest rates.[13] The rules-based exchange rate policy doctrine was adopted widely by politicians and central bankers. The idea of the policy was to fight inflation by creating 'an anchor' for the value of the domestic currency. However, the consequences of the deflationary policy were not properly understood at the time, and the resulting recessions were to a large extent surprising to decision-makers and economists.

Furthermore, it is likely that the Finnish recession was made worse by discretionary fiscal tightening. The recession caused a huge budget deficit. The government attempted to cure this by increasing taxes and cutting discretionary spending during the recession, which made the recession even worse by reducing domestic demand.

Political response to the crisis

The economic crisis coincided with a political crisis. The long post-war tradition of coalition governments of the two major parties – the Social Democrats and the Centre Party (formerly called Agrarian Union) – was broken in 1987. The years of economic liberalisation and the economic boom were governed by a new coalition, an 'unholy alliance' of Conservatives and Social Democrats, both of which were in favour of pro-market economic reforms and rules-based monetary policy. In 1991, at the outbreak of the economic crisis, a new coalition was formed after a landslide victory of the Centre Party in the parliamentary elections. The government of Esko Aho, the leader of the Centre Party, was the first centre-right coalition in decades. Rather quickly it proved to be highly controversial. Aho's government tried to maintain the exchange rate target and support that goal by restrictive budgetary policies. The government also attempted to persuade the trade unions to accept a cut in nominal wages. When that attempt failed, the relations between the government and the trade unions soured. The government tried in vain to introduce reforms that would have weakened the bargaining position of the trade unions.

Economic crisis, mass unemployment and tight fiscal policy made the centre-right coalition unpopular, and it was easy for the Social Democrats to regain power after the parliamentary elections in 1995. A new 'Rainbow coalition' led by the Social Democratic Party leader Paavo Lipponen consisted not only of the Social Democrats and the Conservatives, but also of the Green Party and even the Left Alliance (i.e. the former Communist Party). The coalition reigned over two terms, until 2003. This coalition was very explicitly oriented to co-operation with labour market parties.

The centre-right coalition of the recession years created a discontinuity of the Finnish tradition of consensus-building and over-the-block co-operation. It ignited conflicts and distrust. It utilized the crisis mood to carry through unpopular reforms like reductions in almost all welfare entitlements and public services. Although many decision makers and analysts viewed these measures as necessary, it is possible that the government's inability to create co-operation made the crisis longer and deeper by eroding the confidence of consumers and investors – or the financial market and wider public.

The exceptional character of the subsequent Rainbow coalition manifested a widely desired return to older modes of political co-operation. The unpopular reforms were continued, although more incrementally and negotiated with the labour market parties. Instead of ad hoc crisis management, government policy became more predictable and dominated by long term goals.

The recovery and the Finnish 'miracle'

Turnaround in economic policy

The deflationary pressures caused by high real and nominal interest rates and currency overvaluation ended when Finland – together with many other European countries, most notably the UK – was forced to abandon the policy of exchange rate targeting in the autumn of 1992 and let the currency float.[14] As a result of floating, the Finnish currency depreciated quickly, by more than 30 percent. However, the depreciation was not all that bad because it improved the competitiveness of Finnish exports. Floating also enabled the central bank to cut short-term interest rates by 10 percentage points within a couple of months. Without any fixed exchange rate target, there was no longer any need to defend the exchange rate by high interest rates, and the rates fell.

If we think that the excessive monetary tightening was the main cause of the recession, then it is not illogical to conclude that the biggest macroeconomic change contributing to the recovery was the easing of the monetary policy together with currency depreciation in the aftermath of the 1992

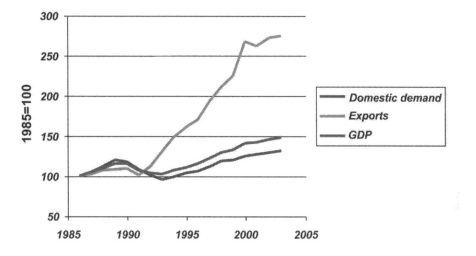

Figure 4.2 GDP, domestic demand and export volumes

EMS crisis. The lower interest rates helped to stabilise and reflate the asset prices, which ended the deflationary process. Private consumption and investment began to grow again in 1994.

The competitiveness problem which constrained Finnish export growth in 1989-91 was solved when the Finnish markka depreciated significantly after it was allowed to float with many other EMS currencies in the autumn of 1992. The currency depreciation in 1992-93 helped Finland to gain a marked and sustained improvement in competitive position. The improved competitiveness led to rapid export growth.

The post-crisis output growth was export-led in Finland, and the rising net exports contributed positively to the growth of GDP in 1994-2000. The export growth was clearly faster than the development of domestic demand, which remained subdued and did not exceed the 1990 level in real terms until 1999. In this respect, Finland differed from all other European countries, in which the growth contributions of external and internal sources have been much more balanced (see Figure 4.2). Rapid export growth together with depressed domestic demand caused an unexpectedly strong improvement in the current account, which went quickly from a deficit of 5 percent of GDP to a surplus of 7 percent of GDP.

Although the domestic demand and investment remained depressed throughout the 1990s, the growth record of GDP in the post-crisis years was impressive. In 1994-2000, the annual rate of economic growth averaged 4 percent, and employment growth was 2.1 percent. In the ten-year period of

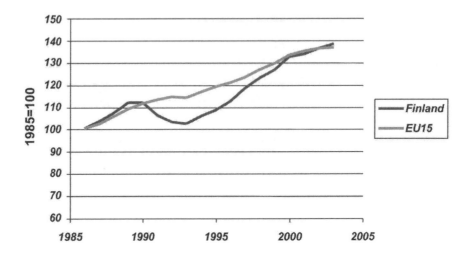

Figure 4.3 The evolution of GDP volume in Finland and EU 15

1994-2003, the Finnish GDP growth surpassed the growth rate of the EU 15 in 9 years (see Figure 4.3). Productivity growth was fast, too. As a result, the unemployment rate was reduced from 17 percent in 1994 to 9 percent in 2001. Total employment rose by 15 percent at the same time, and the employment rate increased 8 percentage points.

The employment record was good, but it was not sufficient to enable a return to the earlier full employment. Employment could have increased more quickly if the economic growth had been stronger in labour-intensive sectors like services and construction. However, until the year 2000, the main contributors to the Finnish economic growth were exports and industrial production. That helped to improve average labour productivity faster than elsewhere, but it also made the economic growth less labour-intensive.

Creative destruction and knowledge-based growth

A decisive improvement in competitiveness was first achieved through currency depreciation. However, the depreciation was not permanent. Part of it resulted clearly from financial market overshooting which was not long-lasting, and after that the Finnish currency appreciated again in 1995-96 before it was irreversibly linked to the euro. More durable factors contributing positively to competitiveness were wage moderation and productivity growth, which together helped to reduce unit labour costs almost every year after 1991. Since 1995, wage moderation was achieved through wide agreements between the government and the labour market parties, and they were supported by tax cuts.

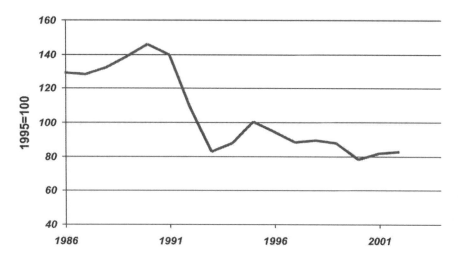

Figure 4.4 The competitive position of Finland in terms of Unit labour costs

The rapid productivity growth of the 1990s was caused by structural change. Finland made a qualitative leap from an economic structure dominated by mostly resource-based heavy industries to one with knowledge-based, mostly ICT industries as a leading sector.[15] That change contributed to a productivity acceleration which also improved the real competitiveness of the Finnish economy. The development of the competitive position of Finland vis-à-vis other industrial countries is depicted in Figure 4.4, which shows the level of real relative unit labour costs. The measure is a combination of relative changes in labour costs, productivity and exchange rates. It is surprising that in spite of the currency appreciation in 1994-96 and improving employment (which should have added to wage pressures), the unit labour costs continued their decrease. At the same time, total factor productivity growth also accelerated.

The accelerated productivity growth which followed the crisis launched a productivity catch-up process. As a result, during the latter half of the 1990s, the average labour productivity in Finland approached the productivity frontier of the USA and EU15 (see Figure 4.5). Recent research has linked that change to something which can be called 'creative destruction' (Maliranta 2001; Jalava and Pohjola 2002). The economic crisis triggered or forced a process of rapid structural change and rationalisation, which first caused a contraction of employment and improvement in productivity. Restructuring of companies at the plant level was the main cause of that; lots of old plants and companies were either closed or bankrupted, and typically they were the least efficient units. The remaining ones were – almost by defi-

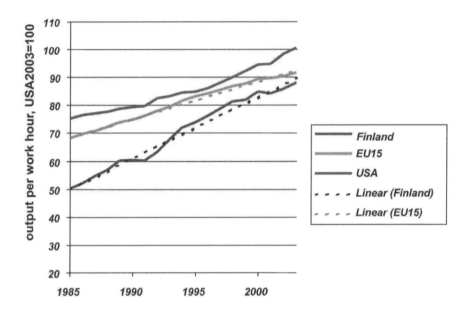

Figure 4.5 Labour productivity in business sector

nition – more productive. It is likely that capacity underutilisation and the existence of slack resources caused by the crisis facilitated organisational re-structuring (e.g. through mergers and acquisitions) and reallocation of re-sources.

That was not the end of the process. In the next phase the improved competitiveness made it possible for the remaining firms to increase their exports rapidly. The growth of industrial production in 1992-2000 was record high, on average 7 percent per annum. The annual rate of labour productivity growth in manufacturing was 6 percent. Due to the accelerated productivity growth, the Finnish manufacturing sector jumped into the group of countries with the highest productivity.

Especially the rise of wireless communication technology (or the so-called Nokia cluster – the leading firms in that field were in the 1990s the Finnish Nokia and the Swedish Ericsson) manifested that change.[16] The spectacular ICT sector growth contributed significantly both to the Finnish GDP and exports growth and to the productivity growth. The share of business sector value-added produced by the ICT sector increased by almost 10 percentage points in the 1990s. Moreover, the rapid growth of the electronics and elec-trotechnics industry was largely based on productivity gains and increased use of intangible inputs. The national technology policy played an important if not decisive role behind that phenomenon. Innovation policy and a long-term approach in building a national innovation system were already active in the 1980s. Industrial R&D spending grew throughout the 1980s and 1990s faster than in any other OECD country. Today, the Finnish R&D spending is more than 3 percent of GDP, which is among the highest figures in the world. These investments have also been supported by public sector support to higher education, and especially increases in high-level technical education. For studies on the Finnish ict cluster: see Jalava (2003), Koski et al (2001), and Paija (2000).

Still in 1990 Finnish industrial production and exports were dominated by paper, pulp, metal products and machinery. By 2000 the electronics industry had become the biggest export industry, mainly due to the growth of mobile communications revolution. In 2000 the Finnish Nokia Group was the world's biggest manufacturer of mobile phones. The Finnish production of telecoms equipment had a global market share of 7 percent. The growth of the electronics industry in the post-recession years was truly spectacular. The output of that industry was multiplied more than six-fold and its relative share grew from 8 percent to over 27 percent of total industrial production – at the time when the total production also almost doubled. In 1992 the electronics sector was smaller than the metal, paper and pulp, food and chemical industries. In 2000 it was the largest sector of them all.

The growth of the Finnish ICT cluster made a crucial contribution to the productivity gains achieved in the 1990s. The direct impact of the growth of Nokia had a large macroeconomic impact on the Finnish economic growth. Finnish producers benefited also from worldwide trends in prices: decreasing prices of semiconductors and machinery improved the profitability (and value-added) of many Finnish ICT firms (not only Nokia), which contributed positively to the measured total factor productivity.

Table 4.2 shows the difference made by the 'new economy' or the Nokia sector to the Finnish manufacturing productivity. Total factor productivity, labour productivity and the productivity of fixed capital all increased by double-digit rates in the 1990s.

Role of policy reforms

It would be intriguing to argue that such good growth, productivity and employment performance as experienced in post-recession Finland would have been caused by a wave of institutional reforms. However, there is not much evidence of any radical changes (cf. Blanchard and Portugal 2001, Blanchard and Wolfers 2000). There are only a few signs of any kind of supply-

Table 4.2 Productivity in Finnish manufacturing industry in the 1990s; annual average growth rates

	Total manufacturing	Electronics (the 'new economy sectors')
Labour productivity		
1991-1995	6.9	10.9
1996-2000	6.4	20.3
Capital productivity		
1991-1995	2.2	10.6
1996-2000	7.4	14.9
Total factor productivity		
1991-1995	5.3	11.2
1996-2000	6.6	16.7

Source: Junka (2003)

side changes or institutional reforms – in addition to the aforementioned public support to R&D and higher education – which could have improved the productive potential and work incentives.

It is evident that all European countries went through many minor reforms and adjustments during the 1990s. Still, in the end, most of them remain examples of the so-called European social model with regulated labour markets even after the 1990s. The same applies to Finland, too. Perhaps the biggest change which took place in the 1990s in Finland was the adoption and wide acceptance of a policy of long-term wage moderation. However, that was a quite natural response to high unemployment even in unionised labour markets, and for the unions it was a positive alternative compared with their marginalisation or exclusion from decision-making. A shift in political power launched some attempts for an institutional reform. The usually dominant Social Democrats were in opposition after an electoral defeat during the recession years (1991-95). The centre-right government which was in power in 1991-95 expressed intentions to diminish the role of trade unions and to get rid of the old corporatist wage bargaining system dominated by central organisations of trade unions and employers. These initiatives were successfully opposed by the trade unions, which threatened twice to arrange a general strike. The center-right government lost the general elections in 1995 and the Social Democrats were able to retake their position as the biggest party and to hold the position of prime minister in two coalition governments in 1995-2003. These governments[17] were careful to maintain the corporatist model and the strong position of trade unions in the Finnish economic and social policy.

There were some changes in taxation and welfare benefit system in 1990s which probably supported the economic recovery and improved public finances. The boldest change took place when the corporate and capital income taxation was reformed in 1993. A new system was introduced where profits, capital income and capital gains were taxed by a proportional 25 percent rate. At the same time the tax base was widened by abolishing several deductions. The reform improved the after-tax profits of firms and the incentives of entrepreneurs. Another part of policy was a gradual reduction of labour taxes in the latter half of the 1990s – after increases in taxation in the first half the same decade. To a large extent that meant only a return to pre-recession tax rates.

The work incentives were improved by a new earned-income tax deduction and by reductions in the levels of welfare benefits. Most entitlements programs were subject to savings measures throughout the 1990s. A usual way to erode the value of entitlements was to reduce their relative and real value by not making full adjustments to inflation. As a result, the replacement ratio of unemployment benefits and old-age pensions declined. More drastic cuts were made to child benefits and other family support programmes. Health care subsidies were also reduced and the user fees increased. In the end of the 1990s the relative level overall level of social spending (excluding the unemployment-related expenditures) was about 10 percent lower than in the beginning of the decade although the number of pensioners had increased (Kiander 2001).

Figure 4.6 shows how the volume of public consumption (i.e. the public services) was reduced in the midst of the recession. At the same other expenditures increased. That was mostly due to increased social spending caused by higher than expected unemployment. Later on, when unemployment declined, also transfer spending started to decrease.

Motivation for the budgetary cuts was twofold: first the cuts were justified as necessary savings, but later also as a way to improve work incentives of the unemployed. The cuts were not popular. However, the majority of voters accepted them reluctantly as the only way to save the basic structures of the Finnish welfare state.

In the 1990s fiscal policy was more or less pro-cyclical in most European countries, and Finland does not make an exception. In the first half of 1990s fiscal policy was tightened with discretionary tax increases and spending cuts. These policies aimed to fiscal consolidation and to fulfilment of the EMU convergence criteria. There was a relatively deep fiscal deficit (7 per-

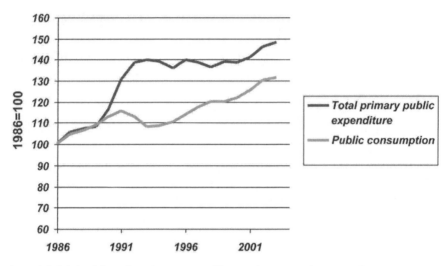

Figure 4.6 Total public sector primary expenditure and consumption expenditure

cent of GDP) in 1992-94 when the rate of unemployment was highest. The deficit was not much cured by the spending cuts made in the same years; higher taxes and reduced public spending increased unemployment, which lead to higher than expected social spending and lower than expected tax revenue.

In the latter half of the 1990s the opposite took place; lower interest rates and earlier budgetary savings created new leeway for policy-makers, who used the higher than expected tax revenues to finance tax cuts and some increased public spending. In the environment of decreasing real interest rates, improved competitiveness and growing employment expansionary fiscal policy did not threaten fiscal stability. Instead, fiscal balances were improving. Thus the improvement in fiscal balance achieved in 1995-2000 was not caused by higher taxes but instead by strong growth, lower interest payments and declining unemployment-related expenditures. After six years of rapid growth and falling unemployment, Finland had a record high (7 percent of GDP) fiscal surplus in 2000. The huge improvement in fiscal balance was achieved at the same time with steadily increasing public consumption and reduced taxes. That fiscal miracle (which resembled very much the famous Laffer curve) was made possible by rapidly increasing tax bases (due to output and employment growth) and by decreasing transfer payments (caused by lower unemployment-related and interest expenditures, and by erosion of the relative value of some transfer programs).

It can be argued that pro-cyclical discretionary fiscal policy had a positive impact on employment growth after the recession of the early 1990s. The growth contribution of fiscal policy may not necessarily have been very important but still it was clearly supportive for growth.

Structural issues: welfare state and labour market institutions

The recession and the subsequent output and employment losses helped to make the case that the crisis and slow growth were not results of a mere macroeconomic co-ordination failure but instead a deeper systemic malfunction ultimately caused by the structures of the welfare state. In the midst of the recession, it was argued that the Nordic welfare state is generally bad for growth because it creates bad incentives.[18] According to such views, overly generous benefits, labour market rigidities and high taxes will finally discourage investment, job creation and labour supply. Many critics used the dismal growth record of the first half of the 1990s as evidence supporting the negative diagnosis for both Sweden and Finland. During the crisis it was widely thought that the large budget deficits would be incurable without abolishing the welfare state. It was easy to find expressions of an 'orthodox' view which emphasises the dismal economic consequences of redistributive welfare ('tax and spend') policies.[19] The analytical background to such a view is provided by mainstream economic theory on the one hand and by the seemingly permanent economic problems of many EU countries since the 1970s on the other.

Since both countries recovered from the crises within a couple of years, they cannot be used any more as ultimate evidence of the failure of the Nordic model. It is now more widely admitted that the recessions were mostly related to financial factors and policy failures, not to serious systemic malfunctions. Both in Sweden and Finland, the sudden rise of unemployment turned out to be largely a temporary shock. The unemployment in the Nordic countries was much less persistent than that in the large EU countries. In Finland, the sudden rise of unemployment in 1991 was not a result of a long-term deterioration of employment but a consequence of a drastic destruction of jobs within a period of three years. After the crisis, employment recovered quickly, supporting the view that the Finnish labour market was relatively flexible, after all. The relation between employment and output did not change much after the surge in productivity in the mid-1990s.

The Nordic welfare state: Good to economic growth?

The relation between advanced welfare state and competitive economy is a complex one, at least in theory. There is a classical trade-off between equity and efficiency in economic thinking. It is also easy to find expressions of such an 'orthodox' view which emphasises the dismal economic consequences of redistributive welfare ('tax and spend') policies. During the Nordic crisis in the 1990s it was widely thought that the large budget deficits of 1992-95 would be incurable without abolishing the welfare state. The analytical background to such a view was (and still is) provided by mainstream economic theory on one hand and by the seemingly permanent economic problems of many EU countries since the 1970s on the other.

The good standing of the Nordic countries – Sweden, Denmark and Finland – in the various measurements of growth, employment, high tech indicators and R&D (OECD 2003d, Koski et al 2001) have even given rise to a new positive evaluation of the economic impact of the Nordic welfare state. The rapid growth and especially the strong performance in new technologies improved the image of Finland as a dynamic, innovative and modern economy. It has even been argued that the Nordic welfare state model may actually have been good for such knowledge-intensive growth because it supports research and education and enables individual risk-taking (Castells and Himanen 2002).

The high taxes of welfare states may be harmful to private sector employment, but the high level of public sector employment more than compensates that (see Rosen 1996, Stemrod 1998, Freeman 1995a). The Nordic welfare states are systems which create incentives and possibilities to increase the labour supply, and particularly that of women. Taxation based on individual (instead of family) incomes together with many incomes-related benefits (most importantly pensions, but also maternity and sickness benefits) favour a family model where both parents work. Publicly provided and heavily subsidised day-care for children makes that an easy option even for the mothers of small children and for those with low incomes. Furthermore, the large-scale public provision of social services offers lots of employment opportunities, especially to women. As a result, the Nordic countries have labour markets where men typically work in the business sector and women in public sector jobs.

The large public sectors of the Nordic countries seemingly do not crowd out much private sector employment. The number of business sector employees as a share of the population in Finland is roughly the same as in other European countries. The impact of the large public sector is that it has created new jobs in public services and shifted a part of unpaid household work (mostly done by women) to the market (Kiander 2005).

The Nordic welfare states have traditionally been good in improving the well-being of their citizens and equality between them. The Nordic social policies are by their nature egalitarian and universal in order to create inclusive systems. They aim to promote equality not only in regard of income distribution but also between genders.[20] Some of the benefits are universal and independent of family income like basic pensions, child and student benefits, while some benefits decrease with income, like housing benefits, and some are earnings-related, like unemployment insurance and occupational pensions.

The low overall poverty rates and especially the very low child poverty rates of the Nordic countries are due to deliberate social policies which help to maintain the disposable incomes of families notwithstanding their labour market position. The egalitarian outcome is helped a lot by subsidised social services like day-care provided by the public sector. The effect of these policies is most visible when one compares the poverty rates of families with single mothers. In most countries the poverty risk of such families is very high, but not in the Nordic countries.[21]

Denmark and Sweden have the most generous welfare state systems with regard to the provision of public services and income transfers, while the Finnish system is more modest and less ambitious. Due to the fiscal belt-tightening in the 1990s the differences between Finland and the more generous Swedish and Danish welfare systems have increased.

Labour market institutions and corporatism

Finnish society can be described as a parliamentary democracy with a Nordic welfare state system and highly corporatist labour market institutions. The unionisation rate in Finland is one of the highest in the world (more than 80 percent) and the coverage of collective agreements is almost 100 percent. Wide union membership is supported not only by political tradition but also by deductible membership fees and unemployment insurance system run by the unions. Employers are also highly organized.

The strong voice of the unions and employers is partly due to their co-operation and continuous dialogue. An unexpected and probably unintended consequence of the economic transformations of the 1990s was the strengthening of the corporatist system (cf. Kettunen 2003). All post-recession governments have been eager to emphasize the importance of the cooperation of the labour market parties. A positive result from that consensus has been continued wage moderation and improved competitiveness. Union members have benefited from low inflation, lower taxes and improved employment. Wage moderation has resulted from biannual centralized bargaining between the confederations of trade unions and employers.

There seems to be a strong continuity in the Finnish corporatist institutions. The recession of the early 1990s was a tough test for that system, and it was challenged by the centre-right government. However, that attempt failed to ignite a systemic shift. Since 1995 the governments have (like in the 1980s) co-operated with the labour market parties and relied on their support in big decisions, like ones on reforming pension system and joining the EMU.

The decision to join the EMU was seen risky on the ground that in past Finland had experienced many asymmetric shocks which were cured by using exchange rate flexibility (indeed, that was the main argument why Sweden decided to not join the EMU). Trade unions were ready to accept Finnish membership only after the government and the employers agreed to establish so called buffer funds (i.e. surplus funds in the social insurance system) to be used to stabilise labour costs in a case of asymmetric shock in future. The buffer funds decision effectively gave part of the control a fiscal policy into the hands of the labour market parties, and further strengthened the institutional basis of the corporatist system.

On the prospects of the Finnish model

Starting from poverty, Finland has in the 20th century succeeded first in catching up with other (more advanced) European countries and finally in surpassing the EU average GDP per capita level. The 'new economy' phase of the 1990s enabled the Finnish manufacturing sector even to achieve the global productivity frontier. In light of such a performance, the Finnish economy can be viewed as dynamic. The trends of output and productivity growth are still stronger than those of other EU countries and the USA. If they can be maintained, then Finland will surpass most other European countries in GDP per capita and productivity, and approach the American productivity and output frontier.

Thus, the economic prospects of Finland are bright; together with Sweden, Finland is the only EU country fulfilling the Lisbon targets of high level of R&D spending. As a consequence of the deep financial crisis of 1990-93, the Finnish unemployment rate is still relatively high. Yet the employment rate is 67 percent,[22] higher than in most other EU countries and reasonably close to the Lisbon target of 70 percent. The Finnish welfare state model and even the corporatist labour market institutions are supportive of wide labour markets participation and full-time work. That is why we can expect the employment rate to continue its growth and to finally achieve the level of almost 75 percent which prevailed in the 1980s.

In the longer term, the biggest challenge for the Finnish economy will be caused by demographic changes. The Finnish labour force is ageing rapidly, and it is expected that the labour supply will start to shrink after 2010. If strong economic growth is to be continued, Finland is going to need immigration and a higher average retirement age (i.e. longer careers). The greying will increase public pension and health care expenditure in the future. However, Finland is prepared for that change better than most other countries; the public finances have a surplus, and the government sector has more financial assets than debts.

Conclusion

In recent years Finland has received much attention as an economic star performer. That view has not been based on traditional economic indicators like income level but on other indicators measuring wider competitiveness and the development of a so-called new economy. Much of that success is very closely related to the Nokia phenomenon. The emergence of the world's biggest producer of mobile ICT in a small country has clearly made a difference. In macroeconomic terms, the biggest change has been a productivity revolution – sustained and exceptionally rapid productivity growth in manufacturing industries in the 1990s.

The odds of such growth were very low in the beginning of the 1990s. As a result of a financial crisis, Finland suffered a serious shortfall in growth and employment in 1990-93. However, that crisis turned out to be only temporary. In spite of the macroeconomic turbulence, the long-term growth record of Finland (even in the 1990s) has not been bad. On the contrary, Finland has been able to catch up with the most advanced economies. The economic crisis forced the Finnish economy to go through a period of painful adjustment and restructuring. The crisis launched a period of 'creative destruction'. The rationalisation processes together with the unexpected rise of mobile ICT technologies created the productivity miracle of the 1990s. It was based not only on technological advances but also on open sector growth and a huge improvement in competitiveness induced by currency depreciation in 1992. In the rapid rise up the quality ladders – from resource-based to knowledge-based production – the role of intangibles and the knowledge base has been indispensable. Finland has clearly benefited from the long-term policy of investing in national innovation system development and supporting R&D.

In spite of rapid growth, the most burning social problem in the 1990s was mass unemployment. Although the rate of job creation in the post-crisis period (i.e. since 1993) has been rapid and the unemployment rate was reduced by 8 percentage points between 1994 and 2001, there is still underemployment. Employment has not returned to the level achieved in the 1980s. However, due to high labour force participation, the Finnish employment rate has always exceeded the average level of the EU (even in 1993-94 when the unemployment rate was more than 16 percent), and it is likely to continue its growth.

The Finnish economic development – from boom to bust, and from creative destruction to technology-driven prosperity – makes one wonder about the roles of social corporatism and welfare state in that process: were the institutional characteristics of the Finnish society an advantage or a hindrance? In the 1980s Finland was clearly one of the small European welfare states with large public sectors and corporatist labour market institutions. As usual, such institutions tend to be resilient and slow to change. They survived the crisis period more or less unchanged, although the replacement rates of most welfare programs were cut in the 1990s. By accepting wage moderation, the trade unions were able to maintain their traditionally strong position, and the corporatist system survived.

In spite of mass unemployment and fiscal problems in the mid-1990s, the Finnish political governance and corporatist institutions remained relatively stable. There were short-lived attempts by the centre-right government in the first half of the 1990s to introduce more radical institutional reforms, which would challenge the corporatist system. Without sufficient electoral support they did not succeed. Rather quickly the political decision making returned to its old mode of consensus building and incremental reforms. Although the structures of the Finnish welfare state survived the crisis of the 1990s, they were subjected to many small incremental changes, which reduced many entitlements and widened the difference between the Finnish and Swedish variants of the Nordic welfare state.

The prospects of the Finnish economy are relatively good. Given the strong technological base and abundance of skilled labour, Finland still has a potential to grow faster than other Western European countries. The main challenge is the ageing population. Demographic change is expected to reduce the labour supply and put public finances under stress between 2010 and 2020. However, the Finnish public finances are in good shape to face that change.

Notes

1 See e.g. IMD (2003) and WEF (2003) and the many indicators in EU (2003). In most comparisons Finland ranks among the top three, whether it comes to competitiveness or indicators of technology and knowledge-based growth.

2 This point has recently been emphasised e.g. by Fitoussi et al. (2000) and Ball (1999).

3 To the wider international public, Finland was not known at all.

4 At that time EFTA member countries were: Austria, Finland, Iceland, Norway, Sweden and Switzerland.

5 It is most likely that the differences in unemployment developments between countries reflect corresponding differences in macroeconomic policies; cf. Blanchard and Summers (1986) and Ball (1999), who emphasize the role of macroeconomic shocks.

6 Unlike most other industrial countries, Finland did not suffer from a recession in the beginning of the 1980s.

7 However, it is interesting to note that some other countries which enjoyed an employment miracle in the 1990s did not suffer from asset price bubbles in the 1980s.

8 That was a bit curious choice since Denmark was the only Nordic country which was a member of the EU. Finland and Sweden joined the Union in 1995.

9 In the mid-1980s the Soviet Union absorbed more than 20 percent of Finnish exports. In 1989-91 that market was lost almost totally due to the internal problems of the Soviet Union.

10 All figures, if not indicated otherwise, are based on diverse editions of the OECD's *Economic Outlook*

11 The concept of debt deflation was originally introduced by Irving Fisher (1930) who tried to explain the Great Depression. In debt deflation, declining asset prices increase the real value of debts, which puts the debtors under financial stress by decreasing their net worth.

12 For literature on the Finnish crisis, see e.g. Kiander and Vartia (1996), Honkapohja and Koskela (1999), Bordes et al. (1993), Jonung et al. (1996), and Kalela et al. (2001).

13 Under fixed exchange rates, high interest rates are needed to defend the exchange rate if investors think it is overvalued, which was the case in most European countries in 1990-92.

14 The European countries were forced to change their exchange rate regime because the market pressure against the fixed parities grew too great. Abandonment of the restrictive monetary policy was not actively sought.

15 In 1990 Finnish exports were dominated by paper, pulp, metal products and machinery. By 2000 the electronics industry had became the biggest export industry.

16 The role of 'new economy' in the Finnish productivity miracle has been studied by Daveri and Silva (2004). For reviews of the growth of the Finnish wireless technology sector and Nokia corporation, see Ali-Yrkkö (2001), Rouvinen and Ylä-Anttila (2003) and Paija and Rouvinen (2003).

17 The Social Democrats were in opposition during the recession (1991-95). After that, they held the position of prime minister in two coalition governments in 1995-2003.

18 An eloquent piece of such criticism and an assessment of the 'Swedish experiment' are provided by Lindbeck (1997).

19 It is easy to find examples of such opinions by reading e.g. *The Economist,* or the country reports of the IMF and the OECD. A good example of a theoretically sound argument showing how excessive social protection can lead to persistent unemployment is presented by Ljungqvist and Sargent (1998).

20 Tanzi and Schuknecht (2000) argue that increasing the size of public expenditure above 30 percent does not yield any economic gains. Such a view seems to neglect the equity-improving impact of welfare states, of which the Nordic countries offer ample evidence. It can also be said that there is no compelling empirical evidence that large public sectors as such would be harmful to growth.

21 Kangas and Palme (2000) show that differences in social policy explain the low family-related poverty rates in the Nordic countries. The same pattern is reflected by the results of Haataja (1999), according to which poverty in the Nordic countries is not connected with unemployment. Forssen (1998) has analysed the Nordic family policies and their distributional impacts.

22 That was the average level of years 2001-2003.

5   The Swiss Miracle: Low growth and high employment

François Xavier Merrien and Uwe Becker[1]

Introduction

Switzerland does not occupy a prominent place in comparative political economy. One reason is probably that this proudly independent country is not part of the EU and therefore missing from many comparative statistical sets. This relative neglect leads to a generally rather superficial knowledge about the peculiarities of the Swiss form of capitalism and the development of its welfare system. It also obscures a specific interesting question: how did Switzerland in the 1990s maintain its very high employment rate in the context of the lowest productivity and GDP growth in the OECD? Switzerland's employment rate was essentially stable at 78.2 percent from 1990 through 2000, second only to tiny Iceland (OECD 2003a, p.298). In a very specific sense, this is also a 'miracle'.

In the following pages we will describe the Swiss political economy, which has been inconsistently characterised as both corporatist as well as liberal. Then we will examine recent developments, including the unrecognised and peculiar Swiss employment miracle, as well as the main features of the Swiss welfare system which, contrary to international trends, has been expanded in recent years.

Corporatism in a fragmented polity

The Swiss political economy is often described as liberal because of, among other things, its relatively low level of employment protection (cf. Table 9.3 in the contribution on Germany). A second feature suggesting a liberal coding is the Swiss central government's low capacity for action. The country is a federation whose cantons are in turn divided into considerably autonomous counties and cities with a strong tradition of bottom-up politics. On the other hand, one cannot deny that the Swiss political economy contains a variety of corporatist characteristics as well. This made Peter

Katzenstein (1985) present the country as a case of 'liberal democratic corporatism'. In this model, the state sets only very general rules but does not intervene actively in the economic process (see also Armingeon 1987). In a bipartite structure, macroeconomic negotiations are dominated by employers' associations and unions, although the former possess the stronger position. Employers' associations are much more centralised than the unions, whose fragmented character reflects the Swiss federation and whose organisation rate is rather low (25 percent). Katzenstein argues that functional effects of Switzerland's position in the international economy explain these corporatist arrangements. Once the imperative of successful competition in the open world markets is accepted, actors are pushed to find a national consensus that facilitates the handling of international change. In a small country, corporatist arrangements are supposed to guarantee continuous adaptation to economic changes as well as industrial peace. It has to be seen whether the first assumption has turned out to be correct in the years after the publication of Katzenstein's seminal work.

There can be no doubt, however, that peaceful industrial relations are a special trademark of Switzerland. The strike volume between 1970 and 2001 has been negligible and lower than in any other country. Annualised, the loss of working days per 1000 employees was only 1 day compared with an OECD average of 219 days (Lesch 2003, p.31). The 'social peace convention' of 1937 between capital and labour is the keystone of the Swiss system of industrial relations. Since 1937, most collective agreements set out an absolute obligation to maintain 'industrial peace'. The convention (cf. Humbel 1987) 'forbids all acts that are detrimental to the partner, whatever the purpose of the restriction. In particular, the signatory of the agreement must not inflict any damage on his partner in order to force the latter to behave in a particular way in relation to matters not governed by the agreement. He also must not inflict any damage on his partner to force a third party to behave in a particular way (strike, lock-out)'. In case of a lasting conflict, a court of arbitration rules in the last instance. However, it is rarely used. In most cases conflicts are resolved at the first level by negotiators between work council and management. If this produces no solution, the case is submitted to the associations of capital and labour. It is only when they do not reach agreement that the court of arbitration will be involved. This court first draws up a conciliation proposal. If one or both of the parties refuse this proposal, then the court settles the conflict in the final instance.

Although the state has developed employment law and a number of protective measures in relation to social insurance, the gradual conciliation procedure has been so effective that since 1937 more than three-quarters of industrial disputes have been settled within the company context through direct negotiations between the interested parties. Those cases which have had to be brought before the bodies representing the interest groups have been rare, and the conciliation bodies have hardly ever been consulted. For this reason, the number of strikes in Switzerland is very low. Until the 1990s collective agreements were usually valid for all workers in the same professional sector in the region the agreement is valid for. There is no statutory performance-related pay, no obligatory pay linked to company profits, and no national minimum wage limiting the bargaining space. And by European standards employment protection is rather relaxed, rendering it relatively easy to fire and hire workers.

This pattern – collective conventions set by the social partners, within a general legislative framework set out by the liberal central state – characterizes most employment matters. Collective conventions can be negotiated at the national, regional or local level by the competent professional organisations, and every enterprise is invited to conform to the agreements. Such a system privileges the negotiation between the social partners, and every partner respects the terms of the agreement (according to the Convention of Work Peace of 1937). Negotiations determine working conditions, periods of notice, modalities of notice, working hours, salary and holidays. When economic conditions change, new negotiations have to take place. In case of disputes, a referee's court with parity composition has to be consulted. Fifty-four percent out of 3.5 million salaried people are covered by this global work agreement, 18 percent of whom are under obligatory agreements. Almost all collective wage agreements contain an inflation indexation clause that regularly adjusts salaries to increases in the national index of consumption prices. Some companies propose their own agreement. In 1992 these accounted for 11 percent of the wage earners in the private sector.

The legislative stipulations governing fixed-term contracts of employment are more flexible than those in most other developed countries, apart from those in the USA and the UK (BIT 1999, p.37). The use of interim work has few legal limitations. It is possible to conclude fixed-term contracts of employment (CDDs) for any duration, while in most countries in the EU, a fixed-term contract cannot extend beyond a period of time ranging from 18 months to 3 years. Similarly, while the legislation in many EU countries imposes limitations on the renewal of such contracts, in Switzerland it is possible to conclude successive CDDs as often as the employers and workers wish to do it.

A coordinated market economy?

The Swiss economy has sufficiently strong enough corporatist characteristics to be considered a case of what Soskice (1999) calls a "coordinated market economy" rather than the "liberal market economy" type dominant in the Anglo-Saxon countries. The level of cooperation between banks and industry is just as high as that between employers and unions. The direct links between the four main economic systems – the financial system, the industrial relations system, the inter-company system, and the education and training system – are strong. The degree of coordination between firms of the same sector is also high. The institutional framework tends to encourage cooperation at all levels and between social actors.

Switzerland exports diversified quality goods, the production of which depends on skilled and experienced employees on whom responsibility can be devolved (Kappel and Landmann 1997). As in Germany and Austria, the Swiss production regime is largely based on the dual system of education and an apprenticeship system based on practical knowledge combined with theoretical education in a specific technical teaching establishment. The dual system works on a corporatist basis of consensus formation between the concerned professional groups and teaching institutions. In such matters, Swiss federalism leaves a large margin of autonomous action for the cantons and the professional organisations. Federal influence is limited to two tasks: it sets quality standards and subsidizes the vocational schools. The legal frame is set at the federal level, but implementation is largely left to the cantons. Enterprises are forced to respect guidelines in technical teaching. Thus, the regulation of professions leads to a sound education adapted to regional economic disparities and cantonal differences. The strong apprenticeship system appears to ensure a steady supply of young, skilled and highly productive labourers. One side-effect of this system is that youth unemployment has never reached the levels seen in other EU countries.

Switzerland's industrial specialisation permits a niche strategy that is supposed to have brought about comparative economic advantages. Traditionally, Switzerland produces and exports machines and tools, chemical goods, and its famous watches, acts as a centre of international financial and insurance services, and also provides an important destination for tourism. In the course of the past decades, services have become the dominant economic sector. In 1965 the service sector represented 40 percent of the economy; today it represents 70 percent. And while the industrial trade balance is neutral, it is positive in services.

This picture presents only a partial view of the Swiss economy, however. A large internally oriented and protected sector exists alongside the externally oriented and competitive sectors. For decades, agriculture and some industries producing for the domestic market were subsidised and sheltered from international competition by private and public arrangements: cartels, price maintenance, and monopolies (Sciarini 1994; Mach 1997). Switzerland is ranked first in transferring resources to agriculture.[2] This explains why prices of goods produced for the internal market are very high, and also why over a long period of time, workers in these sectors were protected against external competition. Recently, however, Switzerland has faced internal and external pressure to open up the protected parts of its economy, with the usual inevitable consequences for the economic and social structure of the country. In particular, a new discourse about competitiveness targets and flexibility has emerged since the late 1980s – despite the fact that in this country wages are traditionally more flexible than elsewhere in Europe, and hiring and firing are relatively easy.

Recent developments

Most economic textbooks present the market option as the only viable one in the long run. They argue that countries should have a flexible labour market (a low degree of employment protection, large wage flexibility, low generosity of unemployment insurance, etc.), a weak welfare state, low taxation and a deregulated economy in order to create employment. But some analysts insist that governments face a more complicated trade-off between jobs and equality. As Iversen and Wren (1998) argue, governments face a trilemma among earnings equality, full employment and a balanced budget. As a result, governments have three choices: two 'regulatory' policy options or the market policy option. The liberal policy choice is to let markets operate, creating a society with full employment but large earning inequality. If they choose the other options, governments either will have to expand public sector employment and as a consequence generate large public deficits, or contain deficits but face a 'welfare without work' trajectory (Esping-Andersen 1996).

Sociologists and political scientists have generated analyses that highlight the institutional configurations (welfare regimes, employment regimes) that constitute this trilemma (Esping-Andersen 1996, 1999; Scharpf and Schmidt 2000). The continental model (and its southern variation) is considered to be less able to cope with the economic pressures stemming from globalisation, and thus inevitably exposed to labour market problems and budget deficits. High taxes on labour depress labour demand and increase unemployment. In turn, a contraction of the active labour force narrows the labour tax base and forces governments to raise taxes even further, reinforcing the spiral of welfare without work. The Scandinavian way, based on high public employment as well as high employee-based taxes, appears to be relatively robust against the new economic pressures (Scharpf and Schmidt 2000, p.89), but requires a centralised, high-capacity state structure. Finally, the flexibility of the labour market in the liberal, Anglo-Saxon model enhances employment growth, but is detrimental to equality.

These are the alternatives Switzerland has faced in the past decade. In the 1990s, neo-liberal ideas, hardly recognised by the Swiss political elite, spread very rapidly into economists' networks, high-ranking officials' circles, employers' associations[3], and the parties of the right. OECD reports, notably the 1992 country report on Switzerland as well as other expert reports[4], exerted a strong influence on the Swiss politico-economic elite circles. Most of the economists, economic advisors and economic civil servants[5] agree on the idea of implementing a more deregulated market, suppressing cartels and other obstacles to economic competition, following strict monetarist policies, limiting public deficits and the growth of the welfare state.

Despite this, the elites are not unified around a liberal project. On the one hand, employers' associations and right-wing parties call for a policy of welfare reorientation and retrenchment, and for more labour market flexibility, while pleading against the extension of unemployment insurance. On the other hand, another group of elites, influenced by Christian democratic ideas or by members of the conservative Radical Party, defends the idea of a Swiss 'social model' with high wages, high regulation of the labour market and social pacts between unions and associations of employers. In addition, just as in other EU countries, trade unions, the socialists, green parties and churches advocate a stronger welfare state, better social protection of the workers, more generous unemployment benefits and a serious fight against poverty.

Furthermore, as Switzerland is a federalist and 'consensual' democracy, it is very difficult to implement radical policy changes (Kriesi 1995; Papadopoulos 1997). The most remarkable feature of consensual politics is arguably the composition of the federal government. The four main parties [Catholic Conservative Party (e.g. the Christian Democratic Party), the Swiss People Party (formerly the Farmers' Party), the Radical Democratic Party, the Socialist Party] together rule the country, sharing ministerial posts and administrative departments between them. Government policies thus tend to be moderate in order to be acceptable to all coalition partners.

These groups argue that development towards the 'uncoordinated market economy' liberals prefer would produce an economic revolution and result in fierce wage bargaining, competition among firms and workers, and a higher dispersion of wages. It would require a complete transformation not only of the welfare state and of the sheltered economic sector, but also of the politico-economic system as a whole – in a country that is already considerably liberal by European standards. Even if they ideologically agree with the neo-liberal ideas, and if they wish more autonomy in the fixation of working conditions, employers do not have strong incentives to change an economic and social system that has made Switzerland one of the most prosperous countries in the world with an unparalleled level of social peace. Is a decade of near-stagnation enough incentive to risk changing this equilibrium? In addition, for historical reasons, even rightist parties such as the Christian Democrats and the Radical Party are opposed to a shift towards a US style of society.

The questions in Switzerland have been how to change working conditions to face the intensification of competition in the world markets without breaking down the historically developed system of industrial relations, how to implement new measures to combat unemployment, and finally how to limit social exclusion. From this perspective, the Swiss case gives support to the 'compensation hypothesis' drawn by Geoffrey Garrett (1998), which is that globalisation does not induce governments to roll back social expenditures, but gives them incentives to respond to political demands for protection against risks. In this spirit, the unemployment policies of the mid-1990s were characterised by the serious attempt to combine labour market and social security targets. One can define these measures as progressive measures. They include higher replacement rates, a longer duration (where relevant) of and easier access to benefits for the unemployed, the poor, the sick and families (Merrien 2002). On the other hand, the architecture of the reforms shows the strong influence of new ideas and practices diffused by the experts.

Economic and labour market development

Two main periods characterise the post-war performance of the Swiss economy and labour market. The first period (1950-1973), the usual 'golden age' period, saw continuous GDP growth that made Switzerland into the

third or fourth richest country in the world and caused employment to increase up to a level of nearly 80 percent. The country also hosted a large foreign labour force whose size could be flexibly adjusted to the business cycle.
After 1973, Switzerland experienced three decades of inconstant economic
developments. The deep crisis of the mid-1970s was followed by a few years
of recovery, then the recession of 1982-83 was followed by more than half a
decade of strong growth that in turn preceded a decade-long period of stagnation in the 1990s. Finally, a few years of strong growth gave way to the
very recent phase of economic downturn in the beginning of the new millennium. Although Switzerland maintained employment at a very high level,
unemployment surpassed the 1 percent mark in the 1990s for the first time
and recently again. Also, female labour market participation and part-time
work have become much more significant in this second period, while the
possibility of managing the foreign labour force has declined.

   Among the factors that might explain the Swiss economic expansion after
World War II, we should highlight the fact that, during the war, Switzerland
was a 'neutral' country. With its industry intact and its unique blend of
goods (drugs, prepared food, watches, special tools and machines), it was
ideally placed to meet the growing demand emanating from a devastated
Europe (helped by the Marshall plan). Neither capital nor labour shortages
interfered with the progress of the unparalleled post-war boom. During the
cold war, capital flew to 'secure' Switzerland from all over the world. The
stability of the Swiss franc, its unique convertibility, and 'bank secrecy' offered a security not matched by any other country. At the same time, an end-
less supply of cheap labour flowed into the country from southern Europe
(Italy, Portugal, Spain), resulting in a labour force of which nearly 30 percent was foreign.

   In the mid-1970s, after the first 'oil shock', Switzerland entered into a severe depression, like most other Western countries. One particular factor
explaining the specific Swiss position in those years was the flow of financial
capital to Switzerland and the strong appreciation of the Swiss franc against
the currencies of its main trade partners. Swiss industry lost competitiveness. In particular, the watch industry and similar branches declined rapidly. Since those difficult years, the trajectory of Swiss growth became much
more erratic than it had been during the 20 years following WW II. Nevertheless, even in periods of economic trouble (1975-1976, 1982-1983, 1986-
1987), employment could be kept at a high level, and the unemployment rate
remained very low.

   It is not easy to explain why Switzerland was able to reach an employment
rate that already approached 80 percent in the 1980s. A high percentage of

public employment, as in Scandinavia, is not part of the explanation, and the search for a particular employment policy is fruitless. Part of the explanation might be found, however, in the liberal Swiss labour market and system of social security. Benefits are not as low as in the USA, where people are forced to look even for badly paid jobs as the only way to escape poverty, but Switzerland is a country of tough means tests, and a country where local municipalities enjoy considerable discretion in awarding benefits (cf. Gough et al. 1997). Another factor explaining the high Swiss employment rate is part-time work, particularly for women. The Swiss part-time rate is the second highest among the OECD countries, and the higher the part-time rate, the bigger the gap between the actual employment rate and the virtual employment rate in full-time equivalents (FTES). In 1999, for example, the employment rate of Swiss women was 71.8 percent, but in FTES the percentage was only 50.5. In Denmark and Sweden, by contrast, actual employment rates were as high as in Switzerland, but measured in FTES their rates were about 8 percent higher. And in France the actual female employment rate was nearly 20 percent lower than in Switzerland, while the FTE employment rate was only about 5 percent lower. In France, as well as in Scandinavia and many other countries, part-time work is much less frequent than in Switzerland (not to speak of the Netherlands, where part-time jobs inflate the employment rate even more; cf. Zürcher 2003).

The increase of part-time jobs continued in the 1990s, but most other economic indicators pointed to stagnation or decline – at least until 1998. In the context of a near-global recession in the early years of the decade, Switzerland underwent a new round of economic difficulties that lasted the entire decade. From 1990 to 1998 the average annual growth of GDP was only 0.4 percent, the weakest in Europe (OCDE 1999; from 1990 to 2000, reflecting the growth sprint of the late 1990s, it was 0.9 percent; OECD 2003e). The high interest rates resulting from an anti-inflationary monetarist policy and fiscal stringency aimed at bringing down the public deficit could be seen as the causes for this development. These measures are supposed to discourage productive investments. If this were always true, however, investment and GDP growth would also have declined in the Netherlands, Denmark and other European countries that prepared for the EMU by raising interest rates and reducing public spending. Therefore, we have to look for a specifically Swiss cause for the malaise of the 1990s.

The first specific factor to be mentioned is that tight monetary policy strengthened the Swiss franc relative to the DM and other European currencies by 15 percent just between 1993 and 1995 (SNB 1997). This in turn could have limited export growth and penalised tourism – though these

Table 5.1   Change of employment 1990-2000, annual averages, and average unemployment
rate from 1990 to 2000

	Employment	Labour Force	Unemployment
Australia	1.4	1.3	8.4
Austria	0.4	0.4	5.1
Denmark	0.2	0.0	6.7
Finland	0.7	0.0	
Netherlands	2.1	1.7	5.5
Sweden	-0.8	0.4	6.1
Switzerland	0.3	0.4	2.9
France	0.6	0.7	10.9
Germany	0.4	0.5	7.5
Italy	-0.4	0.1	10.7
UK	0.2	0.2	7.7
USA	1.4	1.3	5.6
oecd average	1.0	1.0	6.4

Source: OECD 2003a: 22f

things also depend on the question of how price-sensitive Swiss products and services are.

A second specific factor that is very important for the relatively long period of recession and near-stagnation has probably been the sharp decline of Swiss house prices, with their corresponding negative wealth effect and negative consequences for the construction industry. Here, Switzerland's trajectory paralleled Germany's, but not those of the other 'model economies' (with the exception of Sweden and Finland, though there the crisis terminated in the mid-1990s). Just as in these Scandinavian countries, housing prices rose sharply in Switzerland in the late 1980s – in 1989 alone by about 20 percent – before they started to fall dramatically. After a slight increase in 1990, housing prices fell about 10 percent in 1991, 5 percent in 1992, and 10 percent in 1993. Prices levelled off in 1994/95, but began falling again in 1996, by 7 percent. Prices did not start to rise again until 1998 (Credit Suisse 2003, p.9). As a consequence, the construction industry suffered shrinking annual turnover – for example, from 1995 to 1997 the decline was about 10 percent (SNB 1997, p.13 and 2002, p.21). So the Swiss did not participate in the bubble that was so characteristic for the model economies in the final decade of the millennium, and thereafter their share of that bubble was rather modest. Moreover, in comparative terms productivity growth was very low (see below).

As a result of economic stagnation, standardised unemployment rose to the record level of 4.1 percent in 1997 (see Table 5.1 for average unemployment figures of the years 1990-2000). This was still low by international standards, but it created a completely new situation for a country used to rates of about 1 to 2 percent. The OECD (OCDE 1997, p.7) asked whether the era of exceptionally low Swiss unemployment was over. Subsequent years appeared to give a negative answer. The economic recovery starting in 1998 created new jobs and unemployment declined to 2.5 percent by 2001 (OECD 2003a, p.297). This is the point at which Switzerland finally benefited from the euphoric and expansionist, but heavily debt-induced, global business cycle of the years up to 2001. Thereafter, growth slowed down, and Switzerland did not escape from the recession. The employment situation worsened again, and unemployment is back at a level of 4 percent (*The Economist*, December 20, 2003: 152), which however is, just as in the mid-1990s, a comparatively low figure.

Disentangling the Swiss 'miracle'

The most striking feature of the Swiss development is not unemployment, however. It is the stability of the employment rate at a level of 78 to 79 percent throughout the 1990s (Table 5.1 indicates that the changes have been very small). How has this been possible in the context of the very low rate of Swiss GDP growth in this decade and, although to a lesser degree, the previous one (see Table 1.2 in the Introduction)? In per capita terms, the difference between Swiss growth and that of comparable countries is even more accentuated: Annual average GDP growth per capita was only 0.2 percent in the 1990s, while it was 1.7 percent in the EU15, and in the 1980s the figures were 1.5 and 2.1 percent, respectively (OECD 2003e, p.32f).

A quick answer could be that Switzerland maintained its high employment rate because its productivity growth was also very low (Table 5.2). This is probably a good answer and part of the explanation. In fact, however, it only displaces the question, because now one has to ask how a country can stay competitive with such low productivity growth over a long period. Moreover, there was an immense increase of relative unit labour costs from 69 in 1982 to 106 (indexing 1995 as 100; OECD 2002f, p.223). Only Denmark approached this poor performance with a rise from 82 to 107. So, what we have to explain is not only a) why unemployment remained comparatively low and b) why the high Swiss employment rate, which is not entirely the pendant of low unemployment, could survive the decline of productivity growth, but also c) why Switzerland could remain relatively com-

Table 5.2 Labour productivity (output per hour) growth and GDP growth per capita; annual averages

	SPD/capita Productivity		GDP/capita	
	1985-91	1992-01	1980-90	1990-00
Australia			1.7	2.3
Austria	2.7	2.2	2.1	1.8
Denmark	0.9	2.5	1.9	2.0
Finland	3.2	2.9	2.7	1.8
Ireland			3.3	6.4
Netherlands	1.1	1.0	1.6	2.2
Sweden	1.4	2.6	1.9	1.4
Switzerland	0.6	0.5	1.5	0.2
France	2.4	1.1	1.8	1.4
Germany	2.5	1.3	2.0	1.3
Italy	2.2	1.6	2.2	1.4
UK	1.3	1.6	2.5	1.9
USA	1.0	1.5	2.2	2.2
Total OECD	1.9	1.8	2.3	1.8

Source: OECD 2002a: 32f and 150

petitive and did not experience an even severer decline in GDP growth. It is remarkable that the latter two questions are nearly never asked (Werner 2002 is an exception).

In so far as employment and unemployment are in a reverse reciprocal relationship to each other, Swiss unemployment has of course been kept down by high employment. Unemployment, however, also depends on the participation rate. When the latter is rising more than the employment rate, unemployment will also rise even if the employment rate is stable or slightly increasing. This is what happened in a number of Western countries in the second half of the 1970s and the first half of the 1980s when large groups of women entered the labour market. Prior to the cultural changes of the 'Sixties', these women would have become full-time housewives. The policy reaction in most countries of the European continent was to limit unemployment by keeping in check the (growth of the) participation rate. The means most frequently adopted for realising this target were early retirement and disability schemes.

In Switzerland these strategies have not been important for a long time, however. The Swiss employment rate is as high as it is because all groups of the working age population, juveniles, women, and people older than 55 years are participating in the labour market. Instead, Switzerland made use of its large and flexible foreign labour force. For decades, low unemployment was largely based on a capacity to adjust the supply of labour downwards by pushing thousands of migrant workers out of the country. The use of strict migration policy is a well-established feature of Swiss policies to control the labour market (Bonvin 1996; Flückiger 1998; Merrien 2000). From the mid-1960s, foreign workers always represented between 20 and 26 percent of the labour force. When the economy needed workers, the number of work-permits would be enlarged.[6] When a recession occurred, the number of annual, seasonal and cross-border workers would be limited. For a long time, this was the explicit government policy to regulate the labour market.

During the global downturn from 1974 to 1976, Switzerland was hit harder than anywhere else in Europe (Danthine and Lambelet 1987) because at that time the effects of the oil crisis and the loss of market shares (of e.g. watches) to Japanese competitors went together (Schmidt 1985, p.34f). Some 258,000 jobs – about 8 percent of total employment – disappeared. Unemployment did not spectacularly increase to 8 percent, however, because the job loss was largely compensated by the contraction of the non-permanent foreign labour force, particularly of workers whose annual permits were not extended. Foreign workers lost 196,000 of these 258,000 jobs (Table 5.3; Schmidt 1985, p.61, presents slightly different figures). As a result, although labour market participation for the working age population of about 4 million people declined from 3,203,000 in 1973 to 2,951,000 in 1978 (Madison 1982, p.209), the unemployment rate could remain at a level of nearly zero (ibid, p.208; it 'climbed' from zero to 0.7 percent). The Swiss government demonstrated an ability to push a large part of the working population across its borders. In subsequent years to 1982, the economy and the labour market recovered, and foreign workers got back one-third of the jobs they had lost in the previous period. Most new jobs, however, went to Swiss women (Table 5.3).

In the recession of 1982/83, which was relatively mild in Switzerland, it was again foreigners who lost the most jobs, and in part they were again barred from the labour market by immigration policy, but this time the total job loss was very limited. The recovery in the 8 years afterwards created 635,000 new jobs, most of which went to Swiss women and foreign men, but also to foreign women. This new pattern, of a labour market advantageous to women, was also visible in the long recession and stagnation period

Table 5.3 The development of Swiss employment in recent recessive and expansive periods in terms of nationality and gender (in thousands)

	1973-1976	1976-1982	1982-1983	1983-1991	1991-1997
Swiss men	-40	+42	+8	+79	-39
Swiss women	-22	+139	+8	+218	+34
Foreign men	-148	+53	-10	+215	-92
Foreign women	-48	+8	-5	+123	+8
Total	-258	+238	0	+635	-89

Source: Weber 2001, p.6

of the 1990s. Foreign men were the biggest losers, while 'Swiss' men also lost jobs. But for 'Swiss' women and, though only slightly, foreign women, employment increased. This reflects the trend towards part-time work, which is largely a female affair. Part-time employment increased by 2.5 percentage points in the 1990s (OECD 2003a) and has been an important contributor to the maintenance of the high employment rate in Switzerland in this period of economic stagnation.

Nonetheless, the unemployment rate breached the post-WW II level of 1 percent for the first time. The labour market participation rate continued to increase, and so the gap between participation and employment, that is unemployment, became larger. This was due to a) the increasing number of women entering the labour market, and b) the fact that the number of permanent foreign residents/employees in Switzerland had strongly increased since the 1970s, when only 21 percent of foreign workers had permanent permits. In 1983 the respective percentage had already risen to 53 percent, and in the 1990s it reached its current level of nearly 60 percent (Table 5.4). These workers with permanent residence permits can no longer be legally pushed out. It is still possible, however, to limit the entry of annual, seasonal and cross-border workers. This happened in the 1990s – seasonal workers were particularly hard hit – but the total impact was not as dramatic as in the 1970s (Flückinger 1998, p.385; BFS 2003, p.4).

In the stagnation years of the 1990s, the development of generous disability and early pension schemes became a substitute for the flexible use of the foreign labour force. Now Switzerland definitely joined the ranks of those continental European welfare systems that had already fought unemployment with these measures since the late 1970s. The number of disability pensioners increased by 37 percent between 1990 and 1998 and nearly 50

Table 5.4 Categories of foreign workers in Switzerland in 1975 and 1993 in percent

	Permanent	Annual	Seasonal	Cross-border workers
1975	21.0	52.1	18.6	9.0
1993	57.6	18.1	7.6	16.7

Source: OFS 2002

Table 5.5 Number of persons in disability and early pension schemes

Years	In disability scheme	Early pensioners	Together
1960	25,609	9,674	35,283
1980	123,322	79,706	203,028
1985	144,582	89,841	234,423
1990	164,329	93,556	257,885
1995	199,265	114,111	313,376
2001	241,952	160,877	402,829

Source: OFS 2002

percent between 1990 and 2001 (Table 5.5), while that of recipients of the early pension benefits rose by 70 percent. Although the growing use of these schemes weakened the finances of the social security system – in 1997 the cost of the disability scheme alone was 3.20 percent of GDP, versus 4.6 in the Netherlands, 2.7 in Denmark, 1.7 in France, and 1.3 in the USA (OECD 1999b) – the costs in terms of reputation, from an overall public perspective, would be much higher if instead unemployment benefits were paid to these people, and the full employment country par excellence revealed an unemployment rate of about 10 percent.

Summarising, unemployment was held down by the management of the number of migrant workers and later by opening the gates of disability and early pension schemes in order to reduce labour market participation growth. The shift from full-time to part-time jobs also contributed to the limitation of unemployment as well as to the maintenance of the high employment rate – though the latter declined in FTEs. The most important factor explaining the maintenance of the high employment rate is the very low pace of productivity growth. This nexus implies that employment has only marginally been rationalised by technological renewal, and that unemployment has been "stored up" for some future burst of technological upgrading.

As already indicated, this raises the question of how Switzerland could stay competitive and not decline even more. Since this topic has not yet been systematically researched, we can only touch upon features that we find relevant. The first is the industrial specialisation of Switzerland. The country is known for its tourist industry, its chocolate and its watches. Statistics of (merchandise) exports partially confirm this picture: Instruments, watches and jewellery formed 16 percent of Swiss exports in 2001 and food and agricultural products 3 percent (OSEC 2003, p.7). The bulk of Swiss exports came from chemical and pharmaceuticals (30 percent) as well as machines and electronics (26 percent). The export of metal and metal products (7.5 percent) and precious metals and stones (4 percent) also has some significance. Since heavy industry is negligible, this specialisation means that Switzerland, just like southern Germany and northern Italy, is strong in special instruments, mechanics and equipment overwhelmingly produced by small and medium-sized enterprises (54 percent of Swiss employment is concentrated there; Flückinger 1998, p.372). In part, this is a specialisation in middle-tech niches where price competition is not particularly fierce, and for another part it is a specialisation involving maintenance services where quality and reliability instead of price are decisive.

This is not a sufficient explanation, however. For in the past Switzerland has lost market shares in its fields of specialisation (from the mid-1960s to the mid-1970s its world market share in watches shrank by 50 percent; Schmidt 1985, p.34f). Why should this not happen again? Perhaps the answer is that Switzerland has built up a protective quality image. In the case of watches, this would mean that the production of ordinary examples has been lost to competitors, but that expensive, positional quality watches are still a Swiss domain. According to a research study conducted by UBS bank among 500 EU citizens (Pauli 2002, p.4ff), Switzerland has become 'a brand name that sells'. Images are based on simplified and relatively stable concepts, and the 'made in Switzerland' image is associated with quality – an association made by almost 100 percent of the respondents – exclusiveness, above-average levels of environmental friendliness and precision. And crucially, 'many customers are prepared to pay hefty premiums for a product in order to connect directly to its image'. It seems that Switzerland's image has compensated for its lack of productivity growth.

Table 5.6   Gross Public Social Expenditures as a percentage of GDP 1980-1998

	1980	1982	1984	1986	1988	1990	1992	1994	1996	1998
Australia	11.32	12.34	13.30	13.38	12.45	14.36	16.38	16.25	17.92	17.81
Austria	23.33	-	-	-	-	25.00	25.89	27.98	27.91	26.80
Belgium	24.18	26.48	26.07	26.77	26.04	24.60	25.43	25.96	25.53	24.54
Denmark	29.06	29.57	28.65	26.99	29.20	29.32	30.72	33.06	31.69	29.81
Finland	18.51	20.29	21.83	23.49	23.29	24.78	33.92	33.04	30.97	26.54
France	21.14	22.87	23.46	26.41	25.99	26.45	27.88	29.07	29.31	28.82
Germany	20.28	21.12	20.40	20.88	21.21	20.29	25.56	26.19	28.06	27.29
Ireland	16.92	17.71	17.24	22.20	20.00	19.02	20.12	20.21	18.52	15.77
Italy	18.42	20.33	20.91	21.25	21.56	23.87	25.52	25.45	24.38	25.07
Netherlands	27.26	29.85	28.89	27.09	26.96	27.92	28.56	26.85	25.29	23.90
Sweden	29.00	30.18	29.19	30.22	30.87	31.02	36.39	35.21	32.99	30.98
Switzerland	15.17	15.81	16.43	16.46	16.77	19.80	23.35	25.44	27.53	28.28
UK	18.19	20.24	21.15	21.38	19.38	21.62	25.75	26.10	25.79	24.70
USA	13.13	13.70	13.12	13.04	12.92	13.36	15.11	15.34	15.30	14.59

Source: OECD 2002g

An expanding welfare system

The most striking fact of the Swiss system of social security is its expansion in the past 20 years, and especially the last 10. Total social expenditures have expanded in most Western countries, even when, as has regularly happened, welfare and social security benefits have been cut. The reason for this development is a) the process of demographic ageing and the related increase of the total sum of pensions – to which more than half of all social expenditures in most countries go – and health care costs and b) the rising number of welfare recipients in other categories such as early pensions, disability schemes and also unemployment and social assistance. Switzerland stands out, however, because it has nearly doubled its gross public social expenditures from 15 to 28 percent of GDP between 1980 and 1998. By this increase, Switzerland has reached the level of the other small countries discussed in this volume (see Table 5.6; the picture would not fundamentally change if we were to include private social security expenditures).

Simultaneously, taxes and social contributions as a percentage of GDP have risen, though here the increase is not as spectacular as in the case of social expenditures (OECD 1999c). Spending less on defence and education, Switzerland is still not a high-tax state. Furthermore, it should be noted that two-thirds of public expenses are done at the cantonal and local level of the Swiss confederation.

The first attempt to create a Swiss welfare system aimed, as in Germany, to cope with the 'Arbeiterfrage'. The introduction of social insurance by Bismarck in the 1880s was widely seen as an example to be followed (Gilliand 1990). But ruling elites and government were not able to introduce important welfare reforms of the German sort. Their capacity for action was limited by consensual politics and referenda. These two limited the development of social insurance and social programs already agreed upon by Parliament and led to the implementation of schemes that, by European standards, were minimal (Immergut 1992). Because of the resulting residual character of the social security system and the restricted range of state intervention, the Swiss social system was characterised as liberal (Esping-Andersen 1990) for a long time. The low level of employment protection added to this picture.

In fact, however, confessional, conservative *and* liberal parties have been the main political forces creating the Swiss 'welfare state'. For this reason, its features also have a strong Christian Democratic flavour (Van Kersbergen 1995) and can be characterised as approaching the corporatist-conservative model, particularly in recent years when disability and early pension schemes were extended. At very least, one can say that the Swiss system has to be located somewhere in the middle of the axis between the conservative and liberal ideal types. For the institutional reasons mentioned, Switzerland has been a welfare laggard in comparison with other continental welfare states until the 1990s (Gilliand 1990, Gilliand and Rossini 1997; Bonoli 1997), when the disability scheme was extended and public insurance programmes for health care, unemployment and basic pensions were implemented by the federal government. Globalisation did not push towards more liberal-oriented policies in this country. On the contrary, the move was toward an extension of social rights and protection (cf. Garrett 1998 for the general argument connecting globalisation and welfare extension). For some policy-makers, experts, and commentators (Lane 1999), this development explains the deterioration of the Swiss labour market in the 1990s. But it cannot explain, however, the rapid decrease in unemployment from 1998 to 2001.

A special factor is the implementation of the unemployment insurance law. Until 1977, unemployment insurance was not compulsory, and few workers were affiliated to unemployment insurance funds. In economic downturns it pressed several workers, mainly women, to leave the labour market. The crisis of the mid-1970s changed the views of the policy-makers and pushed them to modernise Swiss social security legislation. A bill to make affiliation to unemployment insurance funds compulsory was initiated, passed parliament and made part of the constitution in 1977. Then, the Federal Law on the compulsory unemployment insurance (LACI) was enacted in 1982 and came into effect in 1984. This law prescribes that:

- unemployment funds have to be financed by contributions from employers and employees (0.8 percent of the payroll equally distributed between both);
- these funds have to be administered by the cantons;
- benefits have to be granted up to an amount of 70 percent of the last salary for unemployed people without children and up to 80 percent for those with dependent children;
- the maximal duration is 85 working days for childless unemployed and 250 days for those with dependent children (in comparative perspective, this was not very generous at that time);
- the fund employees have to examine whether the unemployed fulfil the legal eligibility conditions (relating mainly to the length of the contribution period; this element of means-testing is rather 'liberal' in Esping-Andersen's classification).

In 1995, the Federal Council adopted and subsequent referenda confirmed a number of Federal Urgent Decrees (AFU) aiming at quick adaptation of the provisions for unemployed people. The maximum duration of the entitlement to benefits was progressively extended to 400 working days, but the notion of suitable work became an explicit part of the law as did a provision that unemployed people had to accept any job with a salary amounting to at least 70 percent of the last wage. Contributions were increased to 3 percent of the payroll, equally distributed between the employer and the worker. The result of these changes has been that the initial (1st week) net replacement for unemployed Swiss rose from 75.5 percent in 1977 to 76.5 percent in 1999 while it declined in most other countries (e.g. from 69 to 63.5 percent in Denmark; from 85 to 75.5 in the Netherlands, from 62.5 to 32 percent in Britain). France and Italy, where benefits rose from 46.5 to 71 percent and 13 to 46.5 percent, respectively, are the other main exceptions to this trend (Alan and Scruggs 2004).

The development of national welfare and social security schemes at a generous level has probably prevented the increase of poverty and perhaps has helped keep the level of inequality relatively limited. One has to be careful here, however, because Switzerland is not included in most comparative statistical surveys conducted by the OECD or Eurostat. As a result, the comparative data we have are relatively old. In Table 1.3 the data for Switzerland are for the year 1992 when most of the extensions of the Swiss welfare system had yet to occur.

The table shows that income inequality in Switzerland (in 1992) is higher than in both the social democratic welfare systems of Scandinavia and the rather conservative systems of Austria, France, Germany and the Netherlands, but that is lower than in the more liberal UK and USA (as well as Italy which, pensions excepted, has a rudimentary welfare system). The Swiss poverty rate[7] reveals the same pattern by being located in between the northwest-European rates and those of the Anglo-Saxon countries (and Italy). So, both data sets confirm the intermediate position of the Swiss welfare system.

Conclusion

For a long time, Switzerland was presented as a successful example of an export-oriented development (Katzenstein 1985). Nowadays, Switzerland is no longer particularly successful. Therefore, the Swiss 'miracle' is quite different from those in Australia, Ireland, the Netherlands and, for that matter, the USA. These countries present strong employment increases in the 1980s (especially after 1983) and 1990s. The second half of the 1990s presents vigorous economic growth based to a considerable extent on a stock market and, particularly, house price bubble triggering new private consumption. A house price bubble also occurred in Denmark and Sweden, although the latter experienced a harsh crisis until the mid-1990s. Switzerland did not share in this bubble, and the growth rate of its GDP was low. A similar story has to be told about productivity, which also developed very slowly. Nonetheless, Switzerland was able to stay competitive and maintain one of the highest employment rates in the world. This is the Swiss 'miracle'.

The 'miracle' has to be related to the shift from full-time to part-time employment, to the Swiss industrial specialisation and to the country's very strong image of being a reliable quality producer. Much detailed research to explain the 'miracle' still has to be done, however. In terms of luck, 'stuck' (conscious action conditioned by routines developed within the existing institutional context) and 'pluck' (action strategically responding to a perceived misfit between given structures and the changing environment; Schwartz 2001a), the latter is difficult to discern. Unemployment has always been managed by a flexible immigration policy, but its impact has diminished since the late 1970s, and it cannot explain the high employment rate in a context of slightly increasing labour market participation. Perhaps until 25 years ago immigration policy was a matter of 'pluck' – an innovative response to labour shortages in an economically booming Switzerland and a nationalist measure to restrict unemployment in cyclical dips as well as in the downturn of the 1970s. But today it represents only 'stuck' – a continuation of the usual policy routines. The rest of the 'Swiss miracle' is a matter of luck: a specific industrial specialisation and a strong quality image that does not necessarily reflect reality. Other countries cannot copy this luck, but they can learn that image is an important factor in international competition.

Meanwhile, 'liberal' Switzerland has developed a relatively generous, and to some extent 'conservative', welfare system in the past two decades and kept its levels of inequality and poverty clearly below Anglo-Saxon standards. In this respect, it is slowly converging towards EU norms, despite its unwillingness to enter the Union. Given an unwillingness and inability to expand budget deficits, this suggests that unemployment may well rise to continental European 'standards' in the coming decade. Certainly, any prolonged revival in productivity gains can only imply labour shedding as Switzerland defends its product niches from quality gains made by other producers.

Notes

1 For statistical and bibliographical assistance we thank Maud Adriaansen and Franca van Hooren; Herman Schwartz provided editorial assistance.
2 Changes occurred only recently. Following negotiations in the Uruguay Round of the GATT and with the EC, Switzerland has begun to reform its agricultural policy (Sciarini 1994; Mach 1997).
3 Notably those of the export sector (e.g. the machine and chemical industries). By contrast, the associations of the sheltered sector (USAM, USP) were largely opposed to the liberalisation of the internal market.
4 Some academics such as professors Borner and Brunetti have been very influential experts. The thesis of their (together with T. Straubhaar) book, *Schweiz AG. Vom Sonderfall zum Sanierungsfall* (1990) produced large ripples in the mass media and particularly in the publications of employers' associations (cf. Mach, 1997).
5 Notably high officials of the OFAEE (Office fédéral des affaires économiques extérieures), the administrative department, which conducted discussions with the EC and did the Swiss preparation work for the GATT Treaty. Management consultants (in Switzerland the Arthur Andersen group has been consulted very often) also played an important role in selling new policy ideas.

6 Four kinds of work permits exist: the A, B and C and the frontier worker permit. The C is 'permanent'. Workers must have worked in Switzerland for a minimum of five years without interruption. Even in this case it is very hard to obtain Swiss naturalisation. The B is limited to one year but eventually re-con-
ducted. The family of the worker has the right to come to Switzerland only one
year after he received the permit. The A is the seasonal permit. The worker can
work only 9 months a year. He has no guarantee to obtain a new permit and no
right to unemployment benefits. His/her family cannot join him or her. The
cross border or frontier worker has to return home every night.

7 Alternative sources present somewhat different percentages, even if they are
based on the same criteria. According to the OEDC (2002h), for example,
Scandinavian poverty rates and child poverty rates in particular are lower than
in the Luxemburg Income Study. The child poverty percentages for the mid-
1990s are: Finland 2, Denmark 3, Sweden 3, France 7, Switzerland 10, Germany 11, Italy 19, UK 19 and US 23 percent. Such alternative sources do not
present a fundamentally different picture, however.

6   Recasting the Story of Ireland's Miracle: Policy, Politics or Profit?

Mary Daly

Only at one's peril would one underestimate the extent and pace of change occurring in Ireland. Over the space of just six years in the 1990s, the country saw phenomenal growth in jobs, output and incomes as well as significant changes in consumption, lifestyles, values and patterns of political and social organisation. Indeed, it may not be unreasonable to claim that Ireland changed as much in the last decade as in the preceding century. Gainsaying many predictions and the experience of most other countries, 'Ireland.plc' prospered hugely as trade and markets became more globalised and supranational political and economic blocs more established. Ireland is generally regarded as a model case of how a small European country has benefited particularly from the current stage of the globalised competitive economy. The picture which this chapter paints of Ireland is somewhat different: an economy-oriented (and within that competition-oriented), carefully managed model of national modernisation which has self-consciously built a capital-friendly economic policy, a consensus-oriented political culture and a model of society in which the 'social' is subservient to the economic. This piece distances itself from much of the existing literature which is quite polarised in how it interprets and explains the Irish case. Growth tends to be attributed *either* to economic factors (international but also national) *or* to political factors. Here I argue for a more complicated analysis, claiming that the story of Ireland's 'success' needs to be cast in terms of an interaction between policy, politics and economics. Furthermore, the attribution of 'success' to the Irish model in implying significant change may be premature. A more guarded interpretation is called for when one considers how recent Ireland's growth and its sustainability are. Developments in the last few years not only indicate Ireland's vulnerability to recession in the USA but also reveal endogenous challenges, in terms of the management of public finances and the likely continuation of policy consensus.

This article has three main objectives, organising it into three parts. The first is to identify the nature and scale of the changes involved in Ireland's economic fortunes in the last decade or so. The phenomenal nature of Ireland's recent growth pattern is revealed, especially in the context of the longer run of Irish economic development. The second objective is to look for an explanation. The range of possible explanatory factors are pared down to three: the role and nature of public policy, the form and nature of political organisation and political culture, the accommodation reached with international capital. Here I demonstrate that economic change has been accompanied (and in part occasioned) by a transformation of politics and a continual adaptation of policies. In its third part the article devotes attention to the sustainability of the economic progress. Drawing on economic, political and social factors, this section interrogates the sustainability of the growth and hence the characterisation of Ireland as a 'miracle economy'. The main thrust of the argumentation is that the Irish case is not an example of transformation or a miracle but rather of the conjuncture of a set of circumstances which, while it allowed Ireland to reap the dividends of its long-term growth strategy, was underpinned by significant adaptation of political institutions, compromises among interest groups, a polarisation of winners and losers, and a series of economic/social trade-offs.

The constituents of economic growth and development

After the expansionary 1960s and 1970s and very difficult 1980s, the 1990s delivered an economic bonanza to Ireland. The Irish growth experience of the last eight to ten years has not just been phenomenal in scale but is also remarkable by virtue of its depth. It is this growth that has earned Ireland the metaphor of Celtic Tiger. Not only was there extensive growth (growth in the size of the economy, in population and in numbers at work), but intensive growth (rise in living standards of the resident population) also took place (Barry et al. 1999, p.15).

The following table shows the pattern in average annual growth rates for Ireland as well as for the UK, Europe and the OECD over the last half-century.

The data[2] underline both the particularity and exceptionalism of the recent experience in Ireland. Between 1987 and 1998 the country recorded an annual average growth rate of 6.7 percent, almost double the average achieved in the post-war period as a whole. It is important to note that the most intensive growth period occurred from 1994 to 1999, GDP growth averaging 8.4 percent annually between these years. In international comparison, Ireland's 'golden age' occurred during a period (1987-1998) when growth rates elsewhere were modest. Looking at the period as a whole, the

Table 6.1   Average annual growth rates, GDP per capita, 1950-1998, Ireland, UK, Europe and
            OECD

	Ireland	UK	Europe	OECD
1950-1973	3.0	2.4	4.3	3.8
1973-1987	2.5	1.8	1.9	1.8
1987-1998	6.7	1.6	1.8	1.7
1950-1987	2.8	2.2	3.4	3.1
1950-1998	3.7	2.1	3.0	2.8

Source: O'Grada and O'Rourke 2000, Table 7.1, p. 190

rate of expansion of the Irish economy compares favourably with that of the
UK, Europe and the OECD over the last 25 years but not during the 1950-
1973 period. The latter 'relative failure' is important, for one would have
expected Ireland to have been growing rapidly in this period, given its very
poor starting position in 1950. The evidence indicates that Ireland was an
important outlier during this period, with a growth rate significantly behind
what would have been predicted by its initial income situation (O'Grada
and O'Rourke 2000, pp.191-2). In other words, Ireland failed to perform
up to par for most of the post-war period, and its economic growth level began to converge with that of the more developed countries only from the
'mid- to late-1980s' on. It is important, therefore, to bear in mind the recent
nature of Irish 'success'.

One of the most remarkable features of recent developments was the job-
intensive nature of growth. This is significant against the backdrop of international sluggishness in job growth and also in the context of Ireland's long-
term inability to create sufficient employment. The latter left a legacy of
high unemployment and forced up to a quarter of a million people to emi-
grate (O'Hagan 2000, p.176). The country's sustained job creation failure
was overturned in the 1990s, however. In the ten years to 1996, employment
grew by an average of 1.9 percent per annum. It was the later years of the
1990s that saw the most staggering increase though: in 1997, for example,
the numbers at work grew by over 8 percent and in 1998 by 6.4 percent. In
fact, employment expanded by over 34 percent between 1993 and 1998.
This last fact underlines the recent nature of the boom. For all that employment has grown, employment rates in Ireland are still lower than the EU average, the gap for women being especially marked. While there was an increased labour supply, unemployment was also affected, dropping from
over 15 percent in the early 1990s to about 4 percent in 2000. Most of the

fall occurred from 1996 on. Long-term unemployment was especially affected. So buoyant was labour demand that Ireland began to experience significant labour supply constraints. In 1990-2000 the potential labour supply[3] was down to around 9 percent, and current vacancy rates were equivalent to 6 percent of total employment. Both skill shortages and job vacancies were spread across the skills' spectrum.

As might be expected, women have played a major part in the changes in the labour supply. The female labour force participation rate increased by nearly 10 percentage points in the ten years between 1991 and 1999 (from 35.9 percent to 44 percent). Between 1993 and 1997, the number of women in regular employment grew by 26 percent, and between 1997 and 1998 alone the proportion of women in the labour force grew by 7 percent. Such growth is driven mainly by increases in the married women's employment rate, which rose from 20 percent in 1983 to 37 percent in 1997, an increase of almost 87 percent over the period. It may be difficult to appreciate the significance of this from outside Ireland. Such a level of growth in female employment (in fact of any population group) is revolutionary (rather than evolutionary), and I cannot find any precedent for such a growth rate anywhere in Western Europe at any time in recent history. It is worth noting that, while there was some ambivalence about it, increased female labour force participation encountered little resistance. Women themselves seemed to welcome it, regarding it as an opportunity. Nor was there much organised resistance from men or male interest groups. This might be because, from a male/female perspective, the situation was not zero-sum in which female workers displaced male workers. Rather, as women were moving into the labour force, men were moving into better paid jobs and, as will be referred to below, generally improving their class position.

In terms of the sectoral distribution of employment growth, manufacturing employment did not, as elsewhere, fall but actually rose by an annual average of 3 percent through much of the 1990s (O'Connell 2000, p.67). Given that such a rate of expansion is similar to that of employment as a whole, manufacturing maintained its share of total employment (22 percent) over the period. Manufacturing job growth is located in both foreign-owned and indigenous firms. As one might expect, it is the service sector that has seen the greatest job growth. Between 1991 and 1997, there were 100,000 (an increase of 23 percent) new jobs in market services (mostly in professional, business and personal services) and 60,000 in non-market services (mainly in public sector-based health and education activities) (ibid, p.68). As a result, the proportion of total employment located in the service sector overall increased in the period from 57.9 percent to 61.1 percent. Most of the job growth in the 1990s involved full-time jobs, although the share of part-time employment in total employment continued to rise (doubling between 1990 and 1998 when it reached 17 percent of all employment) (ibid, p.77). As measured by fixed-term contracts and atypical and part-time employment, the Irish labour market is becoming increasingly flexible. However, it is again important to note that the rate of flexibilisation in Ireland is slower than the EU average and that the prevalence of part-time and temporary work is below the EU average.

There has been some concern expressed about the nature of the change in the labour market and whether or not the new employment is of poor quality (O'Hearn 2000). In seeking to address this issue, O'Connell (2000, pp.72-76) looks at the class structure as manifested by occupational and employer/employee status. He finds no evidence of deterioration but suggests to the contrary that there has been a general upgrading of the quality of positions in the labour market and that the more advantaged positions in the class structure accounted for a disproportionately large share of the recent employment growth. Apart from the structural transformation involved in a steady shift from agriculture to industrial and service-sector employment, it is suggested that the new types of employment involved qualifications or skills that either had not been required by traditional employment or were unnecessary to inherit the family business or farm. In addition, strong growth occurred in both upper and lower middle-class positions, the former especially among men.

To complete Ireland's 'miracle' there was significant productivity growth. Such growth, whether measured by GDP or GNP per worker, was substantially higher than the EU average since the 1960s. In the 1970s the Irish manufacturing industry enjoyed an annual average growth in productivity of 4 percent. In the 1980s this increased to about 7 percent, and it grew to 10.6 percent between 1994 and 1998 (O'Sullivan 2000, p.262). In addition, unit labour costs decreased by 20 percent in Ireland between 1985 and 1998, compared with a fall of 10 percent across the EU.

Possible explanations

Although some literature might indicate otherwise, it is not easy to identify the exact reasons for Ireland's recent economic growth. As mentioned above, there is a general tendency in the literature to isolate out individual factors. A variety of factors have been considered in this regard, including for example an elastic (and plentiful) labour supply, a well-educated and

English-speaking work force, the existence of a class of entrepreneurs and technical professionals, the single-mindedness and appropriateness of public policy. It is my view that while these all played a role, they are not in themselves a sufficient explanation but are part of a larger explanation. We need to think in terms of broad categories of explanation rather than individual factors. As the title of the chapter indicates, I am of the opinion that the following three factors have been hugely significant for Ireland's recent growth: public policy, political culture and the accommodation reached with international capital.

Public Policy

Although the state has tended to be under-elaborated in explanations of Ireland's development,[4] there is no doubt that the state, and especially its agency with regard to economic development policy, played a huge role. Successive Irish governments have employed what could be called a 'strategy of development' which privileged economic development policy and carved out and resourced a consistent and vigorous promoter role in this regard for the public authorities. A key part of Ireland's story is of a long-standing, relatively highly resourced and fairly consistent set of policies that sought to overcome disadvantages associated with Ireland's peripheral location and its lack of an industrialised core (or past). If Ireland could not develop its own industry, it would substitute foreign industry for it. For around 40 years now, national sights have been firmly fixed on a growth strategy that centred on the attraction of export-oriented foreign, manufacturing companies. Against this background, Laffan and O'Donnell (1998, pp.157-8) suggest that the development of the Irish economy, policy and society since 1960 can be seen as a case study in how to manage internationalisation and the emergence of international governance.

The 1960s were a watershed in terms of economic development policy in Ireland, the time when the country broke with its protectionist approach and embarked on a policy of internationalisation and foreign direct investment (Bradley 2000, p.6). Economic development policy loomed large, and the state placed itself at the centre of this arena by virtue of its efforts to continually upgrade the factors of production and by assuming the role of 'hunter and gatherer' of foreign direct investment (O'Connell and O'Riain 2000, p.315). Economic development policy was marked by a number of features.

- A generous and (at that time) quite innovative set of policies was put in place, offering tax relief and grants aimed at attracting foreign industry to Ireland. Its signature piece was a policy on profits: there was 100 percent tax relief on the profits of manufacturing exports which was followed by a preferential 10 percent corporation tax rate on all manufacturing and internationally traded services profits.
- The strategy of making Ireland an attractive business location was pursued very consistently. From the 1960s to the 1980s an almost singular focus was placed on the attraction of FDI. Later policy became more diversified while retaining the predominant focus on FDI.
- Wage restraint was another, if until the 1980s somewhat under-developed, component of industrial policy. In the 1970s wage bargaining was centralised, and from the 1980s a broad-ranging national planning process was implemented in which wage restraint was a central feature (to be discussed below).
- A further feature of the Irish approach was a very positive (as well as liberal) stance on trade.[5]
- In addition, a state-led restructuring of the educational system towards technical education was undertaken from the 1970s.
- A final notable component of the Irish policy constellation was active participation in the Europeanisation project. Ireland's strongly pro-European stance was remarkable by any standards but especially in relation to its nearest competitor for international investment – the UK.

The year 1987 marked another watershed in that it saw the introduction of fiscal retrenchment policies. Over the course of the 1970s and 1980s, attempts had been made to force growth on the domestic economy (through a combination of tax cuts and increased government expenditure) despite international recession. This led to a crisis in the public finances – fiscal deficits pushed the Exchequer Borrowing Requirement to almost 16 percent of GNP in the late 1970s and early 1980s. This began to be addressed in 1987, under the pressures associated with a fear of public meltdown and impending EMU. According to O'Donnell (1998, p.9), the failure of fiscal policy during the 1970s and 1980s led to a period of intense reflection on the meaning for Ireland of EU integration and internationalisation. This was a climate in which, as O'Connell and O'Riain (2000, p.338) point out, there was space for experimentation and innovation.

The significance of public policy in the Irish case derives not only (or so much) from the orientation and content of policy but also from the adaptations which were (capable of being) made. Successive changes in the nature and content of policy intervention over time underlined the adaptive capacities of the Irish policy apparatus. The search for FDI became increasingly selective, focusing more on growth industries and targeting particular industries. Only potential winners were wanted in Ireland. Secondly, the almost singular focus on attracting foreign industry came to be counterbalanced by a concern to support indigenous industry (as the weaknesses of the indigenous sector and the lack of local and national embeddedness of foreign-owned firms became more apparent) and to increase the linkages between the two. Towards these ends, the public authorities charged with development set about creating a network of industry and trade associations, innovation and technology centres and other forums which provide an associational infrastructure for information sharing, co-operation and innovation (O'Riain 2000). Thirdly, a focus on internationally traded services was put in place to complement the traditional emphasis on manufacturing. Fourthly, financial and other forms of state assistance became more closely tied to the characteristics and performance of companies, and there was a shift away from grants to support capital investment in favour of financial incentives for employment, research and development and training. Moreover, in place of the zero rate on manufacturing profits (long-term politically unsustainable), a 10 percent tax rate on profits of this sector as well as those of internationally traded services was put in place until 2010 (to be followed by a 12.5 percent rate until 2025).

All of this proved a successful strategy for, as we shall see below, foreign direct investment provided the growth engine for the manufacturing sector which proved a very important component of Irish economic growth. The high proportion of FDI in the Irish manufacturing sector and its export-oriented emphasis make the Irish economy quite unique among peripheral EU member countries (Fitz Gerald 2000, p.37). O'Hagan (2000, p.176) suggests that the policy of attracting foreign investment, much of it in the high-tech sectors, allowed Ireland to cope with the trade and technological effects of globalisation. O'Hearn (2000, p.74) goes further in claiming that Ireland bought 'tigerhood'. Huge sums were spent on enticing Intel to come to Ireland, and once it located its European site for the production of computer chips near Dublin in 1991, an agglomeration effect was engendered whereby within a short time nearly every major information technology company followed Intel to Ireland.

Politics

If there was continuity in industrial policy, the structure and practice of economic and political management witnessed considerable change. From a political economy perspective, Ireland is an interesting case for it could be said to be redrawing its political institutions and reconfiguring how politics and the relationship between politics and the economy are organised and managed.[6]

A most significant element in the Irish case, descriptively and causally, is the new corporatism. This has led to an alteration in the mode of governance. After decades of cleaving to the Westminster model, Ireland, under the influence of international developments and as a result of the evolution of its own political culture, has acquired one of the most inclusive forms of interest-based governance in Europe. A new system of political/economic management has emerged over the last 15 years. This involves a corporatist form of planning which has over time become ever more expansive. Initially confined to the state's old partners – trade unions, employers and farmers – 'partnership' has been broadened (for the last eight years or so) to include the community and voluntary sectors – the 'social pillar'. With representatives of the unemployed, women's groups and some church interests now included[7], it seems apposite to apply the term 'social corporatism' (even if Hardiman (2000) prefers Martin Rhodes's term of 'competitive corporatism'). A process akin to a 'national planning process' was initiated in the 1980s and not only survived the 1990s but was strengthened (judged on the basis of increasing breadth of the policy domains and issues covered) under successive governments. Much broader than a pay deal, the usually three-year agreements set down the tracks for national development policy incorporating such matters as regional development, infrastructural development, health policy, the management of the public finances (and sector) as well as social services and welfare. The current national programme is the sixth national agreement since the first one in 1987.[8]

Partnership is highly prized as an element of Ireland's 'winning formula'.[9] It is generally agreed that the national planning process was a key enabling factor for recent economic development. For a decade and a half, it delivered both wage moderation and relative industrial harmony. While social corporatism was born out of the severe financial difficulties experienced by Ireland in the 1980s, the resultant national agreements have always been closely oriented towards the promotion of growth and managing the demands of the different sectoral interests so that they neither lead to inflation nor threaten the country's appeal to foreign investment. In other words, competitiveness dominated as the central consideration in successive national pacts (which were negotiated under different governments). Within this framework, however, they have addressed an increasingly broader set of issues such as local partnerships to combat long-term unemployment, some privatisation of state-owned companies, a programme to combat poverty and social exclusion, the provision of childcare, the modernisation of the public service and partnerships at the enterprise level (O'Donnell 1998, p.12).

There are a number of features of Irish corporatism which merit emphasis. While it brings together a diversity of interests, it is strongly consensual in that, as O'Donnell (1998, p.18) points out, it is generally grounded in a shared understanding of the problems facing the Irish economy. Moreover, the process of social partnership and the nature of the agency involved in it are to be emphasised. In this regard O'Donnell (ibid) stresses the 'deliberative' character of Irish social partnership. Consultation and negotiation have figured prominently alongside bargaining, and the inter-dependence of the partners is recognised, as is the pivotal role played by the government. Since corporatism in Ireland is not a product of (the recent) economic success but of the economic crisis of the 1980s, the results tend to bear out the point made by Castles (1994) and others that historic compromises are effected in the wake of economic crises.[10]

It is interesting to consider why social corporatism should have become so firmly established in Ireland. One reason is undoubtedly the fact that it involves a form of politics that finds fertile ground in the Irish political culture. This is a very consensual political culture in which networking is widespread. Clientilism pervades Irish politics – indeed one could say that a key historical tension in the Irish political landscape has involved marrying the Westminster model with the more personalised, clientilistic pattern of Irish politics. Furthermore, the absence of a left-right political cleavage has meant that Ireland has no great ideological divides in relation to economic and social policy and that all political parties can and do represent the different sets of interests involved. The kind of pragmatism involved in social partnership is not therefore impeded in any major way by ideological factors on the part of any of the main parties. Even the trade unions do not represent a radical constituency. In their case, involvement in social partnership lent them added legitimacy and a leverage in national politics beyond that which the size and influence of their membership would otherwise allow them. Third, social partnership could be seen as an attempt to 'reinvent politics'. One could argue that the general malaise that has afflicted politics elsewhere is especially prevalent in Ireland. Not only does Irish politics have to contend with the decline of interest in formal politics and democratic participation that has assailed most of the industrialised democracies, but public confidence in politics and public institutions in Ireland has been eroded by a series of scandals and dodgy deals which come to light on a regular basis. These reveal the existence of a 'golden circle' of businessmen, bankers and politicians and an interpenetration of the political and economic elites in Irish society (Collins 1999). Against this background, the recent moves to bring in non-labour, non-capital actors (the social pillar) may be interpreted as an attempt to reinterpret (or reinvent) politics in the light of decreased trust in conventional politics.

Searching questions have to be addressed to social partnership, however, as we shall see in the penultimate part of this chapter.

Accommodation with International Capitalism

The development policy in Ireland has above all endeavoured to make the country a friendly place for foreign capital. Judging on the basis of the following, it has been very successful in this regard.

Across a range of industrial sectors, Ireland offers more than double the rate of return on investment to be found elsewhere. One can see that it is particularly attractive as a European location, especially for chemicals and allied products as well as electrical and electronic goods. Apart from the favourable taxation regime, Ireland has considerable wage cost advantages also. Average labour costs, both direct and indirect, although rising, are still below the European average. Moreover, the strategy pursued through social partnership has limited wage growth. Wages as a share of GNP have fallen dramatically. For example, wages and salaries accounted for 60.7 percent of GNP in 1985, 51.7 percent in 1990, 52.6 percent in 1994 and 42.8 percent in 1997 (O'Grada and O'Rourke 2000, p.200). It seems, then, that while workers benefited from the boom, so too has capital. In fact, capital has clearly appropriated more of the growth dividend than has labour, as indicated by the sharp fall in the wage share of GDP.

These same authors undertake a growth accounting exercise which breaks down growth rates into a number of component parts (ibid, pp.196-198). They are especially interested in the components explained by labour force growth, capital accumulation and a residual (total factor productivity – TFP growth) which is taken to represent technological progress. They show that between 1987 and 1998 labour grew by 2.0 percent, fixed capital by 2.3 percent, and TFP by 4 percent. Concluding that TFP growth provides an important key to understanding the recent Irish success, they suggest that tech-

Table 6.2   Rate of return on US foreign direct investment stocks in Ireland, Europe and elsewhere 1997

Manufacturing industries:
Total   13.0
Europe   11.9
Ireland   27.2

Chemicals and allied products:
Total   12.8
Europe   12.6
Ireland   35.4

Electrical and electronic equipment:
Total   14.4
Europe   15.6
Ireland   33.5

Source: O'Sullivan 2000, Table 10.2, p. 266

nological transfers from the rest of the world may have been of great importance in enabling Ireland to catch up. US FDI played a huge role in this. Ireland's share of US FDI increased from 0.6 percent in 1984-86 to 0.9 percent
in 1989-91 and 3.0 percent in 1996-98 (ibid, p.197). Clearly, Ireland has
become a significant platform for US high-tech companies competing in the
European market.

Apart from its taxation and labour cost advantages, Ireland has other at-
tractions. O'Hagan (2000, pp.171-3) describes Ireland as having a relatively flexible employment protection environment. On the basis of such factors
as fixed-term contracts, dismissal of regular workers and so forth, Ireland is
seen to operate quite a liberal employment regime. This is true especially in
comparison with other member states of the EU, except for the UK, which
have considerably more labour market regulation than Ireland. In addition,
Ireland operates a very liberal regime for capital. It does not attempt to regulate capital in any meaningful way, as O'Hearn (2000, p.87) points out. It
openly condones or turns a blind eye to (massive) corporate profit shifting
and takes no action to counter the repatriation of profits. Hence, profit out-
flows are huge – equivalent to 20 percent of GNP in 1998 (having risen from
11.6 percent in 1993) (O'Sullivan 2000, p.267). Furthermore, the wage
practices of most of the TNCs remain outside the national agreements, which
means that they benefit from the restraining and flexibility effects of social
partnership without bearing any of the responsibilities or costs (O'Hearn
2000).

One of the main arguments of this chapter is that none of these factors alone can explain Ireland's recent boom. Rather, they layer one upon the other, interweaving into a series of explanatory factors instead of a single 'critical variable'. It is not a simple matter of policy fit or fortuitous circumstances even though there is no doubt that Ireland's mix of policies was well suited to this (latest) phase of internationalisation. Continuous policy adaptation is to be observed, and we can also see evidence of some learning on the part of both policy and political agents. In general, the 'managed' nature of Irish economic development is striking. A pro-active stance crosses the different domains considered and is not explained by the actions of the state alone. In addition, the classic separation between explanations that emphasise the characteristics of the state and those that focus on forces associated with globalisation has to be overcome. What the Irish case shows is that external as well as internal factors are part of the explanation and that it is how these come or are brought together that is critical.

The Costs: Sustainability?

Characterisation of Ireland as a 'miracle' implies that something long term has been achieved. The Irish case can be taken as a model of development only if it can be sustained. Here I argue that there are good grounds to question the sustainability of the Irish rush to economic growth. Political, social and economic aspects are involved.

While Ireland's policy approach is now seen to have paid off economically after more than three decades, a number of features of Ireland's situation cast into doubt the future sustainability of the policy of maximising growth rates. These are either consequences of the approach adopted or factors beyond the control of the actors involved.

The unbalanced nature of both Ireland's industrial base and the sources of its growth is striking. There are a number of elements to such an imbalance. There is, firstly, the scale of dependence on foreign industry, especially given that such firms, led by the MNCs, have driven the growth. Murphy (2000) demonstrates how the bulk of manufacturing growth occurring in Ireland's 'Celtic Tiger' period is attributable to a small group of MNCs (which employ only about 18 percent of the manufacturing labour force). These come from five main sectors: computers, software, chemicals, pharmaceuticals and cola concentrates. High-tech MNCs in these sectors increased their exports by 250 percent between 1988 and 1996 compared with 89 percent for the remaining sectors (ibid, p.19). A further aspect of imbalance resides in the distinctive character of the foreign firms that predominate in Ireland. They are characterised to a large extent by products with high fixed development costs and low unit costs of production (such as pharmaceuticals, retail software and computer products, and proprietary soft drinks) (Honohan 2001, p.29). They are also not major employers, relative to their size, concentrating on profit taking as pointed out by O'Hearn (2000). Furthermore, the dynamic foreign manufacturing base is concentrated in a narrow range of technologies that can relocate quickly (Bradley 2000, p.25). So, most of the employment gains have been secondary to this MNC investment. A related aspect concerns the reliance on US foreign industry. FDI from the USA accounted for more than 80 percent of the overall FDI flows into Ireland in the last few years (O'Sullivan 2000, pp.263-4). Such investment is especially marked in the main growth industries of chemicals and allied products as well as electric and electronic equipment. Hence, US foreign-owned companies generated nearly 70 percent of manufacturing output and over 85 percent of manufacturing exports in 1997. This indicates how Ireland's boom is closely associated with, if not actually a by-product of, the expansion in the US economy in the 1990s. Some have characterised Ireland as occupying a 'halfway position' between a national and a regional (US) economy (Krugman 1997, p.41).[12] The degree of openness and dependence on external trade as well as the mobility of factors of production (especially labour) underpin such a characterisation. Patterns of recent job loss, in both scale and source, lend support to a negative portrayal of sustainability. Viewed in this light, the strategy of enabling industrialisation through the attraction of foreign companies risks leaving Ireland highly vulnerable to decisions and forces outside its own control. It is especially vulnerable, for example, to change in the US economy. In addition, should Ireland be unable to sustain its favourable tax regime on profits – and it has already come under considerable pressure in this regard within the EU – its attractiveness to US and other multinationals is likely to decline if not disappear.

The spotlight then turns on the performance of indigenous firms. In this regard the jury is still out. Some authors (such as O'Riain 2000) consider the development of indigenous industry not just a key part of Ireland's recent success but as a success in its own right. He argues that there has been a transformation in the productive and innovative capacities of parts of indigenous industry. However, his research mainly concentrated on the Irish software industry, one of the most dynamic sectors. Looked at as a whole, while Irish-owned industry performed well in the Celtic Tiger period, shortcomings exist which lead to real doubts about performance. Huge differences separate the output growth rates in Irish-owned as compared with foreign firms. For example, labour productivity[13] in Irish-owned firms in 1997 was only 40 percent of the average of all manufacturing in Ireland and 18 percent of that of US-owned, Irish-based manufacturing firms (O'Sullivan 2000, p.267). As this author also points out, the success of indigenous industry is concentrated in a small number of firms and sectors. Hence, there is still reason today to accept the OECD's (1995) characterisation of Ireland's manufacturing sector as being of a 'dual nature' with a 'modern', highly productive sector side by side with a traditional Irish-owned sector.

If the partnership process has been integral to Ireland's recent programme of development, then factors undermining it fuel further doubts about sustainability. It is difficult to see social partnership surviving when we inquire into how the fruits of growth are being distributed and the kinds of accommodation that have been involved. The fact is that social partnership has presided over one of the most unequal periods in Irish history. Ireland today is marked by deep inequality and polarisation of incomes. There are many indicators that prosperity has been concentrated. Consider the following:

- Compared with output and productivity, earnings increased only moderately through the 1990s. For example, although there have been significant wage increases, the real level of compensation per employee grew by no more than 4.4 percent between 1991 and 2000, and actually declined in 1997 and 1998 (European Commission 2002, pp.70-71). While this represents major growth relative to what was happening elsewhere in Europe at the time, it is only about average when judged in terms of compensation levels achieved by Irish workers in previous decades, especially the 1960s and 1970s. In addition, no brake was placed on the growth of higher earnings in Ireland, unlike say in the Netherlands (Visser and Hemerijck 1997). There was in fact a substantial increase in earnings dispersion between 1987 and 1997 (Barrett et al. 2000). This was driven by rapid increases for those at the top end of the wage distribution. Although the period of greatest economic growth (1994-1997) was not associated with an acceleration of the trend towards increased earnings dispersion, neither was it associated with a decrease.
- Extensive taxation and social welfare changes made during the latter half of the 1990s are an important part of the explanation of what happened. While the privileging of different sectors of the population was not consistent, the changes made tended to favour the better-off. Whereas in the 1987-1994 period the lowest 20 percent of households gained quite significantly from the changes,[14] the lowest 40 percent of households were relative losers from the changes made to taxation and social welfare poli-

cy between 1994 and 1998 (Callan and Nolan 2000, pp.196-7). In fact, redistribution of income from the bottom of the distribution towards the top was effected in this latter period. The strategy of cutting tax rates was especially important in this regard, generally favouring higher incomes.[15] Ireland is now classed as a low tax economy (National Economic and Social Council 2002, p.31). While Ireland did not experience cut-backs in welfare benefits in the 1990s, there were no new major welfare programmes, and changes in welfare payments rates, while selectively generous to some such as pensioners and families with children, did not keep pace with the rise in general incomes. Hence, the unemployment benefit in 2001 was equivalent to only 74 percent of the cut-off threshold for poverty (50 percent of average income), and its relative value had fallen from 82 percent since 1997 (National Economic and Social Council 2002, p.60).

- The relative welfare effort diminished during the country's greatest period of prosperity (see Table 6.3). While the per capita expenditure on social protection increased in aggregate or gross terms by a considerable amount, Ireland's social expenditure/GDP ratio fell during the 1990s. In 2001, for example, Ireland was spending the equivalent of 14.6 percent of its GDP on social protection compared with 20.5 percent in 1993 (Eurostat 2004). Calculated as a percentage of GNP (which is a more accurate basis since it represents the resources available for redistribution), the percentage spent on social protection in 1998 was 18.1 percent compared with 21 percent in 1990 (National Economic and Social Council 2002, p.250). Moreover, while it was always a low spender on social protection in EU terms, the gap between Ireland and the EU as a whole widened over the same period.[16]

- While the average household net income rose substantially over the last five years of the 1990s – by 54 percent[17] – income poverty also grew. The level of income poverty at over 20 percent for both households and individuals is very high – by international standards and with reference to past poverty levels in Ireland. Up to a third of the nation's children are being reared in poverty, and relative income poverty levels increased steadily over the course of the 1990s (National Economic and Social Council 2002, pp.61-64). However, progress was made on some aspects of poverty. Judged in terms of what is called 'consistent poverty' – which is measured by a threshold of 60 percent of average income combined with aspects of lifestyle deprivation[18] – the prevalence of poverty decreased in Ireland in the 1990s. These are the figures that are usually cited by official sources. Data on income poverty suggest, however, that many of the peo-

Table 6.3   Changes in social protection 1990- 2001

	1990	1993	1996	1997	1998	1999	2001
Expenditure on social protection as percentage of							
GDP*	18.4	20.2	17.8	16.7	15.5	14.7	14.6
GNP#	21.0	-	-	19.3	18.1	-	-
Expenditure on social protection per capita at constant prices (index 1990=100)*	100	119	130	137	142	150	151.1
Taxes as percentage of:							
GDP~	32.6	-	-	31.7	1	32.1	-
GNP~	36.4	-	-	36.6	-	36.9	-

* Source: Eurostat 2002 and 2004: Tables 1 and 2.
# Source: National Economic and Social Council, 2002, p. 250 and Table 4.3.
~ Source: National Economic and Social Council, 2002, p. 241.

ple who moved into the labour market over the course of the boom took up low-wage jobs and that benefit levels were too low to lift people out of poverty.

- Economic growth fuelled a huge rise in house prices, leading to further inequality and rising dissatisfaction among lower paid workers. Taking the ratio of average house prices to the average industrial wage as an indicator of housing affordability, increased house prices have rendered home ownership beyond the reach of many. In the ten years between 1990 and 2000, the ratio of the average price of new houses to average earnings almost doubled (from 4.33 in 1990 to 7.4 in 2000) (National Economic and Social Council 2002, pp.46-47). The increases in wages and take-home income compare poorly. All of this is leading to a bifurcation of the housing market in Ireland with home ownership which was up to now a common good in Ireland (with three-quarters of people owning their homes) emerging as another, more entrenched form of inequality.

While we need to be careful about drawing conclusions about the effects of policy (not least because these take some time to be realised and also given time lags in data), the degree to which growth and inequality have been closely coupled in Ireland in the last decade is striking. And yet the different national pacts contained quite strong solidarity elements. For example, a minimum wage was introduced (in 2000), sustained attention was given to making work more attractive (especially for those on low incomes) through tax and welfare reform, and the value of all welfare payments was significantly increased. In addition, Ireland was the first EU member state to introduce a wide-ranging programme to combat and prevent poverty (in 1997). And yet the evidence available at this stage suggests that only the initial period of social partnership (the late 1980s and early 1990s) saw an egalitarian thrust realised in practice. In light of this, it seems inappropriate to apply the term 'social corporatism' to Ireland. Rather, Hardiman's (2000) characterisation of the Irish arrangements as 'competitive corporatism' seems more appropriate.

Clearly, there is a particularity in the politics that underlie the national management process in Ireland and the nature of the trade-offs that have been made. Despite the participation of the trade unions and representatives of the 'social pillar', moderate wage and welfare increases have been traded for significant tax privileging of those on middle and high incomes (the quite erratic nature of tax reform from year to year notwithstanding). In comparison to tax reform, welfare reform programmes and even the minimum wage appear as window dressing. A further distinctive feature of corporatism in Ireland is that it has proceeded without the participation of one of the main economic actors – the MNCs. Since most of these are non-union companies, they are neither represented in nor covered by the national pacts. There is also the matter of the extent of the leeway allowed to the government in the whole process, and how the government has utilised this leeway. While some parameters, such as pay levels, were clearly specified, other aspects were more general in nature. In effect, the government policy often departed from the spirit if not the letter of the social pacts. The leeway in the programmes was exploited especially by the last government (of centre-right orientation), in power between 1997 and mid-2002, which oversaw a very significant tax and welfare spending programme. Despite its blanket rhetoric of equality, it tended to favour the interests of a rising class of international professionals as well as those of the indigenous business class (especially in the construction and agri-business sectors) (O'Riain 2000). So even if they implemented the measures agreed in the different programmes, the government could still (and did) act to favour their preferred constituencies.

In this scenario, the spotlight is turned on the trade unions and the social pillar (although to a lesser extent on the latter because in numbers, might and 'legitimacy' they are but minor partners). Against the backdrop outlined above, it is hardly surprising that the trade unions are finding it increasingly difficult to keep their membership behind the partnership project. The disenchantment that was at one time residual is growing, with public sector workers, who have borne the brunt of the wage moderation, growing increasingly restive. It is interesting to ponder what the trade unions had to gain from participation as well as why the social pillar was included in the partnership process. In the dark days of the 1980s, the trade unions had much to gain from the emerging partnership. Not only were unemployment and job loss running at a high rate, but public sector spending was being severely curtailed in a regime of very high rates of tax on earned income. Labour interests, therefore, had to be represented. The argument can and has been made that the trade unions would have lost more by staying out.

With regard to the inclusion of the social pillar, Hardiman suggests that at least a part of the rationale for this came from the view that economic policy cannot work effectively unless social policy issues are addressed (Hardiman 2000, p.302). I tend to disagree with this. The Irish case suggests that one should be wary of orchestrated attempts at selective inclusion of certain civil society interests. A potent rationale for this kind of 'inclusiveness' is to be found in the current orthodoxy around the global economy. This suggests that the more homogeneous the society, both sectorally and culturally, the more flexible and competitive its economy is in international markets (Streeck 1999). There is, then, an incentive for the governing powers to lessen the number of sectional interests so that the 'general interest' can be represented with greater vigour. It is not too far-fetched to claim that partnership became more social in Ireland for reasons of national competitiveness (the interests of Ireland.plc) rather than, say, out of a concern for the democratic properties of civil society. In other words, partnership has become a national political project and is used especially as a way of generating legitimacy for policies that redistribute upward and outward.

All of this builds into a set of issues about the social model and its sustainability. How much inegalitarianism can there be before national 'settlements' begin to unravel? When do the social costs, which are currently very large in Ireland, become too great? Matters such as the common good, the state of civil society and the well-being of Irish society as a whole are rarely the subject of explicit discussion or political attention in Ireland. Development was traditionally interpreted in Ireland as economic development, crowding out any real discussion or concerted policy-making about societal issues. In terms of values, the predominant ethos is that what is good for business is good for Ireland (Collins 1999, p.86). In other words, society is equated with economy. Is this a sustainable model of society in the long term?

The Significance of the Irish Case

As a case study in economic development, Ireland is interesting in a number of respects. In the first instance, Ireland did not follow the path of industrialisation, instead moving more or less directly from being pre-industrial to post-industrial. It became a high-tech economy without ever having really been industrialised. Thus, Ireland resembles much of the southwestern part of the USA. But there was an important political element to this as well. Murphy (2000) convincingly argues that Ireland was able to capitalise politically on the advantages of being under-developed. The absence of an indigenous industrial sector or class, for example, enabled Ireland to introduce and develop its low tax regime without opposition. Had there been a mature indigenous (and presumably tax-paying) industrial sector, Ireland could not have introduced a low tax regime for foreign industry. In this way, Ireland turned what was one of its disadvantages into an advantage.

The Irish case also raises questions about the relationship between (adapting to) globalisation and welfare reform. Economic and employment growth was accomplished in Ireland without any significant welfare reform and little welfare state retrenchment. This is unusual in an international context where either class interests or the coincidence of interests between business and the state in the shadow of internationalisation forced some welfare reform. There are two factors that may explain Ireland's divergence. The first is that the quality of social citizenship was quite poor, and still is by wider European comparison, consisting of social insurance payments which grant relatively low wage compensation side by side with an over-arching set of means-tested income assistance programmes. Although it has more solidarity elements, Ireland's welfare state more closely resembles that of the UK than those of continental and northern Europe. So an argument about non-wage and welfare costs as an impediment to national competitiveness does not have the same legitimacy or urgency in Ireland as elsewhere. Secondly, buoyant tax revenues meant that welfare reform was not a pressing item on the economic agenda in Ireland.

The case of Ireland also serves to question existing understandings about the nature of social partnership and the conditions under which it takes place. While it is expansive in terms of the range of actors involved, especially by virtue of the fact that it includes the social pillar, social partnership in Ireland has taken place without the participation of the MNCs, arguably one of the most important economic actors. It could be said that their interests were represented by the government, which played a strong role as arbiter of the various interests involved. Hence, foreign capital continued to be major beneficiaries of the agreements reached. The emergence and practice of social partnership in Ireland also serve to challenge our knowledge of the conditions under which corporatist governance functions. Hardiman (1988) found in a comparative analysis that conditions that had facilitated social partnership in Austria, Sweden and Norway did not obtain in Ireland. Included among these were a dominant social democratic party, a high degree of authoritative centralisation in the trade union movement and cohesive employers' organisations. Not only was government the key actor in the Irish case, but traditional roles are being rewritten in the Irish case which is characterised by the state being proactive in policy entrepreneurship, facilitating joint action and communication among social interests, protection of non-statutory interests and supporting interest group formation (O'Donnell 1998, p.21). Study of the Irish case also strongly suggests the need to take account of exogenous and endogenous factors and actors. Just as the surge in economic growth was not precipitated by domestic factors – whether in the economy or in the policy repertoire – the beneficiaries are not confined to the national territory.

There has been no miracle in Ireland. Neither have the fruits of the growth been evenly distributed. While there was some redistribution to all, the overall picture is of entrenched inequality.

Notes

1 Defined to include the 15 member states of the EU as well as Norway and Switzerland.

2 It is important to bear in mind the limitations of GDP data as a measure of living standards though, especially in the Irish case. There is in Ireland a large gap between GDP and GNP (GNP being some 84 percent of GDP in 2000). Ireland's GDP statistics are known to be distorted by the transfer pricing activities of MNCs, which artificially boost their Irish profits in order to benefit from low corporate tax rates. Transfer pricing acts to optimise the global distribution of an MNC's profits and is effected by locating as much as possible of a company's global profits in a low tax location. For this and other reasons, as O'Grada and O'Rourke (2000: 193) point out, using GDP statistics tends to flatter Ireland's economic performance.

3 This includes both the unemployed and groups outside the labour force who indicated some interest in obtaining a job. It is mainly made up of the ILO unemployed, those who are marginally attached to the labour force as well as those not in education but who want to work plus underemployed part-time workers.

4 Interestingly, in Ireland it is sociologists rather than political scientists who have most employed the state in their analyses of Irish development. The problem with much of this work [and see especially Breen et al (1990) and O'Connell and Rottman (1992)] is that the state is treated unproblematically, the interest base of the state being neither questioned nor disaggregated. Recent work has begun to address this matter, however. O'Riain (2000) applies the concept of the 'flexible developmental state' to Ireland, and Kirby (2002) uses the concept of the 'competition state'. While the former is defined by its ability to network post-Fordist networks of production and innovation, attract international investment and link these local and global networks in a fashion which promotes development, the latter is marked by a diminution of the state's control over the national economy and society as economies become integrated into the international marketplace.

5 Exports are hugely significant in the Irish economy, equivalent to 85 percent of GDP.

6 Developments in Ireland have been characterised as an experiment in participatory democracy of international significance (Sabel 1996).

7 There is some evidence, though, to suggest that these were 'second-class citizens' in the negotiations (see Hardiman 1998). Note in any case that some of this pillar split over the most recent agreement, and certain groups, including the National Women's Council of Ireland, withdrew or were excluded from the process and the agreement.

8 The titles of the programmes are revealing about their aspirations if not their ideologies. The six, together with their period of application, are as follows: *Programme for National Recovery* (1987-1990); *Programme for Economic and Social Progress* (1991-1993); *Programme for Competitiveness and Work* (1994-1996); *Partnership 2000 for Inclusion, Employment and Competitiveness* (1997-2000); *Programme for Prosperity and Fairness* (2001-2003), *Sustaining Progress* (2003-2006).

9 As well as partnership at the national level, many local-level partnerships have been set up, initiated by the *Programme for Economic and Social Progress* in 1991. Involving a host of community interests, they focused on involving local communities in a process of planning and analysis about local needs.

10 Even though it was new in itself, the corporatist way of planning drew upon a longer tradition in Ireland, in particular the corporatist ethos emphasised by the Irish Catholic Church in the 1940s and 1950s. Although it never became institutionalised then, the call at that stage was for employers and employees to work out arrangements to their mutual benefit without involving the state.

11 Income (net of withholding taxes and without a current-cost adjustment) as a percentage of the investment position on a historical basis.

12 See also O'Grada and O'Rourke (2000) who suggest that Ireland's success is a local manifestation of success in North America.

13 Measured in terms of £'000s per person engaged.

14 At the expense of low- and middle-income earners, though, rather than those in the four highest income deciles.

15 However, taxation policy has been erratic. For example the 1999 Budget concentrated its benefits on those in the low (although not the lowest) and middle income brackets, whereas the 2000 Budget gave much greater gains to those already most well-off.

16 Judged in terms of the proportion of GDP spent on social protection, the EU average was 25.4 percent in 1990, compared with 18.4 percent in Ireland. By 1998 the gap had widened. At that stage Ireland was spending 16.1 percent of GDP on social protection compared with an EU average of 27.7 percent (National Economic and Social Council 2002: 250).

17 Changes in disposable household income also show rising inequality. While the average disposable income of households in the two top income deciles increased by over 61 percent over the five years, the increase for those in the two lowest deciles was only 37 percent (Central Statistics Office 2001: 8). Moreover, the ratio of the highest to the lowest household incomes was approximately 13 to 1 in 1999/2000 compared with 11 to 1 in 1994/1995.

18 Such as, for example, by whether people have access to a certain number of meals in the day, the kind of clothes they own and their household possessions.

7   The Australian Miracle: Luck, Pluck or Being Stuck Down Under?

Herman Schwartz

Introduction

During the 1990s "economic miracles" in Ireland, Denmark and the Netherlands attracted considerable attention. All three countries reduced measured unemployment and reversed deleterious fiscal and current account deficits dating from the 1970s to a greater extent than their larger European neighbours. Analysts looking for policy lessons that might be applicable to the employment and growth malaise in those larger European economies were particularly drawn to the two "nice", that is, more social democratic, examples of change, or to the superficially high-tech dynamism of Ireland. All this attention obscured another equally interesting miracle story playing simultaneously in the southern hemisphere: Australia.

This lack of attention is curious for three reasons. First, the Australian economy in GDP terms is roughly equal to the combined economies of Sweden, Norway, and Finland. Second, the scale and direction of change in Australia seems to be much more the product of intentional strategic action – pluck – than of endogenously generated change consistent with prior logics of appropriateness or of simple good fortune – stuck or luck. Analytically, Australia should thus have been a more interesting place to learn lessons for those seeking policy solutions for larger countries, because it is hard to see how changes deriving from local logics of appropriateness can be transferred easily. Finally, Australia is one of the few OECD economies besides the USA and Ireland that experienced productivity growth substantially above both its own historical long-term trend in the 1990s and the OECD average. This occurred despite the potentially adverse consequences of the financial crisis in Asia, the location of Australia's largest markets.

In Australia, unemployment fell even while participation rates rose substantially; fiscal deficits gave way to surpluses; and a substantial shift in export profile occurred even though the current account deficit remained stubbornly high. Australia's employment performance in the 1980s was the best in the OECD. Australia created jobs at roughly twice the OECD average rate

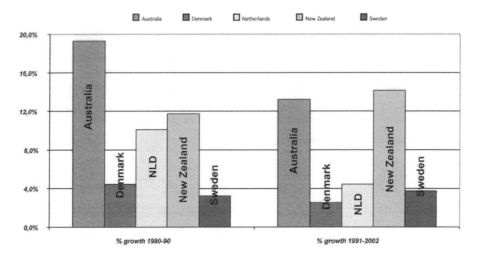

Figure 7.1 Growth in population aged 16-64

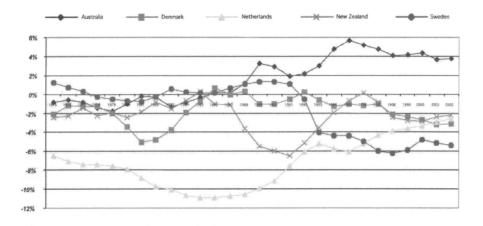

Figure 7.2 Deviation from average ratio of business sector employment to total working age
population, 12 small OECD economies

– a 25 percent expansion – despite rising labour force participation (reflecting strong population growth; see Figure 7.1) that caused the labour force to
grow 1.9 percent annually on average 1985 to 2000. Employment growth
was also substantially above the OECD average in the 1990s, when a 13 percent expansion in employment nearly matched a 14.5 percent expansion in
the labour force, and even more strongly in private business employment
(see Figure 7.2).

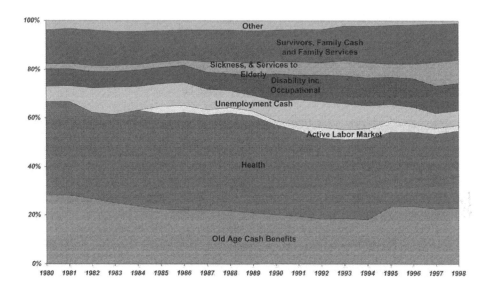

Figure 7.3 Distribution of Australian public spending

By contrast, falling unemployment in Denmark and Sweden in the 1990s occurred in the context of an essentially stable labour force; Denmark's labour force grew only 0.3 percent per year, while Sweden's actually fell by 0.2 percent per year (OECD 2001a, p.222). As rising productivity is the easiest – and perhaps the only – way for any society to make everyone better off, the link between policy changes that occurred in the 1980s and early 1990s and productivity and employment gains merits some examination. And because a high level of employment is generally preferable to having a large portion of the population on social assistance, and makes social assistance affordable for those who must be on it, explaining the sources of employment growth and maintenance is important.

In contrast to Denmark, Ireland and New Zealand, public and mandatory private social spending in Australia also grew in constant dollar terms during the 1980s and then more strongly during the 1990s. Social spending as a share of GDP was lower than in most countries but expanded more rapidly during these time periods. By the end of the 1990s, Australia was allocating more of GDP to social spending than either Ireland or Canada (and more than New Zealand as well – though the data are not strictly comparable). Rising unemployment benefits did not drive this increase. Rather, core welfare programs expanded: pensions, health, and especially disability and

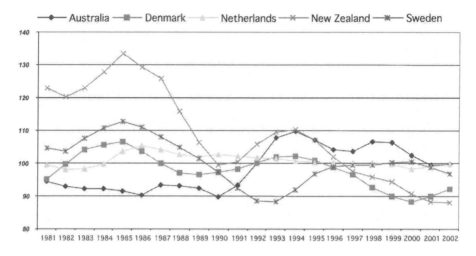

Figure 7.4 Export performence, 3 year rolling average, OECD average = 100

cash benefits to families (see Figure 7.3 for the shares of these programs; for total social expenditures see Table 5.6). However, it should be noted that Australia experienced all of the problems besetting OECD economies: falling rates of male employment, widening wage inequalities among full-time earners, and a parallel bifurcation of employment opportunities between job-rich, dual-income families and job-poor, single or no income families.

On the trade side, Australia's traditionally uncompetitive manufacturing and service sectors increased their exports after changes in the mechanisms for collective bargaining kept wage increases below productivity gains, especially in the sheltered sectors. Decentralisation of the collective bargaining system lowered the wage share of GDP slightly from 62.3 percent in 1983 to 59.5 percent in 1995; this contrasts quite favourably with the more dramatic reduction in Ireland, where the wage share of GDP fell from 60.7 percent in 1985 to 52.6 percent in 1994, and then even further, to 41.8 percent in 1997 (O'Grada and O'Rourke 2000, p.200). Meanwhile, productivity grew twice as fast as wages between 1983 and 1995. Productivity grew faster in Australia in 1990-97 than in New Zealand, Denmark, Sweden and the Netherlands, though not as fast as in Ireland. This permitted relative unit labour costs to fall from 117.8 in 1983 to 83.8 in 1987, before rising to 103 in 1989. Figure 7.4 shows the comparatively sharp and sustained increase in export performance for manufactured goods Australia experienced in the 1990s.[1] This reflected a sharp jump in the trend rate of productivity growth in Australia from roughly 1 percent annually between 1975 and 1991 to 2.7 percent each year after 1991 (OECD 1999d, p.65; Productivity Commission 1999). In short, export growth was not so much an outcome of falling wages as it was of rising productivity that permitted export firms to enjoy higher profits and, in the 1990s, permitted workers to capture part of the increase in productivity arising from changes in collective bargaining as higher real wages. Meanwhile, the state also captured some of these gains as extra revenue for redistribution.

What policies – if any – caused this favourable outcome? As in an earlier analysis of the Danish miracle, this analysis corrects for the implicit privileging of intentional action in causal explanations by explicitly considering the possibility that while actors considered their actions intentional, their policy choices might have been essentially endogenous outcomes of specific institutional structures rather than strategic responses to changing environmental conditions (Schwartz 2001b). If markets, like any environment, select for and reward specific institutional structures and behaviours, then some actors will always appear to have made the 'correct' strategic response to their environment, even if they chose their strategy somewhat randomly. But this may not necessarily be the "optimal" response or strategy. Furthermore, because actors do respond to their environment, that environment is always changing, eroding the degree to which any prior "best" response to a given environment fits the current environment. At any given time, stochastic changes rather than intentional action may create what looks like an "optimal" or "best" response to a given environment. But in this situation causality will be located in the system (in the environment created by other actors' behaviours), not in the choices of specific actor(s) who are usually studied in isolation.

This paper will test luck, pluck and being stuck as competing explanations for Australian "success" in the 1980s and 1990s. To foreshadow the findings, Australia's capacity to preserve the welfare state and expand employment in the face of severe macro-economic constraints, and without generating popular dissatisfaction, is only partly a function of luck or endogenous change that is consistent with local logics of appropriateness. Intentional, strategic reform of Australian political and social institutions did much to ameliorate the Australian macro-economic problems, despite an unfavourable export structure. In other words, pluck or stuck probably accounts for more than luck here, because the Australian case presents a series of changes in which political actors deliberately recast old institutions. These actors naturally enough pursued their own interests in this reconstitution of institutions – this after all is what politics is about. But they did so in ways that comported with the external environment. As a result, the Australian economy stabilized. As with the Danish and Dutch cases, the Australian case suggests that neither environmental change – read 'globalisation' – nor a given welfare state's endogenous dynamics are sufficient conditions for a crisis of a welfare state. Sufficient conditions for economic and welfare state crises rest in the way domestic actors make policy choices about the institutions governing the economy and welfare state. Meanwhile, the Australian case presents some of the few examples where true pluck made a difference in stabilizing a deteriorating welfare state.

The structure of the analysis

Roughly speaking this paper presents nine different explanations for Australian success in the 1980s and 1990s, assessing changes in the Australian current account balance, employment outcomes, and fiscal balance in terms of luck, pluck and being stuck. These three issue areas encompass the core economic foundations for a tax, service and transfer welfare state. Unemployment raises state expenditures, decreases revenues and erodes social solidarity. Fiscal deficits also clearly erode the long-term sustainability of this kind of welfare state as deficits cumulate into debt and as interest payments begin to crowd out services and transfers. Finally, current account deficits and public foreign debt are simply an external and more pernicious version of fiscal deficits. Foreign debt usually carries higher real interest rates than domestic debt and cannot be monetised. Current account deficits are also a proxy for competitiveness, and so are often also associated with higher unemployment as imports crowd out local production or as competitors displace exports from third-party markets.

To put it simply, these three policy areas relate to the following questions: do you make anything anyone wants to buy at a price they are willing to pay? Do you make enough money off of this to employ a politically acceptable number of people? And, are public sector inputs produced at a cost level that is consistent with continued export competitiveness and at a quality level that is consistent with continued public support for the welfare state? This last question means that I must also touch upon narrowly *political* issues of sustainability while discussing fiscal balance. In order to keep the paper broadly comparable with the others in this volume, however, the analysis will concentrate on employment growth.

Luck explanations start from the usual assumptions about institutional stickiness and inertia, and argue that while Australian institutions have been relatively constant throughout the post-war period, the external environment has changed in ways that favour either or both Australian production and public sector institutions. Pluck arguments, in contrast, assume that while institutions are relatively sticky, actors (again in either production or the public sectors) consciously remodelled their own or others' institutions to make them comport better with the external environment. Finally, stuck arguments suggest that endogenous dynamics made Australian institutions change in ways that comported well with a new environment. All nine sorts of explanations thus address both Australian problems before the 1980s and success afterward.

The structure of the luck arguments is transparent: a dysfunctional combination of import substitution policies and a reliance on raw materials exports led to excessive wage gains, a weakening capacity to export and high (imported) consumption in the 1960s and 1970s. But the acceleration of heavy industrialisation in Asia – particularly Korea and China – in the 1980s and 1990s bailed Australia out of its problems. Increased Asian tourism offset interest payments on Australia's rising foreign debt. And global investors blindly rewarded Australians for pursuing what looked like neo-liberal policies of institutional redesign in the 1980s and 1990s.

Stuck arguments would suggest that Australian institutions evolved incrementally according to logics of appropriateness held by actors in those institutions, and that the institutional outcomes were either better than prior configurations or at least less dysfunctional than those into which the competition stumbled (March and Olson 1989). Actors' conscious policy choices were conditioned by embedded notions about the social purpose of their activity and what could be attained given the institutional landscape in Australia. In that sense, they were not perfectly free choices, but rather conditioned by the actors' self-images and their ability to pursue old institutional routines. Because the external environment surrounding Australian production and public sector institutions was also not characterized by optimal organisations, Australian organisations merely had to be less dysfunctional than their global competitors in order to look 'good'.

Note that "stuck" arguments are thus not arguments for convergence towards any optimal organisational form, nor do they offer much guidance about policy transferability. As Alchian and others have argued, markets are like ecologies (Alchian 1950). Firms display a multitude of strategies – expressed as organisational structures – that can be well or ill suited to their environments. Competitive pressures force firms to adapt their strategies (organisational structures), but they do not enforce conformity. Ecologies with multiple niches permit multiple successful strategies, and both successful and unsuccessful strategies change the environment by exhausting resources and generating new resources in the form of wastes, by-products and physical changes to the environment. Moreover, competitive pressure on any given organisation can be diffuse, if it is in an ecological niche (market) with few competitors. Pressures on public sector organisations are even more diffuse, since they have quasi-parasitic sources of revenue (or put differently, something approximating a monopoly in the provision of regulated and common pool services).

Stuck arguments stress three core continuities in Australian economic institutions and practices: the continued reliance on raw materials exports and thus growth impulses external to Australia; continuities in the way the state controls and guides collective bargaining using the arbitration process; and continuity in the targeted provision of relatively low levels of welfare by the state. As in the Netherlands, the stuck argument has a housing component and a collective bargaining component. A relatively flexible housing market, widespread home ownership, and the tax deductibility of mortgage interest combined with disinflation to release purchasing power into the economy in the 1990s, helping to reduce unemployment. In an era of disinflation, Australia's housing market automatically generated an expansionary impulse for the economy. Australia's collective bargaining system also evolved in some ways that could be interpreted as "stuck": the minimum wage continued to set a high floor under incomes, and the arbitration system was used to restrain wage growth, much as the Wassenaar Agreement allegedly did in the Netherlands, and much as arbitration did in the period before 1969.

Pluck arguments are inherently more complex and difficult to sustain. A convincing pluck argument has to show that the Australian political and economic elites assessed the dysfunctionality of Australian institutions and changed them in ways that deviated substantially from prior practices. Pluck arguments would stress that the state comprehensively shifted industrial policy away from the import substitution policies that had characterized policy since the 1920s and towards export promotion for more complex manufactured goods and non-traditional services. Pluck arguments would stress that the social partners and political parties substantially changed collective bargaining practices by abandoning the 70-year-old core principle of comparative wage justice – what Europeans call horizontal wage equity – and by reducing the role of the highly centralized arbitration system in favour of a more decentralized and market-oriented determination of wages. Finally, pluck arguments would stress a departure from traditions of public ownership of enterprises providing infrastructure services reaching back into the nineteenth century, and of control over finance dating from the Second World War, in favour of far-reaching privatisation and market-based regulation of public bureaucracies and finance. Pluck arguments would then causally connect these changes to the rapid gains in productivity that occurred in the 1990s. In short, pluck arguments would stress deviation from almost all the institutional structures and economic trends of the Bretton Woods period, and connect this change causally to the change in Australia's economic fortunes.

Exports and the current account balance

The Problem

Australia's current account deficits arose from the misfit between its export structure and the evolving structure of world import demand, and from the interaction of its collective bargaining system with its system of trade protection. Exports were mostly raw materials, but these faced both volatile and declining prices and, in agriculture, rising protectionism. The collective bargaining system tended to transmit wage increases from the sheltered sector (which included not only the usual services but also manufacturing) to the exposed sector (largely agriculture and minerals). This situation created expanding current account deficits.

Was the stabilisation of Australia's current account just luck? Australia's reliance on raw materials exports created substantial economic problems in the post-war period. In 1961 raw materials accounted for 80 percent of Australian exports, and wool alone accounted for 40 percent (see Table 7.1 for details). Although raw materials exports remained buoyant through the 1960s and 1970s, volatile prices, agricultural protection and Australia's large sheltered sector combined to produce chronic current account deficits.

Australia reversed common European patterns of social and employment policy. *Employment* policy in Australia operated primarily through *trade* policy: high border tariffs and import quotas permitted import substitution industrialisation (ISI). The effective rate of protection for manufactured goods – that is, the share of value added by tariffs – averaged 46 percent in Australia, and reflected deliberate efforts to generate more employment (OECD 1972, pp.29-31; OECD 1989, p.39). The Australian Tariff Board literally told industrial firms, "You make it and [we'll] protect it" (Capling and Galligan 1993, p.105). Protection funded itself by inducing inflows of foreign direct investment into a large, sheltered market. By the end of the 1970s, foreign firms controlled about one-fourth of Australian manufactur-

Table 7.1   Export structure and destination

Goods exports (percent of total)	1961	1970	1997
Raw materials			
Wool	41.4	13.8	7.2
Meat	9.2	10.3	3.2
Dairy, fruit, fish, sugar	13.3	11.7	2.9
Metals, ores, aluminium	7.3	10.0	17.1
Coal, oil, fuels	-	5.8	19.3
Cereals	9.4	12.1	7.5
Raw materials subtotal:	80.6	63.7	58.9
Manufactures			
Commodity-based	18.3	11.0	10.0
Non-commodity manufactures	-	15.0	23.6

Export destinations	1961	1971	2001
UK	23.9	11.2	3.9
Europe (exc. UK)	15.9	9.4	7.8
USA	7.5	11.9	9.7
Japan	16.7	27.1	19.9
Rest of Asia	-	-	38.5
Rest of world	36.0	40.7	20.1

Source: OECD, Economic Survey: Australia, various dates

ing and half of mining as measured by value added (OECD 1972, p.42; UNCTC 1988, p.529).

Social policy similarly inverted the normal European pattern. Social policy operated primarily through judicial regulation of wages and the labour market. For roughly a century, federal and state courts set wages through judicial proceedings. Only labour and employers' organisations could initiate proceedings before the court; individuals had no standing. The courts handed down judicial decisions – "awards" – that set the "basic" or minimum wage, added on skill-based wage premiums for specific occupations, maintained relative wages, determined conditions of work, and mandated occupational benefits. In short, courts rather than state bureaucracies or formal corporatist institutions were the instrument of social policy. After 1907, the federal court set a high basic wage, defined socially by reference to a decent standard of living for a family of four (originally presumed to be male-headed). By the 1930s these wage awards covered roughly 85-90 percent of workers. Relative wage shares were set by awarding additional wages – margins – for skills and enforced via a doctrine of comparative wage justice. The arbitration court defined comparative wage justice to mean that "employees doing the same work for different employers or in different industries should by and large receive the same amount of pay irrespective of the capacity of their employer or industry." Comparative wage justice created an almost automatic transmission of wage gains from one sector to another (CAR 1970; Plowman 1980, p.85).

In short, the **informal** welfare state – the whole range of state policies supporting delivery of a *socially defined wage* in a full employment environment – was thus much more important than the **formal** welfare state – tax-financed, state-provided transfers and services. Social protection and employment strategies based on ISI and informal welfare emerged from Australia's history as a highly indebted primary product exporter (Castles 1985; Mabbett 1995; Schwartz 1998). This combination became unsustainable by the 1970s. The operation of social policy through judicially regulated wages reversed the usual Scandinavian dynamic and pushed up costs in the sheltered sector of the economy, in turn raising costs in the export sector. Meanwhile, the operation of employment policy through ISI constantly expanded the sheltered part of the economy. For a while, foreign direct investment financed ISI, while direct borrowing overseas financed recurrent current account deficits. But eventually, the sheltered sector got too big for the exposed sector to support.

These dilemmas had already emerged in the late 1960s but became acute in the 1970s. Among the most important problems confronting Australian exports was the decline in the raw materials intensity of the economies of its major European customers, and European's increasing protection of their domestic agriculture. British accession to the European Community and its Common Agricultural Policy simply underlined the shift of European consumption away from raw materials.

Exports: Luck

The Australian government responded to these trends by trying to shift exports away from raw materials and towards manufactured goods. To a certain extent this succeeded, and by 1997 raw materials comprised only 57 percent of exports. Nonetheless, the more significant shift was in the direction of trade, away from Europe towards Asia. Europe's share of Australian exports fell from 40 percent in 1963 to only 12 percent in 1996. Meanwhile, industrializing Asia's share grew rapidly, rising from 32 percent (mostly to Japan) to 60 percent in 1996. Indeed, by 1996 Korea alone almost equalled OECD Europe as a destination for Australian exports. This shift in the direction of trade qualifies as luck, because Australian policy had nothing to do with the nature of Asian industrialisation. Precisely because the Asian late industrialisation was raw materials-intensive (think Korean steel or Chinese woollens), Australia easily found new markets for old raw materials exports. Even diversification away from traditional raw materials exports had exogenous origins. Where wool, grain, dairy and meat had accounted for about 68 percent of Australian exports in the late 1950s and minerals only 7 percent, by 1970 the former accounted for only about 32 percent of exports while minerals and fuels jumped to 40 percent, driven by the emergence of Japan as a formidable steel producer. In turn, Korea and China replaced Japan as the destination for iron ores and coal.

Australia clearly benefited from Asian industrialisation. Nonetheless, if the policy had had no effects, one would have expected a fairly constant share for raw materials exports and little change in the level of complexity in manufactured goods exports. But the 21 percentage point decline in the share of raw materials exports occurred precisely at a time when the opportunity to simply keep exporting coal, iron ore, wool and foodstuffs to Asia existed. Manufactured exports grew at an annual rate of 8.7 percent compared with all exports at 6.9 percent, 1984 to 1995, and then slowed slightly to 8.2 percent (versus 8.0 percent overall) after the Asian financial crisis hit in 1996/97 (Productivity Commission 1996, p.41; Department of Foreign Affairs and Trade 2002, p.20). This suggests that policy might have had some influence on the changing composition of Australian exports. Then the question is: was change deliberate and strategic or simply an outgrowth of older policies? Stuck first.

Exports: Stuck

Australian governments in both the 1970s and 1980s tried to boost exports of manufactured goods and to dismantle Australia's ISI policy. Australian manufactured exports faced two hurdles. First, protection created large numbers of inefficient industries, but any single industry pursuing export-led expansion had to purchase expensive inputs from these firms. Second, any given firm's own labour costs were affected via comparative wage justice, so inefficient firms not only passed along their wage costs in the form of inputs, but also in the form of wages that were out of proportion with productivity gains.

The Whitlam Labour government 1973-1975 tried to undo these dilemmas. Institutionally, Whitlam transformed the old Tariff Board into the new Industries Assistance Commission. The IAC was ordered to pursue an efficient allocation of resources in the Australian economy, rather than to erect made-to-measure tariffs based on an industry's costs plus a profit margin. The IAC was staffed from the Ministry for Secondary Industry, which had controlled the Tariff Board but was institutionally separate. Whitlam had the IAC impose a 25 percent reduction in tariffs across the board.

Whitlam's reforms of industrial policy intended a strategic remediation of part of the problems impeding Australian manufactured exports. But strong continuities with prior policy suggest that the policy was stuck. First, the labour-intensive textile clothing and footwear (TCF) industry received A\$25 million to compensate it for tariff reductions. Second, although overt tariffs fell, the onset of the world economic crisis in 1973 led the IAC under both Whitlam and the follow-on Fraser Liberal government to boost non-tariff barriers (NTBS) as a way of offsetting the tariff cuts. Effective protection actually increased after 1975. In effect, the IAC replaced tariffs with NTBS, cutting protection for the most efficient industries while retaining protection for the least. The continuity with 'made-to-measure' tariffs is obvious. Finally, while Whitlam tried to reform collective bargaining to obtain wage restraint, he did not do so in a way that would prevent wage flow-ons from protected industry to exposed sectors. After 1975, the new Fraser government actually revived some aspects of business as usual. The effective rate of protection in the automobile industry, for example, doubled from 1975 to 1984. Most of the policy responses in the 1970s thus continued the original impulse to shelter domestic manufacturing as a way to maintain full employment.

Exports: Pluck

The best evidence for a pluck argument comes from the efforts of the Hawke and Keating Labour governments (1983 through 1996). These governments embarked on a two-pronged industrial policy designed to phase out uncompetitive but sheltered labour-intensive industries in favour of high-tech and human capital-intense industries as well as some scale-sensitive exports (Capling and Galligan 1993; Bell 1993). The intellectual basis for this policy shift came out of the 1979 Crawford Report, which called for a host of new policies promoting export competitiveness in manufacturing: government support for high-tech 'sunrise' industries; tariff reduction as unemployment eased; better skills formation; and easier access to equity and debt markets for smaller firms, which in the context of high MNC penetration of the Australian economy meant locally owned firms.

The political implementation of this policy waited until 1984, when the

Minister for Industry, John Button, launched European-style tripartite bargaining over the reduction of protection. Button set up sector level tripartite forums in three politically sensitive industries (steel, cars and TCF), plus an overarching "Australian Manufacturing Council" encompassing eleven industrial sectors. Button offered carrots (R&D tax incentives, export grants and training schemes) and sticks (pre-planned and extensive tariff cuts) to induce an export orientation in local firms. The automobile and TCF industries were exempted from these tariff cuts, but Button forced an amalgamation of automobile firms' factories to attain economies of scale and so reduce the price of Australian-built cars.

Simultaneously, the Hawke government completely inverted the entire institutional apparatus for protection. In a telling switch, the IAC was renamed the *Productivity Commission*. It turned its analytic skills at making made-to-measure tariffs upside down, measuring instead the productivity and price gap between Australian firms and world market benchmarks, and then suggesting ways for firms to close the gap. Contemporaneous reforms to the system of collective bargaining created incentives for firms and unions to take the Productivity Commission's suggestions to heart. The follow-on Howard Liberal-National Coalition governments (1996 to date) continued the policy of gradual tariff reduction and the work of the Productivity Commission. By 1996 average Australian tariff rates were half those of the European Union (Bean 2000, p.95). They also generated a new anti-monopoly *Competitiveness Commission*, to prevent newly privatised infrastructure firms from abusing their market position.

Finally, the Hawke government also induced an expansion of Australian services exports, primarily in tourism (about half of overt services exports) and education. In education, for example, university budget expansion was keyed to their ability to attract paying foreign students. As a result, in the mid-1990s three of Australia's top "exporters" – i.e. foreign currency earners – were universities. Overall, services exports grew faster than total exports after 1980, and by 2000 Australia had a larger share of world service exports (at 1.2 percent) than of world exports in general (at 1.0 percent), reflecting aggressive forays into the educational and leisure tourism markets (Productivity Commission 2002, p.69).

The last evidence for a pluck argument comes from the floating of the Australian dollar in 1985, which also ran contrary to years of policy. The dollar fell over the 1980s, making some Australian exports relatively more attractive. But most Australian exports – including and especially minerals exports – are priced in US dollars, so the devaluation merely made exporting more profitable, rather than making exports cheaper in world markets. It thus could not have induced buyers to pick Australian goods simply on price terms, although it gave exporters room to manoeuver. A similar but stronger dynamic operated after the Asian financial crisis, when a deliberate easing of domestic interest rates after the Thai financial crisis led to a 25 percent fall in the Australian dollar.

These new policies generated an 8 percentage point increase in the share of technology or human capital-intense exports in Australia's export mix, while also shifting raw materials exports towards higher levels of processing (as with wine, which went from nil to nearly 1.5 percent of exports in 2000, or exports of processed aluminium rather than bauxite). These policy initiatives were based on imported models for industrial policy, and thus represented a telling departure from Australia's more usual policies of made-to-measure trade protection for the manufacturing industry (and especially for labour-intensive manufacturing).

Evaluation

Luck certainly played an enormous part in Australia's ability to continue to export large volumes of minerals into world markets. Moreover, the whole minerals sector remained untouched by policy changes in this period, suggesting "stuck" played a role as well. Efforts to change Australia's export orientation away from raw materials and towards manufactures in the 1970s remained cramped by older policy routines and political preferences favouring continued protection. But the 1980s and 1990s brought a remarkable, wholesale shift in policy. Overall, if we can trust the accounts in Bell and in Capling and Galligan, there was more pluck than stuck behind Australia's export success in boosting manufacturing exports. Furthermore, while Australia was lucky with respect to the possibility of attracting large numbers of Asian tourists and students, the willingness of Australian universities to accept large numbers of students was the outcome of policy changes that forced those universities to be more market-oriented. The *change* in Australia's export structure thus was more pluck than stuck or luck, involving a policy-led shift from metal ores to automobiles and machinery, and from commoditised cheeses to high quality wines.

Employment and collective bargaining

Making things people want to buy is helpful, but it is equally important to be able to price those goods at a level people are willing to pay. In the 1960s, both Scandinavian and Australian economists argued that this means that wage gains have to be in line with both domestic productivity trends and world price trends, not only in the exportables sector but also in the sheltered sector – the so-called EFO-Aukrust model. Otherwise, wage increases in the sheltered sector will price exportables out of world markets, as sheltered sector wage gains and relatively high costs for sheltered sector-sourced inputs flow through to the exportables sector. In Australia, of course, the whole system of social protection worked by deliberately imposing high sheltered sector costs on the exportables sector. This transferred rents from the exportables sector back into the sheltered sector in order to support employment at socially acceptable wage levels. By the 1970s this model was unsustainable. How did Australian elites fix their collective bargaining problem in order to price exportables at the right level and make more goods potentially exportable? How did they get employment back to socially acceptable levels?

Employment: Luck

While luck arguments in labour markets are quite straightforward, they have limited applicability to the Australian case. One lucky source of rising employment was probably the creation of new consumer demand as disinflation allowed homeowners to take advantage of declining interest rates. Australian home prices rose strongly on the basis of falling interest rates and rising immigration. Real prices rose 50 percent in the last half of the 1980s and 41 percent in the five years to 2002 (Reserve Bank of Australia 2002, p.3). Some people undoubtedly were able to cash out part of this gain, given that about 70 percent of Australians own homes, and that 6 percent of Australians own housing real estate for investment purposes (Castles 1998a, p.8). But mortgage interest is not deductible for non-investment housing, and the BIS estimates that the contribution of equity withdrawal to Australian economic growth after 1996 was not significantly larger than for the average OECD country, and substantially lower than in Ireland, Norway, the USA and the Netherlands (BIS 2002, p.21). Thus, while housing was a positive factor, it alone cannot explain Australia's strong employment growth compared with other countries.

A second, and stronger, luck argument would suggest that as unemployment rose, labour markets worked in the normal fashion: real wages, measured as full-time ordinary earnings, fell by about 7 percent from 1984 to 1990, producing an employment rebound that was magnified by increased Asian demand for Australian-sourced raw materials. A near doubling of unemployment in Australia from 1980 to 1984 should have led quite normally to wage moderation and a rising share of income going to capital. In Australia the wage share of GDP fell by about 3 percentage points in favour of capital, largely in the 1980s. Falling employment and wages then permitted the modest export expansions noted above and decreases in unemployment when world markets recovered during the back-to-back US economic booms of the 1980s and 1990s. In Australia this stabilized the employment-to-population ratio in the mid- to late 1990s after a period of growth in the 1980s. Policy changes per se need have had nothing to do with this outcome.

But this luck argument has trouble accounting for both the structure of employment growth and the timing of recovery in Australia. First, Australia's relatively centralized system of collective bargaining could plausibly have led insiders to push for higher wages despite rising unemployment, and the collective bargaining system experienced rising centralisation during the 1970s while unemployment rose, and then was decentralized during a period of robust employment. In the extremely capital-intensive minerals sector, unions could have privileged insider wages over outsider joblessness, and firms could have afforded higher wages. In turn, wage relativities would then have priced low-skilled workers out of jobs in the service sector (Iversen and Wren 1998). Why didn't this happen, given that something similar appears to have happened in continental Europe in the 1980s? In addition, while minerals exports boomed, the minerals sector itself is fairly capital-intensive and cannot account for much of the job growth in the 1980s and 1990s, which was concentrated in the service sector. Much of this sector is characterized by low wage employment, but the Accord stabilized the minimum wage, which had been falling in the early 1980s. Given Australia's high minimum wage, it is unclear why it should have such strong take-up of labour at the low end of the market. In contrast, it is possible to argue that political management of wage levels and, equally important, of the connection between productivity increases and wage growth enabled rapid employment gains.

Second, the 1980s employment rebound occurred despite the double headwind of a growing labour force and rising participation rates in that labour force. Arguably, this should have driven wages down further, while raising unemployment. Participation rose from its average 1974-84 level of 70 percent to 75 percent by the end of the 1990s. The wage share of GDP was fairly constant in the 1970s, during the first sharp rise in unemployment from 1.8 percent in 1973 to 6.7 percent in 1982. While the wage share fell sharply in the 1980s, this occurred at a time when unemployment was moderating, falling from 9.8 percent down to 5.9 percent in 1989. It is not clear why falling wages called more people into the labour market.

So the timing and content of the rebound can be explained as luck only if there is a long lag between the onset of rising unemployment (peaking in 1983) and its effects via falling wages to employment recovery. A "lag" explanation necessarily relies on "institutional stickiness" to have force. But luck arguments don't comport well with the pattern of institutional change, because institutions began to change precisely at the point in time when unemployment moderated, and changed the most while unemployment was low. Moreover, it is not clear why institutions had to change at all. What explains decentralisation of bargaining and wage moderation in the face of rising employment?

Employment: Stuck vs. Pluck

Here it is best to consider pluck and stuck together. As with industrial policy and exports, evidence that actors consciously chose to change collective bargaining structures in the direction described above provides enticing evidence for a stuck or pluck argument. Like Danish and Dutch unions and employers' organisations, Australian unions and employers' organisations all experienced internal struggles during the 1970s that eventually produced a decision in favour of some form of negotiated wage restraint. In Australia this took the form of the 1982 "Accord" (Due et al. 1994; Visser and Hemerijck 1997; Hartog 1999; Schwartz 2000). This first Accord was an explicit pre-election deal between the Australian Labor Party and the Australian Council of Trade Unions, in which the ALP offered up an expanded social wage and efforts at employment creation, while the ACTU promised wage restraint across all sectors.

The Accord was Labor's tool for breaking down old institutional patterns that transmitted wage gains across sectors and was pricing exports out of world markets. The ALP and ACTU wanted the Accord precisely in order to change the automatic, comparative-wage-justice driven link between wages in the exposed and sheltered sectors. They believed that this link generated current account deficits and inflation, while hindering investment. The Accord was a way to try to break this link while still retaining some social definition of wages and thus social equality. The ALP believed it could maintain a decent society by expanding the formal welfare state as a substitute for the informal one comparative wage justice used to maintain (Castles 1988). Successive Accords delineated the precise speed at which collective bargaining was decentralized, and the precise trade-offs between today's wages, today's social spending, and tomorrow's deferred wages.

Under the Accord, and unlike the 1960s and 1970s when the Arbitration

Court largely set wages in one central decision, wages would now be bargained at the sector and firm level, and the Arbitration Court would validate those contracts. After 1987, unions and firms could opt out of the centralized wage system if they presented the Arbitration Court with a joint deal exchanging wage gains for specified productivity gains. The Accord thus facilitated and rewarded productivity growth. The Accord's macroeconomic effects dovetailed with the ALP's liberalisation and desubsidisation of product markets. These "microeconomic" reforms – changes in trade and competition policy – forced firms to upgrade. Decentralized collective bargaining and productivity-based wage increases rewarded competitive firms and cooperative unions that complied with this forced upgrading. This presents a clear break with the past. The Arbitration Court had explicitly based its 1960s economy-wide wage decisions on economy-wide productivity trends; before World War II there had been an implicit link. In the 1980s and 1990s, the wage-productivity equation was relocated to the enterprise level. All this looks very pluck-ish. Moreover, combined with product market liberalisation in the 1980s and 1990s, it arguably produced the sharp increase in labour productivity that occurred in the 1990s. The fastest accelerations in productivity growth in the 1990s all occurred in labour-intensive sectors like retail trade, agriculture, and transport, all labour-intensive sectors in which old work practices impeded the introduction of new technologies, or in sectors like telecommunications and utilities, sectors that had been the subject of tight product market regulation (OECD 2000b, pp.84-85). Indeed, retail and wholesale trade and construction together account for nearly all of the increase in the rate of productivity growth in the 1990s, despite accounting for only 40 percent of hours worked (Gruen and Stevens 2000, p.39).

Second, the evolution of Australian collective bargaining under the late 1990s Liberal-National government also departed completely – in intention anyway – from older patterns of Australian collective bargaining. The Liberals introduced the possibility for individual wage contracts (i.e. "Australian Workplace Agreements") in the 1996 Workplace Relations Act. Simultaneously, the Arbitration Court (now called the Australian Industrial Relations Commission) rejected the notion of a "living wage" in favour of a "Safety Net" minimum wage (Buchanan et al. 1998, p.93). Despite this, by 2000 roughly one-fourth of the workforce remained governed by traditional wage awards of the sort that the ALP itself had tried to phase out, while about two-fifths remained under Accord-style enterprise bargains (Dawkins 2000:328).

Finally, in the 1990s, both the ALP and the Liberal-National coalition governments of the 1990s elaborated new active labour market policies, respectively called *Working Nation* and *Job Network*. This boosted ALMP spending from 0.25 percent of GDP in 1989 to 0.8 percent in 1995, settling at 0.5 percent in 1998 as employment recovered. Active spending rose from 18 percent of total spending on the unemployed to 30 percent (OECD 2002h). The major difference between the two programs was that the coalition government privatised the operation of employment agencies. *Working Nation* offered long-term unemployed (over 18 months) firm job commitments. *Job Network* introduced contractual obligations on job seekers and employment agencies and, later, a form of 'workfare'. *Working Nation* coincided with the creation of over 700,000 jobs 1993 to 1996; *Job Network* with a somewhat smaller 500,000 increase through 2000. Both plausibly helped produce these outcomes.

But the possibility that policy was stuck is evidenced by the ways in which the Accord replicated some older Australian institutions and political strategies. Institutionally, the Accord explicitly and implicitly continued to provide basic social protection through a centrally set minimum wage administered through the Arbitration Court. In 1997, Australia still had the highest national minimum wage, in purchasing power parity terms, of the OECD countries that imposed such a minimum, and the second highest when measured as a percentage of full-time median earnings (Dawkins 2000, p.330). The Accord thus left a floor under wages. Politically, the arbitration system helped the ACTU to externalise conflicts over greater wage differentiation, just as it had in the 1970s. Similarly, the ALP's use of the Accord to expand the social wage was consistent with the ALP's long-standing orientation towards providing the electoral majority at the bottom of society with the cheapest and most robust form of social protection possible. The ALP restored public financing for the health system Whitlam had created in the 1970s, added a new second-tier pension and more social assistance, and created a negative income tax. All of this expanded spending was targeted at the bottom 60 percent of wage earners though, rather than being an expansion of a Scandinavian-style universal welfare state.

Furthermore, as an exchange of wage restraint for tax and social welfare gains, the Accord was perfectly consistent with the model of wage restraint first proposed by the Whitlam government. The 1982 Accord also had support from exactly the same social actors who supported Whitlam's failed 1973 effort: the core metal workers union and the core metal manufacturers employers' association federation. All this suggests that the Accord comported with long-standing notions of what not only what was needed to make things work right but also what was the right way to go about setting things right. This was true even under the Liberal governments of the late

1990s. The government continued to support increases in the minimum wage. The Reserve (i.e. central) Bank head and some large unions met to discuss the details of wage policy and the nature of Reserve Bank submissions on wages to the Australian Industrial Relations Commission (i.e. the Arbitration Court) (Buchanan et al. 1998, p.99). And the take-up of individual contracts was limited – roughly one in seven workers – although they created a potent bargaining chip for management.

Evaluation

In an earlier analysis of Denmark, I suggested that the fact that all three countries started out with similar collective bargaining structures, faced similar problems and produced similar outcomes (wage restraint in favour of employment growth) suggests that there might be some underlying logic of appropriateness that produced this outcome. Danish, Dutch and Australian collective bargaining after all changed in the same ways, and all saw substantial increases in both women's labour force participation and part-time employment. These countries had relatively centralized collective bargaining systems in which the state generalized wage gains and cost of living increases across sectors through "concatenation" in Denmark, "arbitration" in Australia, and "mandatory extension" in the Netherlands. In all three countries the state intervened recurrently in bargaining during the turbulent 1970s, and this frequent resort to legislated or judicially imposed settlements meant that labour market actors conducted their conflicts under the shadow of hierarchy (Scharpf 1997a). All three countries also ran large current account deficits and import penetration. Consequently, organized but market-vulnerable actors sought to re-establish their autonomy in the 1980s by behaving responsibly and using state institutions to punish or discipline potential defectors, rather than suffering indiscriminate state sanctions and an erosion of competitiveness.

By the same token, employers in all three countries sought one firm–one contract type bargains from one industry–one organisation type actors, and all three bargaining systems saw rising proportions of purely locally negotiated labour contracts. In all three countries actors located in the metals industry drove decentralisation following a long established logic of appropriateness present in that industry, which exchanged wage gains for productivity gains and which then let employers and workers adjust local wages to local conditions (Thornthwaite and Sheldon 1996; Due et al. 1994). Finally, in all three countries the "new" forms of collective bargaining cum wage restraint in many ways restored older patterns from the 1960s. Indeed, in retrospect, what seems unusual is not the "centralized decentralisation" of collective bargaining, but the breakdown of collective bargaining in all three countries in the late 1960s and early 1970s. The 1980s were thus something of a restoration of older patterns, particularly in the Netherlands. In Australia, at least, collective bargaining changes reversed the ability of white-collar and especially public sector white-collar workers to push their wages up relative to blue-collar workers. Indeed, through the 1980s and 1990s white-collar workers lost ground relative to blue-collar workers. But unorganised and part-time workers also paid a price for this reversal of fortune. Although the residues of the arbitration system protected them, the concentration of employment into job-rich (dual-income) and job-poor (partial or no income) families meant that poverty particularly affected households with children. So here, stuck explains more than pluck, although there was substantial change in Australian collective bargaining practices under the Liberal governments after 1996.

Fiscal balance

Australian governments reduced general government spending from 38 percent of GDP in 1985 to 32.9 percent in 2000 (OECD 2001a, p.230). On either a percentage point or proportional basis, this decline is nearly twice as large as the comparable reduction in government spending that occurred in the Euro area countries (only 2.9 percentage points from 47.7 percent of GDP to 44.8 percent), is comparable relatively speaking to the decline in Sweden (7.7 percentage points, from 60.4 to 52.7 percent), but is not as large absolutely or proportionally to the decline in the Netherlands (10.3 percent, from 51.9 to 41.6 percent). These reductions occurred despite secular increases in pension and health care costs everywhere. In both Australia and the OECD as a whole, social expenditure's share of GDP rose by roughly 4 percentage points from 1980 to 1997. As with the fiscal deficits, this indicates a larger proportional increase in Australia, because it started (and ended) with a lower ratio of social spending to GDP. Despite this, the general government financial balance averaged a surplus of just over 1 percent through the 1990s, slipping into a small deficit during the 2001-2002 recession. Net Australian public debt remained consistently stable at around 10 percent of GDP in both the 1980s and 1990s, in contrast to the rising and considerably larger public debts of most European nations.

How did Australian governments square rising social spending with declining overall spending? Most of the answer lies in a vigorous effort at commercialisation (i.e. corporatisation) that forced public sector firms to become profitable (thus reducing the fiscal deficit) and allowed them to be privatised (thus reducing public debt). The government also disguised much government spending as private spending, through mandatory private sector spending. For example, private sector employers are responsible for paying 12 percent of current wages into individually owned secondary pensions (earnings-related pensions).

Fiscal balance: Luck

As with other countries, "luck", in the form of the normal working of the business cycle and budget balancing efforts by the Clinton administration in the USA, played an enormous role in balancing budgets in Australia. Falling US interest rates led to declines in nominal interest rates from the early 1980s to the late 1990s. Real and nominal interest rates were quite high in the 1980s, and stayed high in the early part of the 1990s. At the end of the 1980s, real interest rates in Australia were nearly 10 percentage points higher than in the USA. But by the end of the decade, Australian real interest rates had converged with US levels, and the premium on Australian public debt relative to German or US equivalent had disappeared (Gruen and Stevens 2000, pp.60-61). This obviously helped reduce the fiscal burden of public debt, and the timing of the interest rate declines comports well with the reduction of the fiscal deficit. Nonetheless, interest costs for the Australian governments were never that substantial, *relatively speaking*, so the decline in interest rates cannot explain all of the turnaround in the government's fiscal position. Australian general government net interest payments were typically lower than either Euro area or EU area payments as a percentage of GDP despite higher real interest rates (OECD 2001a, p.235). This reflects the substantially lower net government debt in Australia as compared with many European governments noted above. Indeed, bad luck worked against Australia, because the early 1990s recession was particularly deep in Australia, and the Asian financial crisis should also have slowed Australian growth more substantially than it actually did.

Fiscal balance: Stuck

Making a better case for stuck is also difficult, though not impossible. Given that social expenditure rose steadily throughout the entire period being considered, an overall decline in public spending can only have come through cuts or relative stagnation in other spending areas. Otherwise, aside from demographic changes, the distribution of government spending should have stayed fairly constant. On the spending increase side, as noted at the beginning, cash benefits to families increased more (absolutely and relatively) than the usual demographic spending drivers, namely pensions and health care. The biggest declines in spending occurred through the removal of subsidies for the whole range of infrastructure services, and through changes in collective bargaining that worked to the disadvantage of public sector employees.

Adjudicating between pluck versus stuck, however, requires more than just data on raw spending. How money was spent also matters – indeed it might be the only thing that allows us to distinguish between stuck and pluck. In contrast to Denmark and the Netherlands, where changes were quite consistent with old routines and justified by reference to existing norms, the structure of social spending changed markedly in Australia (Cox 2001). Australian welfare changes departed substantially from the country's older tradition of a "wage earners' welfare state", with high minimum wage and full employment obviating the need for all but a minimal formal (tax and transfer) welfare state (Castles 1985). The federal state increased formal social transfers, imposed tuition charges for higher education, and expanded public financing of health care services in ways that all departed from existing norms. However, it should be noted that in what is almost always the single largest area of state spending – old age pensions – the state reinforced the old system of occupational welfare through a mandatory employer-funded second-tier pension. It similarly made training an occupational benefit through a "pay or play" surtax on businesses.

The changes noted in the section on collective bargaining above allowed public sector wages to drift downward in relation to private sector wages, reversing a decade-long compression of wage relativities in the 1970s. Australian public sector wages fell roughly 10 percent in real terms during the 1984-1994 decade, while private sector wages remained constant, and then grew in the late 1990s. By contrast, in the Netherlands nominal public sector wages fell 30 percentage points relative to private sector wages, and public sector employment fell by 7 percent, and in Denmark public sector wage growth remained fairly close to private sector wages (Hartog 1999, p.22; Van Ark and De Hann 2000). Insofar as collective bargaining changes involved a higher proportion of pluck than stuck, this would tend to indicate that this part of the fiscal puzzle is explained in roughly the same proportion. Meanwhile, despite extensive privatisation, public sector employment as a proportion of the working population was constant at roughly 10 percent in Australia from 1980 to 2000, which contrasts with the 3 percentage point increase in the average public sector employment ratio in the other 12 small OECD countries in the same time period.

Finally, the privatisation of commercially viable public entities had an equally large fiscal impact. Starting with a higher level of state ownership of commercial firms in 1980, Australia naturally privatised a far greater volume of entities. Here there was also a marked departure from traditional Australian norms. From their origins as British colonies, the Australian states had been involved in infrastructure investment through state-owned enterprises. But the Australian federal and state governments privatised the whole range of infrastructure services in the 1980s and 1990s. For the most part, privatisation was designed to prevent the replacement of public sector monopolies by private sector ones (the Argentine disease). Privatisation thus took money-losing operations off the states' books, generally resulted in lower prices for consumers, and allowed the direct reduction of public debt. It also facilitated the productivity 'miracle'.

Evaluation

Luck clearly had little to do with the achievement of fiscal balance. Pluck seems to outweigh stuck in several of the areas considered, including privatisation and collective bargaining. Fiscal balance was achieved without substantial cuts in social welfare. Instead, Labour governments in 1984-96 redesigned social welfare programs to address the needs of the bottom 60 percent of the electorate and promoted a gradual expansion of social spending ahead of demographic trends. Some of this followed long established routines, like the provision of pensions through private mandates. But many other programs, including public health care, represented novel developments or better institutionalised versions of earlier forays. Although the Liberal-National governments after 1996 did attack some areas, particularly health insurance, their efforts largely failed.

Conclusion

Changes in industrial policy, collective bargaining and the structure of state spending all played a major part in the recovery of the Australian economy in the late 1980s and 1990s. These changes undid existing institutions that arguably had helped to create the economic problems of the 1970s and early 1980s, and facilitated sharp and simultaneous increases in employment and productivity. To make a very compressed argument, these changes, particularly privatisation and the effort to explicitly link productivity and wage gains at the enterprise level, created an environment that made possible substantial productivity gains in both the manufacturing and service sectors. Australia's rate of total factor productivity growth thus went from 1.5 percent per year in 1960 to 1975 (below the OECD average of 2.2 percent) to 2.4 percent after 1993 (versus an OECD average of 0.7 percent) (OECD 2000b, pp.80-86). Rising productivity created a larger pie, permitting changes in collective bargaining and the distribution of fiscal resources.

In summary then, in Australia the volume of change, the direction of change, and the justification for change all deviated substantially from existing logics of appropriateness. This contrasts with Denmark, where change flowed largely from existing logics of appropriateness. Even so, there were substantial elements of continuity in the Australian case, particularly with respect to how all this was achieved. The raw political mechanisms behind the Australian story also contain large elements of stuck. The ALP forged anew the same alliance between itself and the metals industry that had permitted Labour to govern before World War I, during parts of the inter-war period, and during and shortly after World War II. Each of these periods also saw an expansion of social protection for workers. Similarly, the emergence of essentially caretaker right-wing governments after a period of intensive ALP-sponsored change follows an established Australian pattern. Thus, while the case for pluck in Australia looks stronger in the restoration of fiscal balance than it does in the other two issue areas, overall the Australian case still demonstrates strong elements of stuck. Nonetheless, because stuck is in many ways the default outcome, Australia presents a clear case in which policy directed at a set of employment and fiscal problems led to significant changes in the shape and direction of policies, and to the institutional terrain in which politics takes place.

Note

1 The Dutch curve is somewhat flawed because domestically produced exports have done worse in the period under consideration. Dutch exports were upheld by the increasing share of re-exports (cf. chapter 2).

8 Last Year's Model? Reflections on the American model of employment growth

Cathie Jo Martin

Introduction

Throughout the 1990s (and before the economic tribulations of 2001 and 2002) the American economy was a source of adulation and envy. The stock market demonstrated unprecedented growth, corporate profits surged to double digits as a percentage of national income, and unemployment fell to its lowest point in 24 years (*Business Week*, September 29, 1997, p.3546; Bernstein, September 1, 1997; Commission of the European Communities, 6/93, pp. 11, 40). These features of economic life prompted all sorts of congratulatory self-adulation in the business press; for example, *Business Week* (May 19, 1997) described it as the "wonder economy" These successes also prompted recommendations to languishing European economies regarding the adoption of flexible work regulations, social benefits systems more conducive to job-seeking, and tax incentives for corporate investment (OECD 1996a).

The varieties of capitalism literature classifies the USA as a classic liberal market economy (LME), in which firms' competitive strategies and general employment growth rely on low-wage, low-skilled jobs. This model contrasts with coordinated market economies (CME), in which companies compete in market segments that rely on highly skilled workers and derive economic advantage from human assets and institutional coordination. Analysts in this tradition assert that in CMEs, employers, workers and the state all set a high priority on competitiveness in world markets and develop collective organisational mechanisms to enhance their export position in the areas of wage negotiations, training, research and development, and setting product standards. Thus, a relatively developed welfare state and system of worker skills development are viewed as essential to the functioning of the economy (Estevez-Abe, Iversen and Soskice 2001). According to the model, LMEs have traditionally had less open economies and are less likely to pursue profits through high-skilled production; indeed, LME employers derive profits by squeezing rather than by cooperating with organized labour and have more limited needs from systems of social protection and training (Hall and Soskice 2001; Kitschelt et al. 1999).[1] While those writing in the varieties tradition seldom make normative claims about the advantages of the LME model, the American recipe for economic successes has been promoted widely in the popular press.

This essay calls into question the model characteristics of the US economy, as well as the imputed lessons from this uneasy stereotype. By analyzing the performance of the American model in the latter part of the 1990s, this chapter reflects on the broader questions of the volume as a whole: How well do national economies fit their models, and do the models represent the aggregated strategic choices of individual firms, as Hall and Soskice suggest? Do governments that follow model prescriptions, in fact, fix their economies? Or are economic improvements usually a matter of reverting to trend? At the end of the day, what normative lessons can we derive from the experiences of different models?

Three issues complicate the lessons one might adopt from the American experience. First, a fundamental characteristic of the American economy is its duality, a fact that complicates its easy synthesis and normative value. While its characterisation as a liberal market economy is largely true, the American economy contains many highly productive sectors that resemble those found in coordinated market economies. A stylized view of the USA as a bastion of low-skilled competition is consistent with data revealing a huge share of new jobs in the least-skilled sectors; in addition, low-skilled employment has certainly been driven by the lack of regulatory constraints and low wages found in the liberal market economy. Yet the model seems incompatible with the productivity gains found in high-end manufacturing sectors in the 1990s; indeed, the enormous productivity growth in high-skilled employment occurred despite rather than because of the liberal model. In addition, the focus on manufacturing by scholars writing in the varieties literature tends to neglect the critical contribution of service sector productivity growth to the American economic surges of the decade.

Second, the literature implies that the absence of certain types of public policies reflects the logical dictates of the economic system and the desires of employers in that system, yet many American managers strongly regret the absence of CME-type policies fostering greater coordination. According to the varieties literature, national policy both shapes and is shaped by employers' strategic choices: firms' chosen avenues of competition influence the set of public policies favored by employers. Thus, by characterizing the USA as an LME, the literature implies that managers are happy with the low levels of coordination in skills development. Yet many American employers competing in high-end manufacturing sectors with highly skilled workers, in fact, long for the advantages of non-market coordination. These employers bemoan the inadequate skills of the workforce, the inability of markets to provide collective goods, and the general low levels of human capital investments.

Third, many of the successes of the 1990s have to do with factors quite unrelated to the policy prescriptions of the LME model of economic and employment growth. Bubbles or perhaps time bombs – escalating stock and housing prices and consumer debt – set off a chain reaction in which a rapid growth in demand led to an equally rapid growth in employment. The size of the American economy heightened the economic gains achieved through pumped-up consumer demand. Yet this debt-driven demand has already begun to drop off with recessions in 2001 and 2002. To the extent that the successes of the American model represent a return to trend or an illusion created by transitory conditions rather than by human strategies, it will prove difficult if not downright misguided to try to replicate the model experience. At the same time, the celebration of America's seemingly boundless prosperity – unleashed by unfettered capitalism – is hard to square with the comparatively huge proportion of Americans living under the poverty level.

An American success story

There is no disputing that the US economy has been a veritable powerhouse for much of the past decade and a half in the areas of GDP and employment growth (see Tables 1.1 and 1.2). While growth of real GDP averaged only 2.2 percent from 1988 to 1998 in OECD Europe and jumped to 3.5 percent in 2000, GDP grew on average an annual 2.9 percent in the USA and jumped to 5 percent in 2000 (OECD 2001b, 12). Well-paid American women have especially made great gains in employment in relation to their counterparts in Germany, France or the Netherlands; indeed, two-thirds of employment growth for women between 1979 to 1996 occurred in the income levels that were at least one-and-a-half times the income average (Salverda et. al. 2001, p.12).

Productivity growth rates also started increasing again in the last half of the 1990s after being nearly flat for two decades: productivity grew on average 2.9 percent during the last 5 years, and the trend has even continued during the recent recession (Mandel 2002a). Productivity has grown even more in service sectors such as the retail industry (Koretz 2002). The USA has continued to grow faster than other advanced industrialized countries

Table 8.1   Alternative poverty rates, 1993-95

Country	Annual poverty rate (percent)	Poor at least once (percent)	Always poor (percent)	Permanent income poverty (percent)
USA	16	23.5	9.5	14.5
ECHP average*	11.7	19.2	3.8	7.9
France	9.6	16.6	3.0	6.6
Germany	12.1	19.2	4.3	8.1
Netherlands	7.8	12.9	1.6	4.5
UK	12.1	19.5	2.4	6.5

* ECHP = European Community Household Panel
Data taken from OECD, Employment Outlook, 2001b, p. 45.

in terms of output per employed person in the manufacturing sector (see Table 1.2).

The great strides in GDP growth were matched by rapid gains in employment (see Table 1.2). US employment grew on average at an annual 1.3 percent from 1988 to 1998, and another 1.3 percent in 2000, while employment grew on average annually 1 percent in OECD Europe with another 1 percent in 2000 (OECD 2001b, 14). Much of this expansion in employment occurred in high-wage, high-skilled jobs; indeed, the OECD reports that the USA has a "job surplus" in highly skilled positions, or more of these jobs than the OECD average (OECD 2001b, pp. 107-8). Since 1979, skills have been an important source of productivity growth in the US economy, due to a change in the mix of narrowly defined occupations within many sectors. For example, skills growth in the service sectors occurred as clerical jobs gave way to more professional occupations. Between 1989 and 1997, skill levels as a whole across the economy increased about 1.1 percent, with a 0.2 percent rise in goods and 1.4 percent increase in service sectors, and occupations with higher skills have been growing at a more rapid rate than the average occupational growth (US Department of Labor 1999, pp. 41-48).

The rapid productivity growth of the 1990s enabled wages to increase, again after a two decade hiatus: between 1991 and 2001, private sector workers' wages increased on average a 1.3 percent per year, as opposed to 0.2 percent per year during the prior decade, and between mid-1997 to 2001, the annual growth rate in real wages was 2.1 percent. Even wages for blue-collar workers rose by 12 percent during the 1990s (Mandel 2002b). Household incomes for couples with children have gone up even faster than hourly wage rates, albeit at a price: work effort has increased by 367 hours per year (Becker 2001c).

Yet this impressive picture is marred by the poor showing at the low end of the American economy and a precarious existence for those doomed to low-wage, unskilled jobs, poverty, and social exclusion (Table 8.1). Although skills and education attainment are rising and some industrial sectors have been undergoing rapid technological change, the aggregate composition of the US economy contains a very high proportion of low-skilled jobs in comparative terms. This preponderance of both high-skilled and low-skilled jobs means that there is a comparative job deficit in positions requiring mid-range skills. According to the Bureau of Labor Statistics assessment, over half of the occupations expected to grow most between 1996 to 2006 require less than an associated degree. Requirements are limited to on-the-job training for six of the top ten fastest growing occupations, including home health aids, medical assistants and desktop publishing specialists (US Department of Labor 1999, p. 55, 61). Part-time and temporary jobs (usually without benefits and employment security) also made up much of the recent job growth; indeed, 16 percent of the total work force consists of part-time employees. Part-time workers who lose their jobs are often ineligible for unemployment insurance because they have not been working long enough or contributed enough to the pool, and thus these job losses are not accounted for in the rising unemployment rates (Stodghill 2001). Salverda et al. (2001, p.vi) argue that part-time jobs disproportionately fall in the lower-wage segment of the work force in the USA, while these jobs tend to be divided between high- and low-wage segments in Continental Europe.

In addition, the distribution of skills across the population is highly uneven, resulting in a skills shortage. Compared with other advanced industrialized countries, the USA has a higher percentage of individuals with low quantitative and verbal skills as well as a higher percentage with high skills (US Department of Labor 1999, p. 40). Business managers have been deeply frustrated by a lack of skills in the American workforce. Employers reported in one study that 20 percent of their workers was inadequately trained. Some 57 percent said that the requirements for skills in their companies had increased in the past three years (Applebome 1995). In another survey, firms complained that 40 percent of their new hires needed basic skills upgrading as well as almost 40 percent of their current work force (Managing Office Technology 1995). This skills shortage has meant that even during the period that unemployment rates dropped, vacancy rates remained the same: jobs were being filled, but managers had difficulty hiring for jobs requiring highly skilled workers. In stark contrast, Danish vacancy rates and unemployment rates have declined in tandem, suggesting that vacancies have been filled with individuals with the requisite skills (OECD 2001b).

In order to survive in high-end, lucrative sectors requiring highly skilled workers, employees need to have programs for education and training available to them. Yet US firms spend comparatively less on training than many industrialized countries: only 1.2 to 1.8 percent of total employee compensation (Office of Technology Assessment 1990, pp. 3, 15). Less than 10 percent of all US companies do most of the spending of the $30 billion a year on training, and according to some, most of this is spent on executives and managers (Stanfield 1992). Training in the USA also tends to be more heavily concentrated in job-specific efforts, which are less transferable to new jobs and skills than more basic skills development (Lynch 1994). Some 40 percent of young Americans receive additional training after high school, compared with 75 percent of German youths (Lynch 1993, p.251). The community college system has increasingly become a source for post-high school technical training, and many pin high hopes for the future on this development.

Although the American model offers many benefits to those with the requisite skills, individuals and families without adequate training, good jobs and sufficient resources are reduced to a level of impoverishment seldom seen in other advanced industrial nations. The annual poverty rate (i.e. those who are poor all year) is much higher in America (at 16 percent in 1993-95) than in Germany (12 percent), France (10 percent) or the Netherlands (8 percent). Americans are also more likely to slip into poverty at least once over the course of the year – nearly a quarter (24 percent) were poor at one point as opposed to 19 percent in Germany, 17 percent in France and 13 percent in the Netherlands (see Table 8.1). The proportion of those who are among the poorest with an annual income of less than 50 percent of the median income is also quite high in the USA compared with elsewhere. Differences in the gender distribution of the poor are also quite pronounced on the two sides of the Atlantic: women are much more likely to be always poor than men in the USA but only somewhat more likely among European countries. Changes in family status such as divorces or births caused people to slip into poverty 40 percent of the time in the USA but only 25 percent of the time in European countries (OECD 2001b, pp.45-52).

The skills shortage is partially responsible for the growing gap between rich and poor. Whereas in 1970 male college graduates earned 36 percent more than high school graduates, today a college degree offers on average a 62 percent lead in earnings over a high school education (U.S. Department of Labor 1999, p. 56). Just as the USA enjoys a surplus in high-pay/high-skills jobs, the economy has a surplus in low-pay/low-skills employment with a job deficit in the mid-range category (OECD 2001b, p.107). The scarcity of mid-range jobs in the USA makes the skills premium that much more pronounced.

The welfare-to-work reforms of the 1990s have done little to enhance the skills of former beneficiaries, despite improvements in employment. Albeit, the legislation has been successful in pushing many beneficiaries back into the labour market: the number of caseloads fell by 50 percent, from 4.4 million families in 1996 to 2.2 million by June 2000 (General Accounting Office 2001, p. 3). In addition, not all of this employment gain can be credited to the economy, as strong economic growth in the last half of the 1980s failed to produce a comparable decline (Haskins 2001). Yet sceptics doubt that the reforms have significantly improved the lives of welfare beneficiaries. According to a General Accounting Office study, 60 percent of the TANF recipients continue to be unemployed despite enormous pressures to take jobs. Of the hard-to-place individuals, 30 to 45 percent lack a high school diploma, 20 to 30 percent lack job skills, and 20 to 40 percent have health problems or a disability (General Accounting Office 2001, pp. 5, 16). Beneficiaries exited the welfare rolls much more slowly in urban areas: the top 89 urban counties have 33 percent of the population but 58 percent of the welfare beneficiaries (Katz and Allen 2001). Poverty has not declined with the shrinking of the welfare rolls: Sawhill (2001) estimates that over 700,000 families were worse off in 1999 than in 1995. Those in the poorest quintal of singles saw their annual income drop by 4 percent from 1995 to 1998 (Cohn 2000). Removing poor families from the welfare rolls has made them ineligible for health care and other government benefits: poor families lost 40 cents in benefits for every dollar they gained in earnings. Between 1993 and 1999 the child-poverty gap (the amount needed to bring all American children above the poverty level) only decreased from $59.8 billion to $56.3 billion (*The Economist* 2001). The much-feared "race to the bottom" dynamic has not transpired since the implementation of the bill; however, the legislation has stopped far short of solving poverty, and many families who need help do not seem to be getting it (Nathan and Gais 2001).

The American model

The models literature might argue that the dynamics described above are exactly what one would expect to find from a liberal market economy: employment growth through low-wage jobs, radical innovation in high-tech spheres, and polarisation between rich and poor. This section presents the LME model and explores how it might account for the American economic profile, focusing on two aspects in particular: the labour management system and the social welfare regime in liberal societies.

The varieties of capitalism literature presents a stylized view of the American model as the classic liberal market economy. With regard to financial systems, firms raise investment funding from the stock market. Consequently, corporate decision-making is leashed to a shorter time perspective, a tyranny that can lead to the likes of the Enron and Worldcom accounting scandals in which books are juggled to assure stockholders. In the domain of inter-company relations, US anti-trust law designed to prevent cartels and collusion has also inhibited the growth of collaborative sector associations, close vertical links between producers and suppliers, and other types of industry coordination. Technology transfers in this model occur formally through licensing and informally through employee relocation within the industry (Hall and Soskice 2001).

Industrial relations system

Important to our discussion here is the classic industrial relations systems of the LME model, characterized by limited and fragmented unionisation, little wage coordination, contentious and unstable relations between employers and workers, few worker protections and frequent firings, high strike levels, and little employee input into productive strategies. The USA follows the model with its low rate of unionisation (especially since Ronald Reagan's deunionisation drives that eroded representation to 11.5 percent by 1993). A "substantial representation gap" has denied both firms and workers benefits available elsewhere. In CMEs shop floor workers are given vital information only available to top managers in LMEs. Representative groups strengthen worker commitment to the firm, increase worker concessions in difficult times and provide forums to discuss new solutions. Collective forums have efficiency effects – enabling better decisions, eliminating information asymmetries, and stimulating higher rates of job training (Freeman and Rogers 1993; Osterman 1999). Adversarial labour–management relations can dampen productivity growth because a more cooperative work force is quicker to accept new technology and the elimination of less-productive jobs. Employment security makes it easier for workers to embrace technical change willingly, to give up obsolete work rules, and to participate in the industrial restructuring so necessary to productivity growth (Work in America Institute 1984, pp.323-45).

In the USA the absence of strong unions is one factor that has produced enormous wage dispersion, limited worker protections, and few incentives to make long-term investments in skills development. The weak organisation of labour played a role in the limited movement of wages in the 1970s and 1980s – real wages remained fairly flat even during the period that corporate profits were growing rapidly (*Business Week* 9/1/97). The erosion of unionisation in America also reduced employment security: turnover rates are among the world's highest, and there has been an enormous growth in temporary "contingent workers" (Osterman 1999). Even in the heyday of collective agreements, labour relations were often quarrelsome. Unions were denied much input into the broader productive deliberations of the firm and concentrated on economistic ends. Eager to defend against encroachment on their control over job definitions, unions often rejected technological enhancements to improve productivity and the overall economic competitiveness of the firm (Piore and Sabel).

The US representation gap has also been said to greatly constrain training activities and skills development. Because skills development requires substantial up-front investment, both workers and firms have greater incentives to develop skills in coordinated market economies where there is a higher level of employment security and thus a greater likelihood that returns on investment will be realized (Soskice 1999). Neither firms nor workers have incentives to undertake general training: firms are reluctant to invest beyond narrow, firm-specific training because they fear that workers will go elsewhere (Freeman and Rogers 1993, pp. 13-22). Workers are reluctant to invest in education and training because limited social protections exist to protect the value of these investments in the event of a downturn (Estevez et al. 2001). Employers can easily eliminate positions, and the bubbling, frothy economy so praised during expansions can go flat very quickly during downturns (Storey). Thus, the large number of low-skilled jobs and the skills gap among the workforce can be linked to the absence of a collective voice. Low-wage jobs are easily created, but workers lack the security to train for higher-wage employment requiring higher skills.

Social Protection in the American Model

Another important difference between liberal and coordinated market economies is the role of the social welfare system and its link to economic production. Varieties of capitalism scholars point to the importance of high levels of unemployment benefits in giving workers the security to invest in acquiring skills; thus, social protections are directly linked to the needs for a skilled work force so critical to the CME model. In LMES, however, social protections are generally quite limited in order to deny the (generally unskilled) workers support in exiting the work force (Hall and Soskice 2001). Thus, again this general picture fits with the US economic successes in the 1990s, in which many welfare recipients returned to work, but this work was concentrated in jobs with minimal skills.

The American public system of social protection has always been a small operation, crowded out as it has been by the extensive system of employment-based private sector benefits, the shadow welfare state (Stevens 1990). Overall public social expenditures are low by comparative standards, although when private measures are added the USA begins to resemble European countries (Hacker, forthcoming). (US public expenditures on health also resemble those of other advanced industrial countries.) Yet even taking into account private social measures, Americans workers have fewer protections against unemployment and poverty. The so-called "decommodification" of workers is quite limited, as replacement rates are low. Income supports for poor people are even lower, as individuals on welfare often remain below the poverty level. Therefore, despite conservative claims to the contrary, welfare assistance is hardly a viable alternative to work as a means of economic sustenance.

American public policies in the training and active labour market areas illustrate the limits to social protections in the USA. Early training efforts were tainted in their link to income maintenance program, and many active labour market policies were never seriously considered in the US (Weir 1992; King 1995). Low-income, marginally employed persons have very different needs from displaced workers, but these groups have often been put into the same programs. This goal conflict combined with lack of funding reduced the effectiveness of past government training programs such as the Manpower Development and Training Act, the Comprehensive Employment and Training Act and Job Training Partnership Act (Bonner-Tompkins 1994, pp.1-9; LaLonde 1995, pp.149-168). Kazis and Sabonis (1990, p.7) suggest that employers never followed through with the hard-core unemployed and routinely demand monetary incentives and less red-tape in exchange for their participation in training efforts. The Jobs Training Partnership Act, passed in 1982 ostensibly to help the have-nots of society, ended up benefitting displaced workers and subsidizing normal firm start-up costs. Anthony Carnevale of the American Society of Training and Development characterized this dualism as a "schizophrenia in purpose" (Victor 1990, p.898).

The recent welfare reform, the Personal Responsibility and Work Opportunities Reconciliation Act of 1996, also illustrates the distinctiveness of the American model. Although the reform was a momentous break with social policy in ending the entitlement to social assistance, it built on liberal policy legacies in doing little to alter the low skills profile of the American work force (Weaver 1998; Teles and Prinz 2001). The welfare reform act dramatically scaled back the income support safety net by replacing the existing entitlement program, Aid to Families with Dependent Children, with a new federal block grant program to the states, the Temporary Assistance for Needy Families (TANF). Thus, the law reconfigured the funding base for social assistance, changing it from an entitlement whereby the federal government would fund every eligible person to a block grant whereby each state would receive a fixed sum to allocate as it saw fit. In order to address the issue of long-term dependency, the law set a 5-year lifetime limit on an individual's ability to receive federal welfare benefits and ended benefits altogether for legal immigrants. The bill made deep cuts in the food stamps program and made fewer people eligible for Medicaid, although the Children's Health Insurance Program now funds health benefits for poor children.

At the same time the federal welfare reform act deviated very little from the legacies of a liberal welfare regime, by maximizing the coercive aspects of welfare-to-work by forcing beneficiaries back into the work force while minimizing the incentives such as expanded training and child care opportunities. The liberal character of the act does not merely illustrate a failure of imagination: the Clinton administration originally conceptualized welfare reform along the same lines as active social policy in European countries. The core ambition was to reintegrate the economically and socially excluded back into the core economy and into mainstream culture by giving them the skills and support necessary for entering the work force (Ellwood and Bane). Yet the national bill ended up as a much more narrowly focused, punitive measure that relied on coercion to force recipients into (usually) low wage jobs without offering much assistance to help them make the transition. The original Clinton proposal had no hard time limits and fairly lax work requirements, allowing many AFDC parents to escape work to care for their children. Clinton also proposed including an annual $5 billion to be spent on training, child care and transportation, services to enhance the skills of the beneficiaries and to assist them in making their new jobs a success; however, these expenditures were subsequently dropped from the bill (Weaver 1998; Cohn 2000). As Bane (1997) warned shortly after the bill's passage, by giving the states complete flexibility over the allocation of block grant funds and eligibility requirements, the federal government abdicated all responsibility for poor children and potentially contributed to the disparity among states. Perhaps most troubling, however, was that the block grant approach had different incentives than the old AFDC formula and actually motivated states to spend less on welfare than was available. Under AFDC a state received federal matching funds for its welfare expenditures. Under TANF, however, the state received the block grant up front without stipulation and could choose to apply these funds either to the intended beneficiaries or to a variety of other pressing needs. Given this logic, welfare mothers could lose out to new roads, schools, or other completely unrelated needs (Jencks 1997).

Something closer to the European active social policy models can be found in some states; indeed, the national bill left much up to state discretion in order to create a natural laboratory for regional experimentation. States were inspired to move beneficiaries into jobs and to reduce caseloads by the block grant system, which held states financially responsible for any overload of social beneficiaries. Yet few details were specified, and a thousand flowers have, indeed, bloomed. Some states such as Illinois and Washington have tried to alter the ratio of cash benefits to services such as child care, transportation, and in some cases training; but most states have lengthy waiting lists for these services (Waller 1997). Where Minnesota offers extra cash to welfare beneficiaries for work force participation, Michigan relies heavily on training programs to move individuals into lasting employment. Kansas has invested in other types of services to address the social problems of welfare recipients such as substance abuse programs, while Texas has chosen sticks over carrots in its anti-fraud measures. Some states such as Washington and Ohio offer localities considerable discretion or turn to private contractors for service delivery (Nathan and Gais 2001).

The contour of American welfare reform appears in sharpest relief when compared to the active social policies found in many small countries. For example, the Danish active social policies confirm many of our expectations about social democratic welfare regimes, in emphasizing activation over benefits reduction, autonomy for recipients, and fairly (though now time-limited) high unemployment benefits (Green-Pedersen et al. 2001). Danish social policy extends to a broader group of clientele by including those with reduced working capacities who are currently employed. The effort to bring everyone into an inclusive labour market (*den rummeligt arbejdsmarked*) fits with the universality found in social democratic welfare state regimes; however, some critics worry that active labour market policy strips citizens of their social rights (Cox 1997; Abrahamson 1998).

At the same time Danish active social policy has attempted to eradicate some of the traps of and has deviated in important ways from the legacies of the social democratic welfare states, such as the over-reliance on job growth in the public sector and the problems associated with solidaristic wage bargaining. Devices to end unemployment among specific groups have been part of a larger set of solutions to enhance the skills of the general population and to expand labour pools. The plans have created new low-wage jobs that both alleviate the employment strains of solidaristic wage bargaining and subsidize unproductive jobs within the firm. Confronted with a swelling number of unemployed persons on disability, Danish policy-makers have focused on what these individuals could accomplish – their labour market capabilities and competencies – rather than evaluate them for what they cannot do (*Mandag Morgen* 12-8-97). With these jobs the government has managed to get people off the disability rolls, create new low-wage jobs and solved some of the problems associated with high minimum wages (Teknologisk Institut 2000, p. 11). In addition to benefiting individuals, these jobs have aided firms by putting the organisational slack back into firms and helping them to fill unproductive positions within the firm at lower wage rates.

Limits to the liberal market economy model

Many of the characterisations of the LME model seem to portray accurately the US economy: the tyranny of the stock market, the low levels of unionisation, the incapacities of employers' organisations, the relative neglect of vocational training, and the limited system of social protections. Employment growth through low-wage, low-skills jobs and a relative low skills attainment among blue-collar workers is what one would expect from the LME industrial relations system, and a polarisation between rich and poor is not surprising under a social welfare system that pushes the low-skilled into jobs without much training.

Yet the model seems to be at odds with several features of the US success story. There is more growth in highly skilled jobs than the model anticipates, and American managers have struggled in the past decade to make improvements in process technologies. Managers are much more worried about the skills shortage than the idealized LME low-skills producer; indeed, there has been a tremendous amount of debate in the business community about enhancing human capital investments. Finally, other factors contributing to the recent successes of the US economy are completely neglected by the model. This section explores these issues in turn.

Somewhat misleading about the model is the idea that American managers have chosen (more or less contentedly) a competitive strategy utilizing a minimally skilled work force. That a large share of American firms compete in the high-skills sectors is evident from the dynamism of the US economy, its high productivity levels and the productivity gains of the late 1990s. Indeed, as we have seen in this dualistic economy, half of the job growth has been in the low-skills sectors with the other half in jobs requiring quite high-level skills and educational training. Consistent with this story is a dualistic economy in which productivity levels are quite high in manufacturing and less high in services, although service sector productivity growth has been rapidly increasing. In fact, when productivity growth first began to drop off in the 1960s and early 1970s, the growth of the service sector was an important cause of this decline, while manufacturing productivity remained quite high throughout this period (Thurow).

The varieties of capitalism literature certainly does not deny that LMEs have competencies at the high end, but this literature argues that successes are most likely to be found in cutting-edge technology sectors where product innovations (creating new products and designs) count for more than process innovations (that make incremental improvements to the shop-floor manufacture of the goods). In the former, highly educated scientists and engineers are the architects; in the latter, skilled blue-collar workers on the shop floor often offer ideas. Thus, the skills at the top compensate for the comparative lack of skills in the middle rung of society. Yet while to some extent this is true, productivity gains have not been limited to high-tech sectors as many industries have incorporated advanced production processes, and even services have seen productivity growth (Kask and Sieber 2002; Koretz 2002).

This explanation also ignores the enormous changes on the shop floor in the past 20 years, as American managers have struggled to upgrade process technologies, to implement quality improvements, to reorganize workers into self-directed quality circles, and to incorporate computer technologies requiring a skilled blue-collar workforce. Inspired by the apparent successes of Japanese manufacturing processes, a revolution took place within business thinking (Hayes et al. 1988). Managers were told that the new rules of competition demanded greater worker participation and consensual labour relations, especially because technology can be implemented most effectively under conditions of consensual labour relation strategies (Wilkinson 1983, pp.89-90; Davis and Haltiwanger 1991, pp.115-80). The high performance workplace was said to enhance productivity by using worker expertise and fortifying employee commitment to quality products (Osterman 1995, pp.681-700; Cutcher-Gershenfeld 1991, pp.241-60).

In addition, by placing firm strategies and motivations at the center of the model, the varieties literature suggests that US managers affirmatively decided to compete in low-skills sectors and implies that they have been content with this approach. Yet corporate opinion polls over the past couple of decades consistently suggest that managers are urgently distressed about the inadequate skills of the American work force. In 1986, 80 percent of a *Business Week* 1000 sample wanted new education and training programs, and 65 percent were even willing to pay higher corporate taxes for educational improvement (Harris et al. 1986). In a 1991 NAM study, 64 percent was interested in "a national, business-run remedial education program". Firms rejected five-sixths of their applicants due to inadequate skills and found one-third lacking in essential reading and writing skills (Towers Perrin 1991). A 1996 study found 70 percent of its employers' sample desiring increased federal spending on training. Last year NAM found 59 percent of its members identifying a shortage of skills among blue-collar workers as their most pressing problem, a change from its 1997 survey in which managers were most concerned about finding employees with appropriate information technology skills. (In comparison, only 48 percent of the firms identified a serious shortage of scientists.) Workers' skills deficiencies prevented 43 percent of the firms from implementing new productivity improvements, and 62 percent said that they could not maintain the level of production necessary to fill consumer demands. Some 80 percent of the respondents said that their biggest problem with voluntary employee turnover was among hourly production workers, who in the tight labour market had the luxury of moving elsewhere in search of higher wages (NAM 2001). Reflecting on these sentiments, Clinton's Secretary of Labor Alexis Herman noted that even while the US economy performed "beyond our highest expectations", the new economy demanded a wide range of skills that significant segments of the population simply do not have (Abraham and Klein 1999, p.1). The influential report, *America's Choice: High Skills or Low Wages*, warned:

> America is headed toward an economic cliff....If basic changes are not made, real wages will continue to fall, especially for the majority who do not graduate from four-year colleges....It is no longer possible to be a high wage, low skill nation. We have choices to make (Commission on the Skills of the American Workforce, p. 91).

Somewhat ironically, some of the corporate demand for highly skilled workers has been met with an immigration policy that compensates for the inadequate training system in the US by admitting foreigners with the requisite skills. Since the mid-1980s immigrants have had increasingly higher skills than their native-born counterparts (Jasso et al. 1998). In recent years, there has also been an enormous growth in foreign contingent workers, who come on short-term contracts to fill specific job needs (Martin 2002). Economists and business managers alike have pushed for a liberalized immigration policy that would advantage highly skilled workers, especially those who have been trained in the USA (Tyson 1999). For example, the NAM-led business coalition, American Business for Legal Immigration, joined in urging Congress to pass legislation streamlining visa and green card processing for skilled immigrants (American Business for Legal Immigration 2000).

Firms have also sought to fill the skills gap themselves by internalizing the costs of training and creating firm-specific skills. Although as mentioned above the high levels of labour mobility in the US tend to limit corporate investment in training, many companies have nonetheless expanded their training budgets in recent years. According to a *Training* magazine survey, although the work force has only grown by 35 percent in the past 20 years, expenditures on training have grown by 555 percent (Galvin 2001). The National Associations of Manufacturers survey found that 52 percent of its sample had increased training expenditures since 1997 (NAM 2001). Training in America has become a veritable cottage industry.

The policy efforts of the 1990s also belie this vision of general acceptance of a low-skilled society. Although the welfare reform act ended up very much as a liberal version of active labour market policy, the initial Clinton proposal was much broader in an effort to alter the nature of American employment – to enhance skills and to enable firms to develop high-skills productive strategies that would lead to a greater percentage of highly skilled jobs. Seeking to create the conditions for the high performance workplace, the Clinton administration offered initiatives to improve the human capital available for productive employment. A national health reform act would rationalize health financing, expand access to all Americans, and contribute to a healthy, secure, productive workforce. Frustrated with public sector training programs, the Clinton administration proposed three employment and training initiatives to expand and support workforce development in the private sector (Reich 1983, pp. 248-9). The School-to-Work Partnership Act, although initially a pilot program, was intended to develop a national apprenticeship program. The Goals 2000 Act sought to establish a national framework for education and to make education meet standards of competency: schools would be judged by the knowledge and skills attainment of their students. The Workforce Development Act (initially proposed as the Reemployment Act) would consolidate programs for unemployment, training dislocated workers, and create one-stop retraining/employment centers offering benefits, counseling and training. Thus, the public philosophy and the legislative initiatives of the Clinton administration were not unlike the active labour market policies being proposed on the other side of the Atlantic. Indeed, the major goal of these initiatives was to enable firms to embrace the sorts of production strategies possible in coordinated market economies by introducing greater coordination into the American model.

The great irony is that although national stereotypes portray big business as all-powerful in America, many large firms supported Clinton's high performance initiatives and were disappointed with the limits to the administration's policy successes in this area. These firms are competing in the same kinds of markets as some of the CME differentiated quality producers and logically should desire a highly skilled work force. But while US employers have enormous power to prevent unwanted regulations or to secure selective benefits from the political process, they lack an organisational forum to deliberate and lobby for broader collective goods such as increased skills training. As I have argued elsewhere, US business people have no single peak association to aggregate their interests at a class level (Martin 2000). Rather, the Chamber of Commerce and the National Association of Manufacturers compete to represent the entire business community, and the Business Roundtable claims to represent big business. Competition for members makes groups risk-adverse and unwilling to alienate their constituents with controversial stands. Because umbrella associations lack jurisdictional monopoly, they are unable to make difficult choices and defer to vocal minorities. This least-common-denominator politics makes it hard for business groups to take long-term affirmative positions on policy change. This deep fragmentation makes the American business community less capable than employers elsewhere of thinking about its collective long-term interests. National health reform offers the classic case of large American employers handicapped by their own organisational weaknesses (Martin 2000).

In addition, the low-wage, sheltered small business sectors are much better organized politically than high-wage, exposed large business sectors. Struggling to overcome the bias against collective political action, major small business organisations are a significant powerhouse in Washington today. These groups have developed organisational decision rules to augment the natural advantages of a broad-based, numerous membership. Thus, NFIB avoids the stalemate of the larger umbrella groups by grounding policy positions in regular membership polls. This practice lets them claim a mandate for action and makes it much easier to justify positions that hurt a minority subset of members (NFIB 1995). They have also augmented their power with single-issue coalitions, developed when employers become dissatisfied with the stalemate in large umbrella groups and believe that a new forum dedicated to a single issue can make tougher decisions (Lanouette 1982). Thus, the major small business associations have been able partially to overcome the stalemate that handicaps much of the other business sector. Dominated by domestic-producing, low-waged firms and enjoying close ideological ties to the Republicans, these groups have little interest in expanding worker skills. Consequently, public policy further discriminates against the sorts of social protections that assist productive strategies in coordinated market economies. Thus, where the success stories of countries such as the Netherlands and Denmark partially reflect the ability of their corporatist systems to secure broad collective goals, the glaring gaps in the US economy can be traced to the failure of interest group negotiations (Martin 2000; Visser and Hemerijck 1997; Salverda, this volume).

The Housing/Stock Market Bubble

Another reason the arguments contrasting LME and CME modes of competition have trouble accounting for the success of the US economy is the demand-led nature of the boom, a causal factor unconnected to the LME/CME logic. At least some of the energy fueling the US economy in recent years has been demand-led: demand in the US economy grew at an annual 4.9 percent between 1995- 2000, while demand grew at only 1.9 percent elsewhere. Yet this demand has been of a dangerous kind, built in part on consumer debt made possible by escalating stock and housing prices. Spending propelled by household debt skyrocketed at the end of the 1990s. Where household debt was already 85 percent of income in 1992, it had escalated to 103 percent by 1999, and private saving dropped from 6 percent to –4 percent (Becker 2001c; *Economist* 1-22-00, p. 21). Almost doubling since the start of the 1990s, total household debt stands today at the astonishing level of $7.4 trillion dollars (Bernasek 2002). Although much of this debt-funded buying spree went to satisfy the burgeoning taste for imports, American firms were also able to cash in on the largesse of its buying public.

What has accounted for this Madame Bovary-style mania? Although many factors contributed to our emergence as a debtor society, the enormous rise in stocks and housing prices undoubtedly played a role. The stock market soared during most of the 1980s and 1990s, although as of this writing it remains unclear whether the accumulated gains will last or whether the bubble will burst. The price-to-earnings ratios of stocks are elevated much more than usual due to the intense buying by investors. Yale economist Philip Schiller argues that this speculative bubble has been driven by a mixture of media-driven optimism in the new economy, amplification mechanisms, and the follow-the-leader mentality of the new day trader (Shiller 2000). Whether Shiller's bearish forecasts will prove correct is not yet clear. In November 2001 the National Bureau of Economic Research officially declared that a recession had begun in March: unemployment had risen to 5.4 percent by October, consumer spending was flat, and third-quarter corporate profits among *Business Week*'s 124 bellwether companies showed the biggest profits drop in 25 years (Stevenson 2001; Foust et al. 2001). By the spring of 2002, the recession was declared over, yet by summer the stock market's continuing decline combined with depressed corporate profits dashed hopes for a quick recovery (*New York Times*, 7/8/02).

Housing prices have also been bubbling, rising as much as an annual 8 percent in recent years and as much as 20 percent a year in some major metropolitan areas (Business Week 2001; Bernasek 1999). Those lucky enough to have purchased in more sensible times suddenly feel that they have money to burn. Consumers are rushing to take out home equity loans based on the (new) values of their homes, forgetting, perhaps, that unless they decide to move, the gains in equity have no tangible impact except perhaps for an increase in real estate taxes. Home ownership also increased in the 1990s – from 64 percent in 1991 to 68 percent in 2001 (Mandel 2002a). The Federal Reserve's low interest rates, designed to inspire corporate investment, has fueled both the purchase of homes and the consumer free-fall into debt. With interest rates on 30-year mortgages down to 7 percent, new homeowners feel that they can afford to pay higher prices, and existing homeowners can refinance or take out home equity loans (Bernasek 2002).

One also wonders whether the economic comeback enjoyed by the USA in the 1990s was at the expense of other economies (and former model countries). Thus, Brenner (2001) argues that problems of over-capacity and over-production plague the global economy, and national economies take turns enjoying brief stints of vitality. Economic malaise in the past quarter-century reflects falling rates of profit and employment caused by global over-production and the technological transformation of industry. Firms and nations have struggled to regain profit share at the expense of their workers and global competitors.

Surges in the functioning of national economies have often rested on magical wealth created by housing and stock bubbles spurring consumer demand. Yet as we have seen in Germany, Japan and the USA, these bubbles contain time bombs and are sure to burst when the next winner arises to claim the mantle of miracle. Thus, the rise and fall of national economies has a beggar-thy-neighbor dynamic; thus, the US recovery was aided by lower economic dynamism in Germany and Japan. Unless the underlying problems of over-capacity and over-production are resolved, national economies and models may continue to engage in an elaborate game of trading places (Brenner 2001). Policy reforms may ultimately be able to do little to counteract the fundamental weaknesses of advanced capitalist economies.

Conclusion

What are the lessons to be learned from this survey of the American employment experience? Three conclusions come to mind: success may be transitory, success has redistributive costs, and success may reflect circumstances at odds with or outside the logic of the American model. First, success may be transitory. Although we have now been told that the first recession of the 21st century is over, the downturn dampened praise for the American model and raised questions about disquieting flaws in the American model. Indeed, one can make the case that much of the highly touted employment growth of the 1990s was a somewhat flimsy affair from the beginning, with half of the new jobs in low-skilled, low-wage sectors. These sorts of jobs have a transient, here-today-gone-tomorrow quality that makes for easy disappearance in tough times.

Second, success has not-very-hidden redistributive costs. Enthusiasm for the new economy depends on one's vantage point. Despite gains in employment, those in the poorly paid, unskilled bottom tiers may ultimately be worse off than ever, especially with the safety net of Aid to Families with Dependent Children now an entitlement of the past. The policy legacies of the liberal welfare state reinforced the peculiarly American brand of employment growth. Job growth in the 1990s was partially stimulated by a major welfare reform that severely scaled back already minimal social protections. Indeed, the welfare reform bill eliminated social supports in place for 50 years, leaving many defenseless in the face of future economic downturns. This erosion of the welfare safety net pushed (often unwilling) recipients back into the work force, usually in minimum wage jobs. Issues of compassion or social rights aside, the strategy was far more successful than expected in re-employing welfare recipients during the boom years of the late 1990s. The AFDC caseloads declined by over half between 1994 and 1995, although experts debate the extent to which this reflected the economic boom (Danzinger 1999).

But the goal of employing and retaining (usually) under-skilled, (often) marginally employable persons in the labour market is likely to be difficult to sustain during bad economic times, and many fear for the security of the truly disadvantaged in a time of economic malaise. Because the law turned social assistance into a block grant program, whereby states receive a fixed sum from the federal government, states had the ability to run a social assistance surplus during the recent good economic years. Many states redirected funds targeted for social provision to other (mixed) ends: while some like Wisconsin invested in training, others chose less relevant pursuits such as paving roads or cutting taxes. Those states that spent relatively more on training may have helped recipients make the quantum leap to a more highly skilled level of employment and may actually save money in the long run. Twenty-two states have already exhausted their reserve unemployment insurance funds, and one wonders what will happen when the rolls expand once again with the downturn (Starr 2001; Wilson 1996-7). Thus, the same features of American public policy that inspired rapid wage growth in the 1990s are posing severe risks in the current climate both for individuals and for the broader social fabric.

Third, success may reflect circumstances outside of the American model. Crediting American employment and economic successes entirely to strategies of a liberal market economy may miss the mark. The LME model fails to account for the diversity of the economic system and the impressive employment gains in highly skilled production areas. Nor does it capture the amount of corporate concern about low skills and conflict among sectors about the direction for future economic success. In some ways the impressive aspects of the American model have been accomplished in spite of rather than because of the tendency to engage in LME low-skills competitive strategies. Productivity growth and much of the employment growth have occurred among large firms that have broken with this traditional model (Harrison). Their desperate need for skills has partially been met by factors outside of the model, such as a large number of skilled immigrants who have been trained in their own countries.

The economic boom has been driven in part by the housing and stock market bubbles, a dynamic that limits the extent to which we can and should seek wisdom from the American model. If the employment miracle reflects serendipitous circumstances, the only lesson to be derived is that luck sometimes happens. To the extent that the enormous employment and GDP gains of the 1990s are spurred by bubble dynamics, the economic accomplishments of the decade may be illusionary at best and precarious at worst. Enjoying our transcendental moment of triumph is one thing, trying to replicate it is another.

Note

1 While Hall and Soskice, for example, do recognize that LME firms enjoy certain high-end competencies, for example, in radical product innovation, they suggest that the model's most important contribution to profitability is the numerical flexibility and lack of worker regulations found in CME companies.

9 The German Contrast. On Bad Comparisons, Special Circumstances, Luck and Policies That Turned Out to Be Wrong

Uwe Becker

'Germany isn't working'

'Europe has a problem – and its name is Germany,' according to *The Economist* of January 19, 2002, in a leader titled 'Germany isn't working'. Why? In the decade up to 2000, German economic growth was below OECD average, and in 2001, as the world economy slowed down, German growth slowed to just over half a percent per year, the lowest rate in the EU. By 2002, Germany hardly grew, and growth forecasts were gloomy. Unemployment had risen past the politically important level of 4 million, business as well as consumer confidence was at record lows, and the popular economic outlook was generally pessimistic. Germany had turned from the engine of the European economy into the laggard. What explains this dismal situation?

The usual answer, found in many newspapers and advisory commission reports, claims that the causes of the poor German performance lie in high wages and social security costs, complex taxes and tight labour market regulations. The excuse of reunification costs and shocks no longer has much credibility, according to *The Economist*. Given this diagnosis, most popular analyses suggest the obvious responses: the labour market has to be made more flexible, and the tax and welfare systems have to be reformed! The most prominent voice advising such reforms is perhaps the OECD in its most recent *Economic Survey* on Germany (2002j, pp.5, 13). And company bosses threaten to move activities abroad if tax reform and labour market liberalisation will not take place very soon (*Financial Times*, December 16, 2002, pp.1, 3). The 'proof' that these reforms work is usually made by reference to better performing economies that have reformed their labour markets. Did not the US Federal Reserve Bank Board chairman Alan Greenspan advise the same when he said 'that the greater ease with which employees can be laid off in the US has counter-intuitively created a greater incentive to hire and thus reduced unemployment in the US to levels unimaginable in all but a few countries in Europe' (*Wall Street Journal Europe*, August 29, 2000)?

No question, Germany is not performing well in terms of economic growth and employment. In this sense it is indeed, and particularly was until 2000/01, a striking contrast to the 'model economies' discussed elsewhere in this volume. An additional critical dimension is that demographic ageing is proceeding much faster in Germany than in most other countries and that financing pensions and health care will become precarious in the not so distant future. But leaving apart this specific problem, the current national and international discussion of the German situation is largely based on inappropriate comparisons.

First, the usual miracle stories themselves were not unblemished successes. The economies discussed in Germany as examples are the USA, the Netherlands and, to a lesser degree, Denmark. The US 'wonder economy' has, however, its dark side of mounting inequality and poverty. And its spectacular economic growth in the second half of the 1990s was highly debt-induced, to a considerable degree based on accidental circumstances, and has brought about huge imbalances that have to be judged as a main cause of the current slowdown of the world economy. A story that is similar to some extent can be told about the Netherlands and Denmark. The Dutch 'miracle' started from a very low level of employment, took shape by an explosive increase of relatively cheap part-time jobs, and accelerated from 1995 to 2000 by high economic growth that essentially was based on rising private debt related to surging asset and, particularly, house prices, just as in the USA. Favourable circumstances – house prices again, North Sea oil – have been helpful in Denmark, too. But this country's employment performance also has a clear policy component integrating economic and social goals. Perhaps Danish employment policy could serve as a long-term perspective for Germany. In the shorter run, Germany will have to solve the problems of unification, however. Whereas the model economies have partly been fed by luck, unification has been, in economic terms, bad luck for Germany.

A politico-economic discussion that concentrates on good and bad policies tends to overlook this striking contrast and generally to give no serious attention to accidental, favourable and unfavourable, (national) circumstances. It conceives policy-making as a technical affair, overestimates its importance, and makes comparisons inappropriate. A similar danger emerges from reducing performance differences to divergent institutional frameworks. Institutions do not explain everything, and the very concept has first of all to be defined in a way clearly demarcating it from rival concepts such as structure, organisation, rule and norm. Omitting this brings about the dangers of all-embracing institutionalism and institutional determinism. It is, for example, only a determinist and in this sense 'rigid' institutionalism that constructs an absolute opposition between rigid and flexible politico-economic structures and that is unable to understand that even rigid contexts, as in the cases of Austria and Sweden, can allow for good employment performances (see also Freeman 2000a and 2000b). The analysis of institutional contexts and of policies is important, but reductionism has to be avoided, and lucky circumstances also have to be taken into consideration.

Second, the usual comparisons inappropriately use countries much smaller than Germany. Comparing small and very small countries with large and very large ones without any qualification is a kind of superficial comparative political economy. Germany has 16 times as many inhabitants as Denmark and 5 times as many as the Netherlands, while Upper Bavaria or southern Hesse alone each have the population of Ireland. These two German regions did not experience spectacular growth in recent years but nevertheless approximate Danish employment levels, have relatively low unemployment rates, and are richer than any other non-city region in Europe. And the whole of Bavaria plus bordering southern Hesse, together as large as the Netherlands, outperforms this country in any respect with the exception of GDP growth and registered unemployment in the period from the middle of the 1990s up to 2003 – but the figures of registered unemployment are particularly misleading in the Netherlands. In comparing big and small countries, such regional developments have to be taken into account. Doing this also sheds some critical light on general assertions about the necessity of labour market and welfare reforms.

In the next section I will comparatively sketch a number of central features of the German economy and of its development up to the eve of unification. In section 3, I will discuss the impact of the often-quoted 'rigid' labour market structures and unemployment benefits on German employment. The subsequent subject is the contrast between the 'lucky' housing bubble in the model countries and the burden of unification costs in Germany. This section will also briefly review a few political decisions made in the immediate period after unification that turned out to be wrong. Before concluding and discussing German prospects, section 5 points to the relatively positive performances of some West German regions. Throughout, some attention will be given to the distinction between structural and temporary components of the German situation.

The German economy in comparison

If we want to understand what is going on with German employment, we first have to distinguish between structural patterns and specific developments in the past decade. Regarding the structural component, it makes sense to use Esping-Andersen's (1996, pp. 10ff) distinction between (European) continental, Anglo-Saxon and Scandinavian ways of macro-economically regulating employment and unemployment. A main ingredient of the first route or strategy is to keep measured unemployment low by reducing labour market participation. When it is successful, this strategy brings about a relatively low unemployment rate, but at the cost of a (relatively) low employment rate. In the past three decades, Germany has developed along the lines of this route, with diminishing success (see Table 1.1). Countries of the same category – which Esping-Andersen called 'pensioner states' because a large part of employees older than 55 years have been sent into early retirement – include Belgium and France and, at an even lower level of employment combined with high unemployment, Italy and Spain.[1] Until very recently, the Netherlands also was a 'member' of this club, and when measured in terms of FTEs, this model country still belongs to the low employment group. For in quantitative terms, the Dutch 'miracle' can largely be reduced to the explosive growth of part-time jobs since the mid-1980s. And looking at its extremely high number of disability beneficiaries (14 percent of the labour force in late 2002) and the low employment rate of persons older than 55 years, this country is a 'pensioner state', too. On the other hand and in a specific sense, it has taken over one central component of the Anglo-Saxon way.

Of the other model countries, the USA mostly represents the Anglo-Saxon or liberal way that is characterized by a low level of employment protection, pronounced wage dispersion and correspondingly a significant low-wage segment of employment. As a complement, unemployment benefits are residual (in non-standard households they are even lower than the figures for standard families in Table 1.3 indicate[2]), and social assistance is only rudimentary or even absent. Because of the low unemployment benefits, Americans are forced to look for work, much more so than people in most countries of the European continent, and they have to accept low-paid jobs (but then they can receive tax credits – the EITC – for improving their net income; cf. Appelbaum 2000, p. 15). The result is a higher participation and employment rate than in the countries of the continental route. The Netherlands has also gone some steps on the liberal way of wage dispersion by a drastic employment rise of low-paid jobs for women and juveniles (who are

Table 9.1   Attitudes about gender roles in the EU-12, 1994 (excl. Luxemburg)

	B	DK	W-G	E-G	UK	GR	F	IRL	I	NL	P	S	EU
A)	3.35	2.95	4.01	2.87	3.11	3.91	3.49	3.23	3.55	3.21	3.80	3.13	3.46
B)	3.36	2.65	3.07	2.17	2.73	3.20	3.12	3.12	3.10	2.55	2.97	2.58	2.91
C)	2.93	2.93	2.95	2.01	2.83	3.10	2.78	3.07	2.51	2.50	2.89	2.40	2.71
D)	2.95	1.92	2.98	2.15	2.34	3.02	2.50	2.64	2.62	2.20	2.97	2.31	2.57
E)	2.84	2.26	3.15	2.91	2.57	3.68	2.66	2.84	2.98	2.25	3.68	2.54	2.83

Source: Eurobarometer 42, 1995, B55

often paid the legal youth minimum wages that are considerably lower than adult minimum wages) working part-time. Instead of a residual welfare system, however, the Netherlands still has a comparatively generous one with a benefits level resembling that of the Scandinavian countries (see Table 1.3). The Scandinavian way involves generating high employment by public or publicly financed job creation. This way is also called social democratic because it combines high employment with high social security and equality levels. Denmark has recently replaced Sweden as its foremost example. Other countries have copied Scandinavian-style labour market policies to some degree, but there are no cases outside Scandinavia where public employment counts for more than 30 percent of total employment.

As an aspect of relatively low structural employment, female employment has also been low in Germany, particularly by Scandinavian standards. This is at least true for Western Germany that shares this feature with most continental European countries including the Netherlands. The formerly socialist Eastern Germany is somewhat different in this respect and raises the overall level of female employment in Germany, but it cannot decisively change the picture because it is much smaller (and moreover adapting to West German standards). The relatively low female employment rate in (Western) Germany relates to low scores in emancipation values regarding gender roles in that country. Table 9.1 shows that West German attitudes are similar to those in economically less developed Greece and Portugal and in clear contrast to the respective attitudes in Eastern Germany, Britain, Scandinavia and the Netherlands – though in the last country reality and values do not match. The table scales attitudes from 1 to 5 with 1 as the emancipation-egalitarian pole and 5 as the conservative-traditional pole. The figures reflect answers on statements[3] with respect to women's and men's roles and duties at home and on the labour market as well as their relations to their children.

Another property said to be a structural feature of the German economy is the relatively small service sector and, correspondingly, an oversized industrial sector. The assumption is that as a result Germany cannot optimally profit from the job-growth potential of the former. Most of the time, the comparative yardstick is the USA, although one could also take Britain, Denmark, the Netherlands and a number of other economically advanced countries where the figures are not much different from the American ones. In the USA, employment in the service sector reached 72.2 percent in 1993, while it was only 59.3 percent in Germany. Conversely, industrial employment was much higher (38.6 percent) in Germany than in the USA (23.7 percent). On closer investigation, these differences disappear, however. The figures just presented come from statistics counting employees per sector. This is not a precise way of calculating because there might be different national standards, and service activities sourced out of industry in one country may still be part of the latter in the other one. Therefore, figures counting job activity are more exact. Looking at these figures reveals that 72.8 percent of German employees had a service job in 1993, while the comparable percentage in the USA was 71.6 – and in industry the respective figures were 25.4 and 25.9 percent (the remaining 1.8 and 2.5 percent of employees have a job in agriculture; Lindlar and Scheremet 1998, pp.34f). However, this does not change the general fact that structural employment in Germany has been rather low in the past decades.

Nonetheless, in the second half of the 1980s, Germany, just like Japan, was discussed as a 'model' – while economists (e.g. Thurow 1992) and the media described the USA as rather a problematical case (see generally Albert 1997, p.4). According to Richard Freeman (2000a, p.2), even the early Clinton administration – we are talking about 1993/94 – 'looked jealously at parts of Germany's Rhineland Model'. And nobody talked about the Netherlands or Denmark. Germany had recovered from the recession of the early 1980s, the budget deficit had almost disappeared at the end of the decade, unemployment had declined to a lower level than in most other countries, employment was rising, and nobody seemed to care about the still relatively low employment rate. Moreover, the country, in particular the federal state of Baden-Württemberg, got special positive attention because it appeared to have smoothly handled the changes from Fordism to post-Fordism – as far as these qualifications make sense with respect to Germany – and, quite in contrast to the USA, to have modernised its industry by integrating high-tech elements (Sabel et al. 1987, pp.35f). What seemed to have developed during the 1980s was a German, particularly southern German, 'adjustment path' (Siegel 2004, pp.107ff) towards an economy of 'diversified quality production' that had reached its fame by robust and efficient capital goods as well as positional consumer goods such as expensive cars and that was 'internationally competitive across a uniquely wide range of products' (Streeck 1997, p.41; cf. Boyer 2000, pp.19, 56). However justified the qualification of German high quality might be, the country's industry had managed to acquire an oligopolistic position in certain markets and to receive a quality and oligopolistic 'premium' on many of its goods (Boyer 2000, pp.34ff).

So, the economic sky was bright when the German Democratic Republic broke down in 1989 and when unification of the two Germany's took place in 1990. In the first instance, this worked out positively in the form of the 'unification boom' lasting for two years. Thereafter it went wrong, however-er. GDP growth declined and remained at a lower level than in most sur-rounding countries for the entire 1990s, employment more or less stagnat-ed, and unemployment rose. This negative turn did not come about because the (West) German economy became less competitive in that period. It is just a 'paradox' (Harding 1999, pp.69f) that its export-oriented industries maintained or even improved their competitiveness in the context of a wors-ening labour market (see also OECD 2002j, pp.24ff and Streeck 2001a & b, p.3; this process continued into 2004 when German unemployment soared to nearly 5 million and the country became the biggest exporter in the world; Fels and Christian 2004). So, did German growth and employment decline because of labour market rigidities, because the country missed the accidental circumstances fostering employment growth that other countries had in the 1990s, or because of the costs of unification?

A bad employment record because of labour market and welfare rigidities?

Labour market rigidities, high taxes/labour costs and high welfare benefits are the factors the dominant national and international discussion has iden-tified as the main causes of the German employment misery[4] and what re-form proposals by the German government concentrate on. And it is partic-ularly with respect to these topics that the USA and to a lesser degree also Denmark and the Netherlands are referred to as positive examples. Are the criticisms justified, is the diagnosis correct, and do the model countries re-veal figures on these items that are clearly more favourable for employment? The answer is not unequivocally yes, but rather mixed and complex. Labour market flexibility, defined as the ease of hiring and firing in legislation, is indeed high in the Anglo-Saxon world, particularly in the USA (with an overall indicator of 0.7 for employment protection legislation – 'EPL'; see Table 9.2), and there employment is relatively high, too. A similar constellation is found in Denmark (1.5) and Switzerland (1.5). On the opposite side, rigidity is high, flexibility thus low where employment is also relatively low: in Germany, France and Italy. The subject is more complicated, however. This is because compared with the USA and with the exception of Denmark and Switzerland, all continental European countries reveal more or less high levels of employment protection while their employment records are very different. And one should not forget that labour markets that commonly are described as rigid may have developed their own forms of flexibility such as overwork or the temporary reduction of weekly working hours ('Kurzarbeit').

Germany with its overall EPL indicator of 2.6 is in the same league as France (2.8) and Belgium (2.8) where employment is comparably low and unemployment comparably high (though Flanders, taken separately, would show a different picture), but also as Sweden (2.6) and Norway (2.6) where employment and unemployment figures point in the opposite direction (see Table 1.1). And the Netherlands (2.2) is not far removed from these values. Looking at regular employment, its employment protection legislation (3.1) is even more rigid than of its neighbours, and taking into account that the lowering of the protection for temporary employment (from 2.4 to 1.2) only took place in 1998, one even has to conclude that the Dutch 'miracle' occurred in the context of a pretty rigid labour market (see also Schettkat 2002). Finally, one could mention that the Portuguese employment record is much better, in spite of a very rigid labour market (3.7), than that of neighbouring Spain (3.1) as well as of many countries with a considerably lower indicator.

The indicators taken from the OECD (1999) are open to discussion but sufficiently exact to sustain the conclusion (ibid, pp.48ff and 69f, see also Nickell 2002 and Freeman 2000a) that there is only little or no association between the strictness of employment protection and the overall levels of employment and unemployment. This is at least true as long as employment protection legislation is viewed independently of the larger politico-economic context of which it is an element. By implication, there is no reason to expect significant change from isolated liberalisation of this legislation. This is illustrated by the recent slight move towards more flexibility in the German labour market – particularly with respect to temporary jobs – that has not visibly improved the employment situation. The number of fixed-term contracts increased (*Die Zeit* 49, 2001), but this did not fundamentally change

Table 9.2   Indicators of the strictness of employment and unemployment protection legislation in 20 OECD countries in the late 1980s and 1990s

	Regular employment		Temporary employment		Collective dismissals[1]	Overall strictness[2]	Index of un-employment protection[3]
	Late 1980s	Late 1990s	Late 1980s	Late 1990s	Late 1990s	Late 1990s	Late 1990s
Austria	2.6	2.6	1.8	1.8	3.3	2.3	0.81
Australia	1.0	1.0	0.9	0.9	2.6	1.2	0.22
Belgium	1.5	1.5	4.6	2.8	4.1	2.5	0.82
Canada	0.9	0.9	0.3	0.3	3.4	1.1	0.30
Denmark	1.6	1.6	2.6	0.9	1.5	1.5	0.91
Finland	2.7	2.1	1.9	1.9	2.4	2.1	0.43
France	2.3	2.3	3.1	3.6	2.1	2.8	0.54
Germany	2.7	2.8	3.8	2.3	3.1	2.6	0.77
Ireland	1.6	1.6	0.3	0.3	2.1	1.1	0.37
Italy	2.8	2.8	5.4	3.8	4.1	3.4	0.18
Japan	2.7	2.7	-	2.1	1.5	2.3	0.33
Netherlands	3.1	3.1	2.4	1.2	2.8	2.2	0.89
New Zealand	-	1.7	-	0.4	0.4	0.9	0.27
Norway	2.4	2.4	3.5	2.8	2.8	2.6	0.64
Portugal	4.8	4.3	3.4	3.0	3.6	3.7	-
Spain	3.9	2.6	3.5	3.5	3.1	3.1	-
Sweden	2.8	2.8	4.1	1.6	4.5	2.6	0.63
Switzerland	1.2	1.2	0.9	0.9	3.9	1.5	0.86
UK	0.8	0.8	0.3	0.3	2.9	0.9	0.11
USA	0.2	0.2	0.3	0.3	2.9	0.7	0.10

1) Indicator of collective dismissal rules contained in legislation and collective agreements. 2) Weighted average of the preceding three indicators. 3) Standardized averages of the 'net unemployment replacement rate' for a 40-year-old 'representative worker', the overall generosity of unemployment benefits, and the definition of a 'suitable job'.
Sources: OECD 1999e: 66 for columns 1-6j; Estevez-Abe et al. 2001: Table 2 for the last column.

the German political economy. The flexibility or rigidity of the labour market is not only defined by EPL, but also by and in conjunction with e.g. the coverage grade and character of collective wage agreements, the existence and the level of a legal minimum wage, and the system of social security.

The coverage grade of collective wage agreements in Germany is 92 percent (in 1994), in most continental EU member states it is about or higher than 80 percent, in Denmark only 70 percent, in the USA it is not even 20 percent, and the British figure lies inbetween (Nickell 2002, p.44, Table 12). This means that the space for paying wages below the level written down in collective agreements is very limited in Germany. A legal minimum wage does not exist, however. The agreements as such, negotiated at sector levels, have become more differentiated in the recent past and leave room for exceptions at the plant level (Flecker and Schulten 1999, pp.97f), and in East Germany, where unemployment is particularly high, there is a considerable degree of 'illegal flexibility': about 85 percent of the companies employing 55 percent of all East German employees (Sinn and Westermann 2000, p.18; see also – for somewhat older figures – Thelen and Kume 1999, p.481) pay wages below the level of industry contracts. Perhaps German collective agreements are less flexible than those of countries with comparable degrees of coverage and employment protection that have a higher employment rate, such as Sweden. There is no indication, however, that this could explain the different employment performances. Moreover, a comprehensive and reliable comparative index of the flexibility of collective wage agreements identifying Germany as particularly rigid does not exist.

A conclusion similar to that about the isolated relationship between labour market flexibility and employment has to be drawn with respect to the isolated relationship between the level of employment and unemployment and the generosity of unemployment benefits and unemployment protection in general – also including the definition of a job 'suitable' for unemployed people (see Table 1.1 and the last column in Table 9.2; see also Nickell 2002, pp.40ff). Again, relatively low benefits in the Anglo-Saxon countries correspond with high levels of employment – although 15 percent of all civilian jobs in the USA are subsidised by tax credits (Schelkle 2000, p.5) – but the reverse statement would not be true. After all, high employment countries such as Denmark, Switzerland, Sweden, Norway and also, with employment on a bit lower level, Austria and the Netherlands, have the most generous systems of unemployment protection (even if the generosity of this systems has somewhat been reduced since the mid-1980s). Germany – where welfare retrenchment has been very modest (Korpi and Palme 2001, p.32) – and Belgium are the only countries where a relatively high level of unemployment protection corresponds with only a mediocre employment rate and high unemployment. In Italy, however, an even worse situation on the labour market coexists with a system of unemployment protection that cannot be described as other than poor.

The construction of a direct link between the absence of unspecified welfare reforms and the increase of German unemployment in the 1990s (Cox 2001) is too easy, therefore. The same is true for Streeck's (2001, pp.1f) assertion that the German welfare system has depressed economic activity by producing equality. Equality in Scandinavia and the Netherlands is higher! Neither the level of welfare benefits nor income redistribution reducing inequality automatically result in a low employment rate. What about eligibility criteria? They appear to be more important than replacement rates. Countries where eligibility criteria for receiving unemployment (and social assistance) benefits have been tightened, particularly Denmark (Torfing 1999), have shown a reduction of unemployment (OECD 2000a, p.129; this relation should not be exaggerated, however, because this tightening cannot create new jobs). In Germany, by contrast, eligibility criteria are rather soft (ibid, p.136; Nickell 2002, p.42, Table 10; but see Oschmiansky 2003, p.15 for a different view); therefore the incentive for unemployed people to seriously look for work is not particularly strong (Brixy and Christensen 2002). The popular (but documented) stories about Polish workers who have to do the asparagus and wine harvest in Germany because the German unemployed do not accept the low pay for this work fit exactly into this picture (though one has to admit that similar stories are told in the Netherlands and even in the USA with its low unemployment benefits).

What is the conclusion of the preceding considerations? That labour market structures and welfare systems do not significantly influence employment and unemployment rates? No, that is not the conclusion! Throughout this section the argument has been that simple bivariate relations do not exist between rigid labour markets and generous unemployment benefits on the one hand and a low employment rate/high unemployment rate on the other. There is not even a bivariate relationship between rigid labour markets and generous benefits put together and low employment! One can always point to at least one Scandinavian country where these features are combined with high employment and low unemployment. In fact, however, this only means that such a combination is possible under certain conditions. In Sweden and Norway, this condition involves relatively huge active labour market policies and, most important, the high level of public employment. It is the latter that compensates for the employment-reducing effects of rigid labour markets and generous welfare systems with soft eligibility criteria (cf. Iversen and Wren 1998).

Without this or an alternative (e.g. extra GDP growth) compensation employment tends to be low, and unemployment tends to be high. Cheap labour, easily attracted and dismissed, is hardly available. This is exactly the situation in Germany as well as in a number of other continental European countries. A relatively low employment rate is, as already indicated in the beginning of section 2, a structural feature of these countries' political economy (see however the regional specification presented in section 6). Unemployment can often be kept limited – as in Germany for a long time – as long as economic growth meets expectations and as long as the early retirement of large groups of workers older than 55 years can be financed.

To change this situation, Germany has two options. One is to move radically into liberal directions by reducing employment protection, unemployment as well as social assistance benefits, and the coverage of collective wage agreements to American or at least British levels. To realise this, the unions would have to be fought and other central aspects of the very form of the German political economy – or 'variety of capitalism' – with elements such as co-determination would have to be broken down. The price to be paid for such a move would be increasing inequality and poverty. One may wonder whether such a move could receive the necessary support. And could it be combined with the German specialisation in the international division of labour – particularly the production of quality machinery and cars – that requires, it is said (Hall and Soskice 2001), a large group of highly skilled and motivated workers identifying themselves with the goods they produce and the company they work for? (The so-called Hartz reforms, in 2004 enacted by the Red-Green majority with the support of most of the federal states have not yet seriously cut welfare and liberalised the labour market, and after a few months of popular discontent the majority of the population seems to acquiesce to the reforms or to support the even more radical proposals of the opposition parties).

The alternative move would be in the Scandinavian direction of a large sector of public or publicly financed employment supplemented by measures of a limited employment effect such as a Danish-like selective tightening of eligibility criteria in social security and welfare and a selective loosening of employment protection (the employment threshold at which protection against unfair dismissal applies could be raised again – it was lowered in 1999 – from 5 to 10 full-time employees per establishment). One has to ask, however, whether the politically fragmented German federation would have the institutional capacity to move along the Scandinavian way, how such a move would have to be combined with the maintenance of competitiveness (in a big country this might be more difficult than in a small one) and whether the German population would be willing to pay for raising public employment. If the support for maintaining a given level of unemployment benefits (George 1998; Mau 2001) and for higher taxes (*The Economist*, March 26, 2000) is an indication, then one has to be rather sceptical.

High German taxes, to conclude this section, are already a prominent subject for interest group complaints and academic criticism. Running a generous welfare system with relatively high benefits for a large number of recipients, a large group of early retirees as well as the growing number of pensioners in an ageing society is an expensive affair. So, German taxes are high. They are not exceptionally high, however. Average 'household taxes', i.e. income taxes plus employee contributions, for a family with one earner and two children, are nearly 20 percent in Germany, but this level is not significantly different from those in New Zealand and Norway and lower than in Sweden and Denmark (where it is 30 percent; *The Economist*, March 1, 2003, p.98). These taxes and contributions plus payments for the 'holyday gratification' as well as high employer contributions result in very high so-called non-wage labour costs that according to *The Economist* (July 14, 2001:31) are 'the biggest single obstacle to job creation' (see also Scharpf 1997, pp.7f). Perhaps this is true, and perhaps the German social system should be paid for in a different way. Bringing down employers' contributions and raising indirect taxes would be a possibility. This is the Scandinavian route where total taxes on labour, because of the included indirect consumption taxes, are considerably higher than anywhere else (50 percent for the standard family in Germany, but 60, 61, 62 and 77 percent in Norway, Denmark, Finland and Sweden, respectively; Nickell 2002, p.48, Table 16). The high indirect taxes in Scandinavia include taxes on services and are a basis therefore for a flourishing black economy. Mediterranean countries are the champions in this respect, but the Scandinavian countries are second. In 1998, the estimated size of the black economy was 29 percent of GDP in Greece, 27.8 in Italy, and 23.4 in Spain, but also 20 percent in Sweden and 18.4 percent in Denmark. In Germany it was 14.7 percent, in the Netherlands 13.5 percent, in Britain 13 percent and in the USA 8.9 percent (Schneider 2000, p.18). Everything appears to have its price tag.

Discussing German taxation, one should not forget that the high level of taxes and social contributions can partly be explained by the special burden of financing economic development and social security in the relatively backward East Germany that unification in 1989 brought to West Germany. To finance social security expenditures in East Germany, for example, payroll taxes rose from 36 percent of gross wages in 1989 to 42.1 percent in 1998 (Siegel 2004, p. 117).

Accidental circumstances: housing bubble versus unification

Unification-related costs could be circumscribed as, in economic terms, 'bad luck' for Germany that contrasts to the favourable circumstances that emerged in the 1990s in Denmark, the Netherlands and the USA. Before analysing unification costs and the post-unification German political economy, I want to point briefly, therefore, to these favourable conditions in the 'model countries' where employment continued to increase and registered unemployment further declined after 1993, when Germany went into a period of crisis and slow growth. In absolute terms, employment growth was most spectacular in the USA, while the employment rate, because of an increasing working age population, rose at a lower pace (Appelbaum 2000, p.8f). The employment increase Denmark is noticed for occurred just after 1993 when, as part of a more general crisis of the Scandinavian economies, unemployment soared at more than 10 percent (OECD 1997b). While Finland and Sweden continued their crisis for several more years, Denmark recovered quickly. The Dutch 'miracle' of an explosively rising number of part-time jobs, particularly for women and juveniles, started from an extremely low employment rate in the early 1980s that continuously, except for a slight dip in 1993/94, increased until 2001.

Elsewhere in this volume, the 'model economies' have extensively been dealt with. I only want to highlight a specific, lucky aspect of these economies' recent development that partly explains their positive employment performances: the stock market and, much more important, the house price bubble. Stocks did rise strongly everywhere in the West, but house prices surged not only in Denmark, the Netherlands (by 40 and 119 percent, respectively, between 1995 and 2002; in the Netherlands, the climb started already in the early 1990s) and, somewhat later and less, the USA (by 48 percent), but also in Australia (by 64 percent), Ireland (even by 203 percent) and Spain (by 77 percent) as well as, at the end of the decade, in Britain (by 106 percent) and Sweden (by 60 percent; *The Economist*, March 8, 2003 and March 30, 2002, pp.65ff; for an extensive account see OECD 2004). All of these countries feature a positive employment record, and one should add that house price development, although relatively autonomous, is not completely unrelated to the business cycle. The special thing in Denmark, the Netherlands and the USA, however, has been the wealth effect strengthened by very generous possibilities of tax relief on mortgage interest payments (Haffner 1998, p.171). This constellation has to be characterised as accidental because it was not the result of any policy consciously undertaken to foster employment growth in the years up to the turn of the century. And it has to be described as lucky – at least in the short term – because it stimulated consumer demand and economic activity as well as, as a result, employment growth. In the longer run it might turn out to be a negative development because it was built on increasing private debt.

In the USA, in a context of declining interest rates and tax relief for the full 100 percent of interest payments on mortgages, the wealth effect took the form of a rising number of refinanced mortgages and of loans on the increased value of real estate as well as on the risen value of stocks. Total household debt jumped from 85 percent of personal income in 1992 to 124 percent in 2000, while private net savings went down in the same period from 5.4 percent to –7 percent (Goodley and Izurieta 2001; *The Economist*, July 14, 2001: 76). This 'unprecedented borrowing binge' (*Wall Street Journal Europe*, July 5, 2000) triggered demand to continuously surpass GDP growth (*Financial Times*, April 5, 2000). In 2001 the so-called mortgage equity withdrawal operation created extra space for consumption to the amount of $35 billion (Roach 2002, p.2) and for 2002 it was estimated at $130 billion (*NRC Handelsblad* December 31, 2002: 18; see also *Business Week*, October 28, 2002).

In the Netherlands, the stock and particularly house price bubble was also combined with a 100 percent tax relief for the interest on mortgages (including mortgages on the 'overvalue' of houses), a combination that strongly stimulated demand. Consumptive use of mortgages made private consumption rise in those years above GDP growth, and according to estimates of the Dutch central bank, mortgage money was good for about 0.5 percent extra annual GDP growth in the second half of the 1990s; in 1999 and in 2000 it was even 1 percent (DNB 2001, p.131 and DNB 2002, p.36). Additional growth impulses came from other forms of borrowing that generally increased while saving declined in the second half of the last decade (*NRC Handelsblad*, 19 July 2000). As a result, private debt as a percentage of disposable household income rose from 95 percent in 1990 to 188 percent in 2000 (DNB 2002, p.30) – a percentage much higher than the comparable figures in Britain (120 percent) and the US (110 percent). However, in 2001 and 2002 people started to prefer saving above spending.

In Denmark, strongly rising house prices were facilitated by the possibility of a tax relief on 46.4 percent (reduced to 32 percent in 2000) of mortgage interest payments (Madsen 1999, pp.5, 35). The OECD estimates that one-third of the increase of Danish private consumption between 1994 and 1998 can be explained by this constellation (*Financieel Dagblad*, July 4, 2000). A second accidental factor was the discovery of oil and gas fields in the Danish part of the North Sea, the production of which has increased significantly in recent years and in 1997 has added about 1 percentage point to GDP growth (Andersen 1997, p.46).

Germany did not experience a house price bubble after 1995. On the contrary, from 1990 to 1999 these prices decreased by no less than 22 percent (Neuteboom 2002, p.17; cf. OECD 2002j, p.31 and IMF 2003, chart 12b). Furthermore, Germany (with an ownership rate of 43 percent in 2000; in Denmark this was 51 percent, in the Netherlands 53 percent and in Britain

68 percent) does not provide tax relief on mortgage interest. Germany had a brief house price bubble in 1990 and 1991, immediately after unification (*The Economist*, March 30, 2002, p.66). This bubble did not burst, but it sharply declined after 1992 and flattened off thereafter and left the Germans with a mortgage debt still amounting to 54 percent of GDP in 2000 (Neuteboom 2002, p.17). In Europe, this is the highest rate behind the Netherlands (71 percent), Denmark (61 percent) and Britain (60 percent). After house prices had started to decrease, this debt rate was probably one of the factors explaining the weakness of German consumer spending in the 1990s and also one of the forces that brought down construction (an aspect we have to return to below).

House prices and the lack of a bubble have not been at the heart of the discussion about the German employment misery. The same is true for the costs of German unification. This is very amazing because the financial burden unification placed on the West German economy is considerable. There is much commotion every year in the net payer countries of the EU about their contributions to the budget of the European Commission. In 2000 these net payers spent between 0.25 percent (UK) and 0.5 percent GDP (Sweden) to Brussels with Germany – 0.47 percent and in absolute terms the biggest spender by far – being one of them (*Das Parlament*, June 7, 2002, p.10). This is only a tenth or less, however, of the 4.5 percent GDP – in net terms – that West Germany is annually transferring to East Germany (Priewe 2002, p.709; Bibow 2001). It is not realistic to expect that such a transfer of resources did not have and will not continue to have a huge impact on German economic performances. The reason that this subject has largely been taboo in the public debate seems to be that addressing it was politically unwise because it could have been interpreted as placing the blame with the East Germans – the so-called Ossi's who are culturally still divided from the Wessi's and who still feel inferior.

From its very beginning in 1989/1990, the new Germany was statistically less rich than the preceding Federal Republic because the new eastern part, the richest part of the country before WWII (Sinn and Westermann 2000, p.4), was poor and unproductive by Western standards. The intention of the incumbent government parties put forward in the election campaign of 1990 was to change this situation quickly. The Easterners were promised 'flourishing landscapes' in only a few years, and 'unification was promoted as a "win-win situation" without any costs for the West Germans and huge gains for the East Germans' (Schettkat 2002, p.21). As one of the first steps, the East German mark was converted at an exchange rate of 1 to 1 into the West German mark (the real relation was 1 West mark = 4.3 East mark).

From one day to the next, large parts of the East German economy became uncompetitive by this act and quickly lost their markets in eastern Europe. At the time and later on, this measure was characterised as unrealistic and wrong – the president of the German National Bank (*Bundesbank*) even resigned because of it.

A similar criticism was formulated with respect to the subsequent agreement (in 1991) to equalise contract wages as soon as possible. With the 1:1 conversion, eastern wages had already jumped from less than 10 percent to about 30 percent of western wages, but the 1991 agreement brought an additional and fast increase of eastern wages to 62 percent in 1992 and 75 percent in 1995 (AFW 2002, p.732; Sinn and Westermann 2000, pp.15f; after 1995 the pace of wage equalisation slowed down – see Table 9.3). In part, this course of events might be explained by the (West) German unions' fear of low-wage competition from the east. But wages also came under pressure from the German welfare system into which East Germany became integrated, with slight specifications, which required that wages to be raised (considerably) above the level of social assistance benefits (Sinn 2000, pp.18f). Economically, there can be no doubt that the criticism of an unrealistic and wrong policy is true. But politically one has to ask whether a policy of economic division would have been viable. Would an even bigger migration from east to west than actually happened (Priewe 2002, p.712) have been desirable? Germany was clearly confronted with a dilemma.

The consequence of making an economy consciously uncompetitive was a dramatic decline of employment and an explosive rise of social costs. Many plants had to close, other ones dramatically enhanced their labour productivity by replacing workers with modern equipment. From unification until 1992, East German employment decreased by a third from 10 to 6.5 million (Lindlar and Scheremet 1999, p.5); in manufacturing alone, it shrank from 3.4 to 0.6 million (Priewe 2002, p.708). This meant that East Germany became largely de-industrialised. 'Official' unemployment quickly increased to about 17 percent (where it has remained since the early 1990s), while broad unemployment – registered unemployment plus that hidden in early retirement, disability schemes and a reduced female labour market participation rate – rose to twice this level. Paying benefits for this large group of unemployed people, in the broad sense, required a massive income transfer from the west to the east that started immediately after unification. Social transfers were also necessary to pay the high regular pensions of East Germans, which the one-to-one conversion of the two German currencies had brought about. The East German economic basis was much too weak to finance these costs. Together, social payments added up to 70 percent of the

Table 9.3 East Germany in comparison to West Germany (WG = 100 when indexed)

	1991	1992	1993	1994	1995	1996	1997	1998	1999	2000	2001
GDP/Capita	33.4	41.2	50.8	57.2	59.6	61.7	62.2	61.5	62.0	61.1	61.7
Construction in-vestment/capita	70.2	103.1	131	164.1	175.8	180.8	172.2	153.3	137	120.6	110
Wages	49.3	61.9	69.2	72.6	75.2	75.8	76.1	76.3	77.3	77.5	77.6
Productivity	34.9	48.3	59.4	64.2	65.0	67.0	68.0	67.7	68.3	68.9	70.6

| Registered unemployment in percent | | | | West Germany | | | | 8.8 | 8.3 | 7.3 | 7.3 |
| | | | | East Germany | | | | 16.8 | 16.3 | 16.5 | 16.9 |

Source: AWF 2002: 732-733

total transfer (or 3 percent of the West German GDP) from west to east (Sinn and Westermann 2000, pp.7-11).

The remaining 30 percent of the west to east transfer went into the service of old German Democratic Republic debt, subsidies for private investment and particularly into the restoration of cities and the building of a modern infrastructure. Until 1996 the latter resulted in a hypertrophy of the construction sector, where investment increased from 70 percent of the western level (indexed) in 1991 to 180 percent in 1996 (AWF 2002, p.732; cf. OECD 2002j, p.17). This development explains the so-called unification boom, together with a strong increase of industrial investment as well as savings-based consumer spending, and it also largely explains the continuation of East German economic growth after the initial boom had ended and West Germany had gone into recession in 1993. East German GDP growth was still 12 percent in that year and 11 percent in 1994 (Priewe 2002, p.707). Thereafter, growth rates decreased by big steps, and since 1997, when construction also started its way down, they are lower than in West Germany (see Table 9.3).

West Germany has financed the transfers to the east by two measures: extra payroll taxes and public borrowing. Payroll taxes, as already indicated at the end of the preceding section, rose by one-sixth in the decade after unification, while public debt more than doubled in the same period (Sinn 2000, p.22). Rising public debt made the *Bundesbank* decide to tighten interest rates as early as February 1991. The jump of the discount rate from 6.5 percent to 8.75 percent in July 1992 (Siegel 2004, p.116) not only made unification even more expensive, it also resulted in a crisis of the European Monetary System (EMS) that was abandoned – temporarily – by several of its members (Manow and Seils 2000, p.288) and was a main cause of the West European recession in 1993. And at least in Germany, the 'hard line' of the *Bundesbank* – Bibow (2001, p.24) talks about a 'consolidation crusade' – was an additional factor tempering economic growth for a longer period. After the unification boom had ended in 1991 and with the exception of the year 2000, annual West German GDP growth has never again exceeded 2 percent.

In the second half of the 1990s, the burden of financing unification and the restrictive monetary policy of the *Bundesbank* were joined by a sharp decline in construction (and house prices), particularly in the east but also in the west (Priewe 2002, pp.708ff; AWF 2002, pp.727f), and by low economic growth in the eastern part of the country. Now economic growth for the whole of Germany never exceeded 2 percent (except in the exceptional year of 2000). A lot had changed in East Germany, inner cities became renovated, 800,000 new houses were built (*The Economist* 2002, p.14), and the standard of living of the population approached the western level. But the construction of a competitive economy turned out to be a failure.

Suppose the world does not wait for more of the typical German goods such as cars and industrial equipment, what has East Germany to offer and for what price? Until now, these fundamental questions have not been answered. Manufacturing has radically been modernised, but this sector is small in terms of employment (Sinn and Westermann 2000, p.22) and only good for 15 percent of East German GDP (Priewe 2002, p.708). And an internationally operating sector of business services is not recognisable. That is not enough for developing the export volume required to pay for the necessary imports, and therefore East Germany, just as the Italian Mezzogiorno, will remain a 'transfer-dependent economy' (ibid, p.702). Investment has stagnated since 1992/93 (Lindlar and Scheremet 1999, p.1) and where in the west there are 48 ICT specialists per 1000 inhabitants, in the east it is only 21, and in patents the relation (per 100,000 inhabitants) is 74 to 20 (Priewe 2002, p.710). So, this part of the country is anything but 'flourishing'. Meanwhile, its western part has moved into high debt and high payroll taxes as well as low domestic demand and low GDP growth. Not a favourable climate for raising employment.

On strong German regions

Not everything about employment in Germany is negative. Some states of the Federal Republic perform relatively well. The dominant comparative

Table 9.4 Bavaria in international comparison in 1999

	Population (millions)	Employment rate[1]	Standardized unemployment	GDP growth 1995-1999	Per capita income[2]
Bavaria	12.2	48.5	5.3	8.2	122
Germany	82.2	44.6	8.7	5.9	106
Austria	8.2	46.4	3.7	8.6	108
Belgium	10.2	39.0	9.0	10.0	113
Denmark	5.3	51.1	5.2	10.2	118
France	58.9	39.6	11.3	9.3	105
Ireland	3.7	42.2	5.7	40.7	116
Italy	57.3	36.2	11.3	6.0	100
Netherlands	15.7	46.4	3.3	14.8	113
Sweden	8.9	45.7	7.2	10.1	103
UK	58.7	46.5	6.2	11.5	97
USA	276.2	48.3	4.2	23.3	151

[1] In percentage of the total population. [2] In PPP; EU 15 = 100
Source: BSWVT 2000a: 5

political economy tends to overlook these states because it only compares countries, and treats all of them as equals, independent of their population size. This approach is problematical because big countries may include regions as large and performing as well as small countries. With the exception of the USA (and to a certain degree Great Britain), it is precisely such small countries numbering between just over 3 million (Ireland) to about 20 million (Australia) inhabitants that were noticed for their performances in recent years. Besides Denmark, Australia, Ireland, the Netherlands and Switzerland, one could also mention Austria, Norway and add Sweden and Finland, which in recent years were on their way to recovery from their crisis of the early 1990s. Put together, these countries are less inhabited than Germany.

The German southwest comprises, however, the states of Hesse, Baden-Württemberg and Bavaria whose level of socio-economic development (including employment) is equal to or even higher than that of the small model countries. This region in the southwest hosts the financial center of Germany (banks in Frankfurt, Hesse; insurance companies in Munich), luxury car companies (Daimler, Porsche in Baden-Württemberg, Audi, BMW in Bavaria) and a large part of Germany's high-tech industry (Bosch, SAP, Siemens, aviation industry, foreign subsidiaries such as IBM and Cisco plus many of the small and medium-sized companies in machinery and tool production). Although these rich southern states have to bear the largest bur-

Table 9.5 Regional German Differences in Selective Comparison in 1996/1997

Region/ Country	Inhabitants (thousands)	GDP per head (in pP Euro)	Unemployment	Employment rate
Hesse	6019	147.9	7.4	64.8
Denmark	5763	119.3	5.7	76.1
Darmstadt	3690	171.3	6.7	65.5
Upper Bavaria	3985	156.5	4.8	71.4
Ireland	3626	96.5	10.1	57.7
Bavaria	12,019	124.2	5.9	69.6
Bavaria + Darmstadt	15,709	130.0	6.1	68.6
Netherlands	15,531	106.8	5.2	68.0
Hamburg	1708	192.5	7.5	63.9
Thuringia	2497	61.2	17.6	63.0

Source: European Commission 1999

den of unification by the intra-federal redistribution, the 'Länderfinanzausgleich', they are very suitable for a comparison to the small countries most mentioned as models: Denmark and the Netherlands.

German states have their own education and economic policies, but for the rest they operate in the same institutional and legal framework as the other German states. And neither unions nor employers' associations see these states as primary fields of action. As a rule, their more or less flexible agreements, even if initially negotiated at sub-state level, are valid for the federation as a whole. So, wage differentiation all over West Germany narrowed rather than widened (OECD 1996b, p.61), and the unions have been particularly successful in raising the lowest wage scales, to the dismay of the employers (BDI 1998, p.75). And looking at differences between the states, it is surprising that the well-performing southern states do not belong to the top either in facilitating technological innovation or in active labour market policy (Schmid and Blancke 2001, p.220).

Nonetheless, in Hesse (slightly more inhabited than Denmark) and Bavaria (not much smaller than the Netherlands), economic and employment growth has been considerably higher than in the rest of Western Germany in the entire period of the two decades up to 2002 as well as since unification (Baden-Württemberg performed at the average level of West Germany). Bavaria, the state providing the most comprehensive set of data, has done much better than West Germany. Bavarian economic and employment development roughly reveals the West German pattern of subsequently strong growth, recession and modest growth in the 1980s and 1990s. But Bavarian increases were about 30 percent higher in the former decade, while the slow-down in the latter was about 40 percent less harsh (BSWVT 2000a, pp.5f). In international comparison, Bavarian growth since 1983 was higher than that of Denmark and roughly identical to that of the USA and the Netherlands. From a Dutch perspective one could add that this happened in spite of a wage growth twice as high as inflation (BSWVT 2000a, p.40; excluding the wages of civil servants).

The Bavarian employment rate – as percentage of the population as a whole and including all persons in 'minor employment', in so-called '630 mark jobs' (in 1999, DM 630 was the threshold above which social security contributions are due; currently this amount is 325 Euro) – in 1999 was 9 percent (3.9 percentage points) higher than in the entire German federation, as high as in the USA and higher than in any other EU member state with the exception of Denmark. Standardized unemployment was only lower in the Netherlands, Portugal and tiny Luxemburg (see Table 9.4). GDP growth from 1995 to 1999 (as well as in 1993 and 1994) was at the lower edge, however. This reflects the problems related to unification already mentioned – and that neither Bavaria nor any other part of Germany has experienced a mortgage bubble.

Some parts of Bavaria and Hesse – parts as large as Ireland – performed even better. Table 9.5 therefore includes the sub-state level. This table has a different source and presents slightly divergent figures, but it clearly shows that the 'Regierungsbezirke' (an administrative level between counties and states) of Darmstadt and Upper Bavaria can easily compete with Denmark and Ireland and that the combination of Bavaria and bordering Darmstadt (taking into account their relative weights) provides an interesting comparison to the Netherlands. Including the city-state of Hamburg – the richest place in Europe – as well as East German Thuringia, the table also demonstrates the wide gap between rich and poor in Germany. The general message is that comparative political economy investigating small countries should not ignore such regional differences within the larger ones.

Another point is that the Bavarian development (a similar story could be told about Hesse) indicates that it heavily depended on exceptional economic growth (127.1 percent from 1970 to 1998 compared with 87.3 percent in West Germany as a whole, BSWVT 2000b, p.5) that only slowed down in the 1990s. It is not realistic to assume that exceptional GDP growth can continue forever, not even in a context unhampered by events such as German unification. Exceptional growth is confined to shorter periods or, as in the case

of Bavaria some 35 years ago and Ireland until very recently, to circumstances of relative backwardness. Then it can last longer, but in mature
economies this seems to be just as impossible as a Dutch-like job increase after a high employment rate has already been realized. And at times of slow
economic growth, Bavaria in the 1990s confirms that the GDP growth route
to higher employment no longer works. The employment rate declines. So
Bavaria, just like the Netherlands, has done particularly well, but it is not a
model, not even for the other German states. Competition is not a game
where all participants can be winners.

A certain competitive edge is one of the factors explaining why it is just the
German south that performs better than the rest of the country. But where
does it come from? Policy seems not to be decisive because everything that is
successful in a state is copied by the other states. Is it the political colour of
the state government? For decades, Bavaria and Baden-Württemberg have
been governed by the Christian Democrats, but this is not true for Hesse
where the left is stronger (though since 1998 the state has a conservative
government). Some accidental factors seem to be more important. The
south does not have a heritage of heavy industry, its western part belongs to
the old European city belt, after WWII some big companies such as Siemens
moved from Berlin to Munich, but not to Cologne or the Ruhr area, and currently southern Germany is located within the very large and economically
active zone around the Alps that also comprises Austria, northern Italy,
parts of eastern France, Switzerland and the only rich state of formerly communist Europe: Slovenia. An exhaustive explanation of the south German
economic success is not the intention of this contribution, however.

Prospects and possible lessons from the 'model cases'

To summarise, in terms of export performance, Germany has not lost its international competitiveness, but economic growth has remained below
trend since the early 1990s, and employment has stagnated while unemployment has risen since then. This appears to be not so much due to a rigid
labour market and a generous welfare system, but rather to the high costs of
unification. High employment protection and high benefits (by US standards) related to, in the broad sense, unemployment do also exist in well-
performing countries like Austria, Norway, Sweden and the Netherlands.
The burden of unification makes Germany very special, however. It is as if
the USA were to integrate Mexico and have to raise the latter's incomes to US
levels within a few years, Robert Samuelson wrote in *The Washington Post*

(November 12, 2002). The continuous transfer of economic resources from West to East Germany has seriously indebted the country and undermined domestic demand and public investment; a process that has been enhanced by the restrictive monetary policy of the *Bundesbank* and subsequently the ECB. And where rising house prices, the related wealth effect and possibilities of tax relief on mortgage interest payments gave an extra push to economic and employment growth in the 'model economies', German house prices declined and had rather a negative effect on private spending.

So, Germany has had bad luck with its unification, but for the rest everything is fine? This would be a wrong judgement. To begin with, German employment is structurally low because high employment protection and the relatively generous welfare system are not complemented by the large-scale, Scandinavian-like creation of public or publicly financed employment. Another weakness appears to be education: students are studying much longer than their counterparts elsewhere (*The Economist*, May 10, 2003: 28; in fact, this is a form of hidden unemployment), and in 2002 and 2003 there was much ado about the relatively poor performance of German pupils in the comparative tests of the PISA study (although comparative knowledge and qualification tests among adults are still very positive for Germany; cf. Estevez-Abe et al. 2001). Furthermore, huge demographic problems plus related financial problems of the welfare system will rise in the near future because of the low birth rate of only 1.34 children per woman (in 2000; *NRC Handelsblad,* May 16, 2003; EU average: 1.53; Denmark: 1.76; France: 1.89; Netherlands: 1.72; UK: 1.64; US: 2.06), and there are many inflexibilities – e.g. in the ancient systems of civil servants – that could even be removed in a political economy trying to prevent a further commodification of labour.

It is in this field, just as with respect to eligibility criteria in social security, that Germany could learn from Denmark. From Scandinavia in general it could learn about the connection of high welfare and high employment to a large number of publicly financed jobs. This connection becomes necessary when a country wants to raise employment, but rejects the liberal way of breaking down employment protection and lowering the lowest wages. The required popular support and willingness to pay for the Scandinavian or social democratic route does not seem to exist, however. In surveys, people show their support for keeping a high level of social security, but this support declines when they are asked about the price they are willing to pay for it (Mau 2001), and their willingness to pay higher taxes is limited (*The Economist*, March 26, 2000). It is not for nothing that tax cut proposals do well in election campaigns. Also, if we are not looking at social security in general – the most costly components are pensions and health care in which everybody is interested – but unemployment benefits, then there is no majority willing to pay the price for maintaining its given level, and the more qualified respondents are and the higher their incomes, the lower their support. So, why should one expect them to be willing to pay for publicly financed employment?

Are there any other lessons to be drawn from the 'model economies'? There are probably a number of smaller elements that could help raise German employment such as the Danish leave schemes (but again: who would like to pay for it?), and some jobs could be created by bringing down wages in certain business sectors and raising incomes by, as is done in the USA, allowing tax credits for low-wage earners. If such a measure would be more than marginal, it would involve the same cost problems (cf. Koch et al. 2002) as just discussed with respect to the Scandinavian way. Does the Netherlands provide a solution for Germany's problems? Redistribution of work towards part-time jobs is a serious option at times where productivity increases faster than demand. Germany has, however, already gone the Dutch way of sharply extending the number of part-time jobs. The big difference is juveniles. For the 'teenagers' age group, the Dutch employment rate (about 70 percent in 2003; in 1983 it was 16.5 percent; cf. Table 1.1) is twice as high as that in Germany. Most of these jobs are part-time, often even tiny ones, and held by pupils and students who mostly earn minimum youth wages starting (in 2003) of 2.20 euro per hour for 15-year-olds and progressively climbing by about 40 to 80 eurocents each year of age (until age 23). Perhaps this is fine for teenagers looking for some extra income, but it is not a solution for the problem of low employment, neither in Germany nor in the Netherlands with its huge groups of unemployed hidden in early retirement and, particularly, the disability schemes.

The number of lessons that could effectively shift the German situation in a positive direction turns out to be limited. Meanwhile, governmental initiative and political debate in Germany concentrate on somewhat liberalising the systems of social security and employment protection. In 2002, a number of proposals was made by the 'Hartz commission' (named after a manager of Volkswagen chairing it), in 2003 the Red-Green government launched its 'Agenda 2010' and in 2004 a number of measures (a change of financing health care; a change in the system of unemployment benefits) was enacted. One should not expect too much from these initiatives. They tend to reduce unemployment to a consequence of individual misbehaviour and do not seriously touch the basic problem of the German political economy. This basic problem is the structural weakness of the eastern part of the country that will continue to depend on its western part. In the foreseeable future, the costs involved will weaken and partially even paralyse the latter in a similar way as in the previous decade. The Europeanisation of the required transfers would be desirable but seems not to be a realistic option, and therefore the prospects for German economic development and employment are not particularly rosy.

This also means that Germany will not be able to act as the engine of the European economy. It will only follow the general trend that is determined by the international business cycle and particularly by the US economy, which tends to rather low growth rates in the years to come. Too much debt, as indicated in the introduction to this volume, has been accumulated in the previous decade, and it will take some time before the imbalances of the past will be removed. Perhaps the eastern enlargement of the EU will have some positive effects on East Germany and so on Germany as a whole and Europe, but one has to wait and see whether this will really happen. And perhaps Robert Boyer (2000, p.60) is right that Germany (just like Japan) will profit from the need in future years to 'update' production processes to the technological (ICT) standards developed in the 1990s because of its industrial specialisation. Perhaps.

Notes

1 Although in these Mediterranean countries, particularly Italy, a larger part of employment than elsewhere is hidden in the black economy (Schneider 2000).
2 For the same reason, the table is misleading in the case of Great Britain where poverty among the unemployed is extremely high (45.5 percent in 1988 compared with 2.7 percent in Denmark; Eurostat 1996: 213).
3 The following statements are posed to the respondents:
  A Young children will suffer when mother is working.
  B Employment is good, but most women truly prefer home and children.
  C To be a housewife is as satisfactory as being in employment.
  D The task of men is to earn money and that of women is to care for home and children.
  E It is not good when a man cares for home and children while his wife has a job.
4 It comes perhaps as a surprise that labour market 'rigidity', though it is the target of continuous complaints by business associations, did not trigger any significant capital drain, and in net terms nearly no jobs have been exported (Heise et al. 2000: 339f).

10 Conclusion: the Importance of Lucky Circumstances, and Still the Liberal-Social Democratic Divide

Uwe Becker and Herman Schwartz

What are the main results of the previous chapters? Did the small countries discussed in this volume develop new ways of generating employment and particularly of dealing with the issue of work and welfare that is often supposed to be a dilemma? Are they 'models' other countries can learn from, did they establish a specific form of competitiveness? How important has been deliberate policy? What about luck? These questions have guided the contributions to this volume, and they will be addressed again in this final chapter. Furthermore, we briefly consider the latest developments and the prospects of the political economies of 'our' small countries. The chapter will end with some considerations on the fundamental politico-economic alternatives that currently exist.

In sum

In Table 10.1 the main results of the contributions to this volume are summarised by using very rough indicators. A plus means that a country scores higher than average, a minus means that the score is lower than average (the qualification 'all' indicates a score above the historical average). To keep it simple, we have refrained from using two or three plusses and minuses to indicate the stronger and strongest positive or negative score. One has to be aware, of course, of the, sometimes significant, differences between plus or minus cases. In Denmark and Switzerland, it is rather the maintenance of a high employment level than employment growth; in Ireland, GDP growth has been much higher than in the other countries; the same is true for house prices; in the USA the house price bubble occurred later than and not as intensively as in the European bubble countries and Australia; Dutch and US tax relief on mortgage interest is considerably more generous than the Danish and Australian one; and the number of part-time jobs, particularly tiny ones, has increased more in the Netherlands than in Australia and Ireland. For the purpose of a concluding comparison, the chosen indicators are sufficiently precise, however. For a detailed exposure of the differences between the countries, one has to turn to the statistical material presented in the Introduction and subsequent chapters.

The most striking result is that lucky circumstances have been at least as important as conscious policy efforts (pluck) for the explanation of the miracles. Looking at the countries separately, one can say that

- In Australia, the 'miracle' is somewhat less miraculous when related to the strong population growth and appears mainly to be caused by the lucky circumstances of the house price bubble and an expanding Asian market where it could sell its minerals, basic manufactures and agricultural goods (cf. Table 1.5; in technologically advanced goods, Australia is weak).
- In Denmark, the success has been due to a combination of a house price bubble, the maintenance of the country's quality image, the discovery of North Sea oil and welfare reforms (leave schemes, tightening of eligibility criteria).
- Ireland performed as it did because it was chosen as the European hub of the American ICT industry, but also because it facilitated and enhanced this choice by fiscal and labour market policies. Furthermore, it has been a house price bubble country and enjoyed considerable aid from the EU.
- In the Netherlands, the 'pluck factor' is particularly low. There the explanation comes from the house price and mortgage bubbles, and from wage differentiation resulting from freezing the minimum wage for many years to stop the rise of related social security costs, lowering the youth minimum wages as well as from redistributing work towards cheap female and juvenile part-time work.
- In Sweden and Finland, innovation (see the next section of this chapter) and active labour market policies have been more relevant than elsewhere, while luck does not seem to deserve special attention (at the end of the 1990s Swedish house prices also started to surge and they are still strongly rising – in the 3rd quarter of 2004 by 9,8 percent; *The Economist*, December 11, 2004, p.67 – while Finish house prices increased at a considerably lower pace; Stephens 2003).
- Switzerland, finally, has not performed well, but it kept its high employment rate because of its historically grown specialisation and because of its very positive image. Again, this is rather luck than pluck.
- Of the countries discussed in this volume as a contrast, the USA is a case in which pluck and luck enforced each other, while Germany is not only the country with the bad luck, in economic terms, of the unification costs

and, slightly, deteriorating house prices, but also of unsuccessful policies in the post-unification period.

Summarising this, it is striking to observe how strong the house bubble-induced wealth effect corresponds to positive economic and employment development during the 1990s and the early 2000s. All 'miracles', except Finland and the special case of Switzerland, have been house price bubble countries, and the same is true for the USA and the UK. Conversely, countries with slow GDP growth – such as Switzerland, Italy and Germany – did not participate in this bubble. Wage restraint, by contrast, that was so central in the discussion on 'new social pacts', did not make the difference, because good as well as poor performers tried it. And some good performers – Ireland, Sweden, the USA and the UK – do not even belong to the countries where wage restraint is worth mentioning (the stagnation of Swedish wages in the first half of the 1990s only reflects the country's economic crisis in those years).

Finally, welfare reform (i.e. cuts) and labour market flexibilisation, always put forward by liberals as necessary requirements of raising competitiveness, do not appear to have a causal relation to the Dutch, Finnish and Swedish successes. Despite cuts, these countries' welfare systems still belong to the most generous in the world (the same is true for the Danish one, though it underwent more serious changes), and labour market flexibilisation worth mentioning only took place in the Netherlands in 1999 with respect to part-time and contract work.

Recent developments and prospects

The information contained in the contributions and statistics presented in this volume ends with the years 2000 to 2002, depending on the topic. For as complete a picture as possible, we will add some data on the developments since then. We also want to say a few words about the socio-economic prospects of our 'model countries'.

In late 2000, the Western economy entered a slowdown, and in late 2004 stable, employment-generating recovery had not yet taken place. US GDP growth was up again, though the statistics are controversial (cf. *The Economist*, April 10, 2004: 68), and China has become a second engine of the world economy. A serious question is whether the Western economy will repeat what happened to Japan, which fell into a decade of stagnation after its stock and house price bubble burst at the end of the 1980s. As a result of the

Table 10.1 Summary of socio-economic performances and factors explaining GDP and employment growth 1990-2001/2002 plus schematisation in terms of 'pluck, stuck and luck'

	Aus	CH	DK	FI*	IRL	NL	S*	US	UK	FR	Ger	IT
Performances												
GDP growth	+	-		+	+	+	+	+	+			-
Employment growth/ maintenance high employment	+	+	+	+	+	+	+	+		-	-	-
Productivity growth	-		+	+	-	+					+	-
Growth of export share (domestically produced)			+	+	+	-						
Kept poverty and inequality relatively low	+	+	+		+	+				+	+	
Explaining factors												
Foreign investment					+							
Stock market bubble	All											
House price bubble	+	-	+		+	+		+	+		-	
Generous tax relief on mortgage interest	+		+			+		+				
Reform welfare system and flexibilisation			+									
Lowering taxes					+							
Increase of part-time jobs	+	-			+	+	-	-				+
Wage differentiation	+				+	+		+	+			
Wage restraint	+	+	+	+	-	+	-	-	-	+	+	+
Innovation			+		+		+	+				-
Positive (quality, design) image of goods		+	+								+	s
In terms of Pluck, stuck and luck												
Pluck			+	+	+		+				-	
Stuck				Taken for granted								
Luck	+	+	+		+	+		+	+		-	

*Finland and Sweden are special cases because of their severe downturn in the first half of the 1990s and their strong recovery in the second half. The valuations presented here refer primarily to this second period.
+ = above average
- = below average
Sources: As mentioned in the preceding chapters.

sharp decline of share prices in the USA and Western Europe (particularly of tech stocks), tech investment and consumer spending, mediated by the disappearing wealth effect, have also declined in many European countries. US consumers have kept their spending comparatively upright because many house owners have refinanced their mortgages at lower interest rates in a context of still rising house prices (a similar story could be told about Britain; cf. *The Economist*, June 5, 2004: 64f). This so-called mortgage equity withdrawal operation has created extra space for consumption to the amount of $35 billion in 2001 (Roach 2002, p.2) and of about $130 billion in 2002 (*NRC Handelsblad*, December 31, 2002: 18; cf. *Business Week*, October 28, 2002). Fuelled by the FED lowering interest rates, the refinancing of mortgages continued to boom in 2003, and household debt rose to new record heights (*The Economist*, June 14, 2003: 45f and July 19, 2003: 61; Xie 2004). The same is true with respect to consumer borrowing other than mortgages (*New York Times*, September 9, 2003). At some point, however, real estate prices in the USA, just as in Australia, Britain and a number of other countries, will have to stop their upward move. Houses become no longer affordable for newcomers when their price increase exceeds GDP growth for a longer period (*The Economist*, January 3, 2004: 51ff). At the same time, consumer debt will have to be reduced, and the huge US trade deficit cannot grow forever. And China, which has been extremely important for the world economy in the early 2000s, cannot infinitely continue its overheated growth rates (*The Economist*, April 17, 2004: 71). Together, these aspects are not favourable conditions for stable economic expansion.

In the small 'model countries', recent development has diverged. In Australia, the economic boom and the house price bubble have continued into 2004; Ireland has experienced a year of low GDP growth in 2003 (2,2 percent) but recovered in 2004 to 3,3 percent – though not to the spectacular level of the 1995-2002 period (9 percent on average); Sweden has (just like Britain) shown a stable GDP increase of about 1.5 to 2,5 percent from 2001 to 2003 and then jumped to a rate of more than 3 percent in 2004; the range of Finnish GDP growth in those years has been 2 to 2,5 percent; in Denmark (as well as in Austria and Norway), the pace of progress has become somewhat slower; and Switzerland has continued to perform below average. In all of these countries, employment growth has stopped, and unemployment has risen, because of a still rising participation rate, by about 1 percentage point.

The most striking case is the Netherlands, the 'star performer' (*The Economist*, November 15, 2003: 27) and model country par excellence of a few years ago. There, GDP growth was low in 2001, stagnated in 2002, went into the red (to an even lower level than in Germany) in 2003 (cf. OECD 2004, p.55), revealed the lowest growth rate in Euroland in 2004 and the forecast for 2005 point to the same direction (*The Economist*, December 11, 2004: p.92). After their spending drift up to the years 2000/2001, the Dutch have started to save again, and private consumption has sharply fallen (ibid, p.16; European Commission 2003, p.25; *de Volkskrant*, February 13, 2004:7). In contrast to a number of other 'model countries' (the USA, Ireland, Australia and, since the very late 1990s, Sweden again), Dutch house prices are no longer soaring, and the wealth effect is fading away. Until 2003, the Netherlands has also only slightly shared in the revival of world exports particularly induced by the vigorous growth in China. Moreover, contributions to pension schemes and health care insurances have increased by double-digit percentages in recent years (and will continue to do so in 2005; *NRC Handelsblad*, December 9, 2004: 16) and reduced people's purchasing power. As a result of these developments, Dutch unemployment is climbing more rapidly than in the other model countries.

Talking about prospects, one enters a field with speculative elements. The past has been determined by luck, and there is no reason to expect that this will change in the future. Some indicators of future success already exist, however. These are the industrial and commercial specialisations of our countries and their current efforts to stay competitive in the future. As far as it is true that small European countries predominantly engage in quality- and image-sensitive businesses for their comparative advantages (Denmark, Sweden, Switzerland; partially Finland and Austria) and as far as they will be able to integrate up-to-date technology into their production processes, they have a good chance not only to stay competitive, but also to keep their employment level. For quality- and image-sensitive production is not moving as fast to low-wage locations as is the case with the production of high-tech, but price-sensitive goods (Boyer 2000). Compare what happened over the past 30 years to the production of cars on the one hand and the production of consumer electronics on the other.

Nowadays, the production of computer hardware and software, once it is standardised and simplified, moves quickly to Asia or Eastern Europe. High-tech, the production of which has become low-tech, moves away, while the production of e.g. a brake system working for a 100,000 km or of industrial equipment will stay in Austria, Germany, Sweden and Switzerland (or Japan). This means that employment in high-tech producer countries such as Ireland and the USA could be much more vulnerable in the next decade or so than in middle-tech producers such as Denmark. The following quotation from *The Economist* (April 10, 2004: 63) is illustrative in this context:

Table 10.2 R&D spending (in percent of GDP), employment in medium- and high-tech manu-facturing, and competitiveness rankings

	R&D (%)	Empl. MHT (%)	TII	BCI			GCI	ICI
	2000	2000	2000	99	01	03	2003	2003
Australia				13	14	11	10	7
Austria	1.49	6.6	11	11	11	17	17	17
Belgium	1.78	7.2	12	15	15	15	27	15
Canada				8	12	12	16	10
Denmark	1.97	6.4	6	7	8	4	4	19
Finland	3.09	7.2	3	2	1	1	1	2
France	2.16	7.2	10	9	13	10	26	9
Germany	2.38	10.9	9	6	4	5	13	3
Ireland	1.42	7.3	8	17	22	21	30	16
Italy	1.04	7.6	15	25	23	24	41	22
Japan	2.88		5	14	10	13	11	12
Netherlands	1.92	4.7	7	3	3	9	12	6
Sweden	3.71	8.3	1	4	6	3	3	8
Switzerland				5	5	7	7	5
UK	1.79	7.6	4	10	7	6	15	4
USA	2.54		2	1	2	2	2	1

Sources:
R&D, Empl. MHT (Employment in Medium and High Tech Manufacturing; percent of total em-ployment) and TII (Tentative Summary Innovation Index): ITT 2001.
BCI (Business Competitiveness Index): Porter (World Economic Forum; WEF) 2003:9
GCI (Growth Competitiveness Index): Sala-I-Martin (WEF) 2003:4
ICI (Innovation Capacity Index): Porter and Stern (WEF) 2003:4

'Manufacturers in China would have a dreadful time producing good conventional film cameras, for example, because of the complex opti-cal, chemical and mechanical processes that must be mastered. But Chi-nese factories have little trouble assembling digital cameras: all they need to do is obtain advanced components from Japan that are pre-de-signed to work in harmony when snapped together.'

Solely trusting on the inherited industrial structure is not enough, of course. The data in Table 10.2 reflect in comparative perspective what the small countries have done in recent years to enhance their competitiveness in terms of technological development and the institutional conditions of suc-cessful economic activity. The first thing one has to say is perhaps that the relevance of the presented data should not be exaggerated. Italy, for example, scores miserably on all indicators but still belongs to the richest countries in the world. Perhaps strong industrial clusters and related collective technical memories of regional work forces compensate for low R&D investment and a rigid institutional context that make this country rank very low in the business and growth competitiveness rankings. And why should Belgian subsidiaries of foreign companies (Belgium largely depends on foreign capital) invest in R&D when the mother companies are doing it? The same question can be asked with respect to Ireland.

Having said this, a few striking features should be signalled. One has already been mentioned: the surprisingly low scores for Ireland, the 'European tiger'. Irish competitiveness rankings are low, and employment in medium- and high-tech is not particularly pronounced and might partially reflect the low-tech character of the production of computer hardware. It is also striking that Switzerland, although it ranks high, has not managed to raise productivity in the past one to two decades. And the Dutch position is weak in middle- and high-tech employment, deteriorating in competitiveness rankings (see also IMD 2004), characterised by relatively few efforts to change this situation by R&D investment and, one could add, by a low number of graduates in science and engineering as well as a low level of cluster development (Porter and Stern 2003, p.4). On the opposite side we have Finland and Sweden (and the USA) ranking high in nearly every aspect and investing more than any other country in R&D. Particularly remarkable is the high share private companies take in R&D investment (about two-thirds) (ITT 2001).

Putting these elements together, one gets a mixed picture. Leaving aside future luck and circumstantial factors such as the costs of German unification that might continue to hamper European growth (isn't the solution of this problem a European issue?), one gets the impression that:

- Dutch miracle and model times are over,
- there is no reason to expect that Australia will not continue to fare well with the expansion of Asian, particularly Chinese, markets
- Switzerland will probably remain a special case with a strong image,
- Ireland remains a very special and vulnerable case,
- and Scandinavia, particularly Sweden (Finland perhaps depends too much on one company, and the Danish case is less clear), has once again the best chances to continue its model status – at least for those who want to pay the high taxes required by the level of Scandinavian social security and public employment.

Generally, however, one should be cautious with concepts such as miracle and model. The Dutch development was a miracle because its starting point in the early 1980s was a very low employment rate, Ireland impressed by its Asian-like pace of GDP growth, Finland and Sweden started a very strong comeback in the second half of the 1990s. And Switzerland is an astonishing case because on the basis of the data on GDP growth one should have expected its employment to go down. For the rest, our success stories have never been miracles. Have they been models? In part, this is a question the answer to which involves a strong subjective dimension. A clear yes or no is not possible. 'Models' seems to have their times. In the 1980s for many Sweden was the model; around 1990, Germany and Japan were the models; at that time in the USA economists (e.g. Thurow 1992) and the media discussed the country's economic decline (Albert 1997, p.4), and nobody talked about the Netherlands or Denmark, the models of the second half of the decade. Currently, one gets the impression that their model status is fading away. Is there at least something to learn from these countries?

What is to be learned?

Although the small economies discussed in this volume attracted attention precisely because politicians and analysts sought transferable policy lessons, the chapters in this book suggest that little of what happened in the miracle economies is easily transferable – assuming it is worth transferring. First, the dominance and inertia of once-existing policy routines – of being 'stuck' – in most countries suggests that the precise political and institutional causes for specific policies barely can be implanted elsewhere – even if, as e.g. in north-western Europe, overall politico-economic structures are similar. Second, the importance of 'once only' events in the expansion of aggregate demand and subsequent employment growth suggests that policy-makers who wish to import the successful policies of the 1990s have already missed their opportunity. In particular, it is unlikely that the next decade will experience the secularly falling nominal interest rates that characterized the 1990s and early 2000s. Given the right institutional conditions, falling nominal interests allowed homeowners in many countries – Switzerland and Germany being exceptions – to liberate purchasing power from rising home equity, enabled consumers to take on new debt without increasing their interest burdens, and helped cause a wholesale revaluation of equity markets. All of these contributed strongly to increases in aggregate demand that then turned into buoyant employment in the Netherlands, Ireland, the

USA, Denmark, and Australia and somewhat later in Sweden, too (as well as in the UK and Spain). But the root causes for disinflation have played out, particularly in the US. The US budget is back in deficit, much labour-intensive industry has already moved to China, and increased insecurity makes investors more wary.

Looking for important specific lessons we can say this:

- A first point, to be drawn from the 'bubbles', is that domestic demand is still important for GDP and employment growth.
- For detecting employment growth one has to look at the relatively protected service sector. In manufacturing, even if investment and exports are increasing, long-term productivity growth is outpacing the need for additional employment. Germany from 2002 to 2004 illustrates this more than any other case: strongly increasing exports and rising productivity, but GDP stagnation and shrinking employment.
- A tightening of eligibility criteria in social security, as Denmark has exercised it, may also have a (very) small positive effect on employment growth, but one should not forget that it is not individual misbehaviour that caused unemployment. Tax credits are of the same order as eligibility criteria.
- Labour market programs, particularly leave schemes of the Danish type, which could be understood as a step into the direction of social 'flexecurity', could have a larger effect – but they also have their price, of course.
- From the Netherlands one can learn about the importance of part-time work in situations of shrinking demand for labour, although a formula for a more equal distribution of part-time jobs between women and men has still to be discovered.
- A general lesson to be taken from the corporatist ones of the small countries discussed here is that, with national nuances such as the eminence of part-time (Netherlands, Switzerland) or public employment (Scandinavia), a high level of employment and job growth can be combined with moderate to high levels of employment protection, social welfare and material equality. So principally, an alternative to the dominant liberal recipes still exists. This has to be specified, however.

For the rest, the specific lessons one can draw from the recent development of the small countries are limited, discouraging and problematical: Ireland, Denmark and Finland could be too small to be discussed as models – why not discuss Trentino-Alto Adige, the Italian province of 900,000 inhabitants doing so well economically? Larger countries can neither concentrate on ICT hardware as Ireland does nor strongly depend on just one big company as Finland does on Nokia, and they are not permitted to have Danish unit labour costs. Large economies also cannot specialise in niches largely outside international competition. And small countries such as Portugal, Greece and most of the countries that entered the EU in 2004 have a long way to go before they have reached the level of the Danish or Finnish infrastructure, and the Irish method based on foreign (US) investment can, if at all, only be copied by a very few other countries (e.g. the region of Slovakia bordering Austria is vastly developing a strong car industry cluster based on FDI). Furthermore, only a few countries can have – like the USA and Australia – a huge deficit on current accounts. And demand 'bubbles' triggered by strongly increasing private debt that is based on soaring house prices cannot be created at will.

As indicated, arguments relying on supposed features of some of our small countries' development such as dismissal flexibility are of little value, too. These developments are limited, and more importantly, there is no evidence that flexible, American-like hire-and-fire rules *generally* facilitate employment growth (OECD 1999e, p.47; Nickell 1997, p.72). The Dutch, Finnish, Swedish as well as German-Bavarian (and one could add: Austrian and Norwegian) rules are much more rigid than the American ones, and high employment countries like Denmark – where relatively relaxed dismissal rules are embedded in the context of the world's most generous welfare system and active labour market policies – and Switzerland are located inbetween the rather rigid standard of most countries on the European continent and the Anglo-Saxon world where the commodification of labour has reached a high level (see Table 9.2). Rather than being a general condition of high employment, flexible labour markets seem to belong to the liberal variety of capitalism describing only one possible route to job growth, and this flexibility appears only to be employment-effective when it is combined with pronounced wage differentiation and a residual welfare system. In the corporatist variety of capitalism, by contrast, high employment exists in combination with less labour market flexibility and relatively generous welfare.

'Competitive corporatism'?

This is the proper context to return to the question about the feasibility of competitive corporatism (with corporatism defined as variety of capitalism). Built on extraordinary, beggar-my-neighbour wage restraint, as recently launched in the discussion on 'new social pacts', it would barely be a competitive one. Its diffusion would imply the generalisation of ineffective and counterproductive strategies with respect to wages and taxes, really endangering the world economy to become a zero-sum or, even worse, a negative-sum game because aggregate demand would suffer. And it would strengthen rat-race economic nationalism. In fact, a nationalist, beggar-my-neighbour wage policy has already been a more general feature of the 1990s. A number of countries have formulated guidelines for modest wage development for the goal of price competitiveness, and in some cases – Belgium, Norway – the explicit aim is to undercut the wage increase in the main competitor countries (cf. Schulten 2002, pp.186ff). This might be a viable strategy for emerging economies, but not for high-income, high-wage countries that mainly depend for their competitiveness on their productivity and innovative capacity (Porter 2003).

In an ideal-typical circumscription, the most general aspect of corporatism is the institutionalised coordination of economic and social (plus potentially environmental) goals by agreement and exchange between capital, labour and, in the tripartite variety, the state for the sake of a society's common interest, i.e. what is thought to be good for society as a whole. In 'full corporatism' the goals at stake are profitability, employment, material equality, and social security, and since the late 1980s, under the impact of the latest developments in globalisation and Europeanisation, competitiveness has been added (the Swedish Rehn-Meidner Model of the 1960s – forcing companies to extra innovative activity by specific wage agreements – was an early predecessor). The market cannot (and liberals do not want to) accomplish this coordination.

What, however, can corporatism add to market incentives to raise productivity and to state action to create conditions for this endeavour? Traditional pro-corporatism arguments from a company point of view have been economically responsible wage demands by the unions, accountability of the unions and the long-term perspective it makes possible. These properties appear to render corporatism compatible with competitiveness rather than directly enhance it. The exchange involved is wage development oriented towards macroeconomic parameters, accountability and a long-term perspective for certain levels of job protection, equality and social security. Innovation can be included in collective agreements, but how to exchange it? How could it be connected to an incentive really to innovate? Perhaps a modernised version of the Rehn-Meidner Model is possible, and on the company level, particularly where some form of co-determination exists (Streeck 2001, p.14), incremental shop-floor innovation can be fostered, and flexibility can be exchanged against job protection, leave schemes and perhaps even career trajectories. A look at Table 10.2 reveals that Finland, Sweden and to a lesser degree Denmark, Switzerland and Germany do well in terms of (technologically pronounced) competitiveness, but the link to corporatism is not clear, and other corporatist countries (the Netherlands, Austria) just deteriorate in these terms or in terms of productivity (the Netherlands and Switzerland).

Moreover, one should not forget that corporatism depends on a certain balance of power between capital and labour. When one part is structurally weaker than the other, the existence of corporatism is in danger. The impact of recent globalisation developments – intensified international competition, the removal of trade barriers, and the rapidly increasing mobility of financial capital – on national affairs should not be exaggerated, but it seems plausible to assume these developments are providing exit options for companies. These exit options, then, are an eminent power resource of capital, reducing the threat unions can exercise by strikes (see the excellent account on the different positions in the globalisation debate in Schmidt 2002). Adding decreasing union membership in many countries and the process of social-structural individualisation, one has to envisage the erosion of corporatism because of a deteriorating position of labour. Big changes take time, but there are signs, such as the lack of more than only defensive exchanges between capital, the state and labour in recent times and the strength of the liberal discourse, that suggest that this process is already under way. The Dutch development seems to point in this direction (although in the fall of 2004 the unions successfully mobilised against the intention of the government further to reduce and liberalise social security). And in the Irish 'new corporatism', labour has been subordinated to or even instrumentalised by the 'competition state' (Boyle 2004) from the very beginning. When labour is strong, capital may quit corporatism, as happened in the late 1980s and early 1990s in Sweden (though it came back in 1997 – at least partially; Elvander 2002), indicating by this that corporatism currently tends to be viable only when labour is acquiescing. So, perhaps one has to describe (symmetrical) corporatism as a declining variety of capitalism. This process is not yet irreversible, however.

Finally, consensual patterns of interaction are a condition of what could be called effective corporatism. This is particularly important for countries that want to adopt corporatism. The installation of a formal-institutional framework is not sufficient. France has such institutions (particularly the 'conseil du travail'), and Britain has tried them under Labour in the 1970s (Bamber et al. 2003), but neither of these countries is corporatist. Effective corporatism requires a high level of social trust, a discursive pattern of conflict resolution, the norm of compromising, and a commitment of its players to the common interest (Katzenstein 1985). In Denmark, Sweden, the Netherlands and Switzerland (as well as Norway), these patterns have been emerging in largely evolutionary democratisation processes since early modern times. As Austria and Finland demonstrate, however, the historical process generating the consensual political culture does not necessarily take centuries.

Still the liberal-social democratic divide

What remains after the critical discussion of the current 'models' is the fundamental division between the two principal ways of raising employment: The liberal way of clearing the labour market by increasing wage differentiation, relaxing dismissal rules – particularly at the lower edge – and residual unemployment benefits, and the social democratic – corporatist (incidentally, Christian democratic – corporatist) way of public or publicly financed jobs on a large scale embedded in a generous system of social security. Neither of these ways is totally resistant against fluctuations in unemployment, but both of them lead to an employment rate that is higher than that of the passive welfare systems on the European continent.

The liberal way has strong points in its stress of competitiveness to be raised by market competition and of individual responsibility because it is crucial for democracy. As has been emphasised by classical political economists from Adam Smith onwards and even by Karl Marx, competition between companies as well as individuals has been the main engine of the unique economic progress that took place in the West in the past two centuries. Targeting only quantitative progress, the liberating of markets still seems to be the best recipe, therefore. There is more than technological development and GDP growth, however. And when more individual responsibility is not only the device for democracy and entrepreneurship, but also for the welfare system, it will often have the effect of concentrating the financial burden of social security on the shoulders of those most at risk to become unemployed, sick or disabled. This group, however, has only a limited capacity to pay for it. The argument pleading for more individual responsibility tends to overlook that market risks are unevenly spread and generally assumes an omnipotent individual, as well as a perfectly functioning market bringing a good income to everyone doing her or his best. Because of this blind eye, the liberal way or 'model' has high social costs in the form of considerable poverty and inequality and through the 'walled communities' and the rising number of social workers, police and private security agents in its context.

This is exemplified by the USA more than by any other country. Until now, however, continental European traditions of social integration, whether Christian democratic, otherwise conservative or social democratic, and of scepticism towards the market together with the electoral weight of the unionised population have blocked any radical adoption of this model. The Netherlands has moved some steps towards increased wage differentiation more than other continental countries, but in absolute terms it is still far removed from American standards. And in Germany, the Christian Democratic opposition is launching a liberal attack on the welfare system. Until now, this has only been talk, however, and even if such forces would seriously try to radically change the existing system, they would be confronted with oppositional forces making use of the numerous veto points built into the political structure of continental European democracies. One has to admit, however, that the liberal discourse, in spite of its weak empirical basis, has many supporters and has become common to a considerable degree: time and again, one is told about the necessity of fundamental, liberal reforms of the welfare system and the labour market. The next decade will have to show whether the European continent will, in social terms, become americanised or retain its peculiarities.

In contrast, the social democratic – corporatist way more or less put into practice by the Scandinavian countries and Austria is a costly and directly visible pecuniary affair, just like financing unemployment at a generous level. One may doubt whether low-employment societies have the institutional capacity to go this way and ask whether their populations want to raise female employment. With respect to costs, the question is whether they would pay for a large number of well-paid public and/or publicly financed jobs. In the context of increasing global competition and of companies becoming increasingly mobile in financial terms (Genschel 2001), this question has to be translated into the one of whether wage earners (by income taxes) and consumers (by indirect taxes) will pay the bill. What is at stake is the feasibility of what once was metaphorically circumscribed as 'socialism in one class' and what could be called social individualism. 'Socialism in one class', a slogan once coined to denote the Swedish 'model', simply means that financing social security, material equality as well as extensive public employment is largely done at the cost of the wage earners because capital taxation is low. In relative terms, this would even be true when critics of the globalisation thesis (cf. Schmidt 2002) are right that the exit options of capital are limited.

Social individualism is not a philanthropic device. It means that people would be aware that they are social beings with limited capacities for autonomous personal development. As a consequence, they would be aware that, to a large extent, they are advantaged or disadvantaged by genetic and environmental factors and their own creations only to a small extent. On this basis, they would not only support the principle of individual responsibility, but also solidarity and collective responsibility for work and welfare. Is this feasible? We are living in a period of rapid social-structural individualisation or atomisation. Class boundaries are still important in an economic sense (organisations of capital and labour are based on them) and for the formation of social milieus, but their relevance in the constitution process of individual identity as well as in political action is declining. Moreover, we are living in a period of liberal ideological dominance. In this context, atomisation appears to be fertile soil for the myth of the autonomous individual. Connected to economic liberalism, liberal individualism as the ideological framework of meritocracy is at the same time the legitimisation basis of growing income inequality and welfare cuts.

Looking for the opportunities of turning individualism social, one has to be sceptical. In superficial surveys, people show their support for keeping a high level of social security, but this support declines when they are asked about the price they are willing to pay for it (George 1998; Mau 2001), and their willingness to pay higher taxes is limited (*The Economist*, March 26, 2000). It is not for nothing that tax cut proposals do well in election campaigns. Also, if we are not looking at social security in general – the most costly components of which are pensions and health care which everybody is interested in – but at unemployment benefits, than there is no majority willing to pay the price for maintaining its given level, and the more qualified respondents are and the higher their incomes, the lower their support. So, why should they be willing to pay for publicly financed employment on a large scale? The Scandinavian countries have a particularly strong egalitarian tradition, and they developed their expensive system of public employment in the social democratic tide of the 1960s and 1970s. Since then, times have changed. Principally, however, social individualism and the social democratic employment strategy based on it seem to be the only way to solve the tension between employment and equality.

Being sceptical about the feasibility of social individualism implies that one has to be sceptical about the prospect for substantial employment growth in the larger European democracies as well as in Spain, the Netherlands (with its still low labour volume) and Belgium with their strong conservative or Christian traditions of a passive welfare state. The forces critical towards the market and thus towards employment growth by increasing wage differentiation plus relaxing dismissal rules are (still) very strong there, while the forces that could support the social democratic way are too weak. In the current context of liberal individualisation, this way might even, or already has (Iversen and Wren 1998), come under strain in its Scandinavian homelands.

Perhaps future research could establish a basis for a more optimistic view. Topics like benchmarking and learning are still too extensively related to comparisons between countries, which differ greatly in size. The comparison of small countries such as the Scandinavian ones with regions or states of larger countries is underdeveloped, however. Europeans who are critical about US poverty rates could perhaps learn from US states such as California or regions such as New England excluding New York City where a liberal variety of work and welfare co-exists with poverty rates considerably lower than the US average. And what about the big, trans-national region surrounding the Alps comprising Austria, Switzerland, southern Germany, parts of eastern France and northern Italy and also including Slovenia, the only East European country approaching the wealth of Western Europe? Sixty million people live there. Why is it that the economy is flourishing just there? Is there a way of reconciling employment and (relative) equality that is different from the Scandinavian way? Maybe a comparison between this region and Italy, France and Germany could shed some light on these questions.

Bibliography

Abraham, K. and D.P. Klein 1999, *Report on the American Workforce*, Washington D.C.: US Department of Labor

Abrahamson, P. 1998,'Efter velfærdstaten: Ret og pligt til aktivering', *Nordisk Sosialt Arbeid* 3, 18: 133-142

Aiginger, K. 2000, 'Europe's Position in Quality Competition', *Background Report* for *The European Competitiveness Report 2000*, Brussels: European Commission, DG Enterprise,
http://www.wifo.ac.at/Karl.Aiginger/publications/2000/quality_comp.pdf

Alan, J.P. and L. Scruggs 2004, 'Political Partisanship and Welfare State Reform in Advanced Industrial Societies', *American Journal of Political Science* 48, 3: 496-512

Albert, M. 1991, *Capitalisme contre Capitalisme*, Paris: Seuil

Albert, M. 1997, 'The Future of Continental Socio-Economic Models', *MPIfG Working Paper* 97/6, Cologne: Max-Planck-Institut für Gesellschaftsforschung

Alchian, A. 1950, 'Uncertainty, Evolution, and Economic Theory', *Journal of Political Economy* 58: 211-221

Ali-Yrkkö, J. 2001, 'The Role of Nokia in the Finnish Economy', *The Finnish Economy and Society* 1: 72-80

Allen, R.L. 1995, 'Food Service Industry Reps Rally in DC, Vow to Aid Welfare Reform', *Nation's Restaurant News*, January 23

Amable, B. 2003, *The Diversity of Modern Capitalism*, Oxford: Oxford University Press

American Business for Legal Immigration 2000, 'Letter to Congress', June 6,
http://www.nam.org/tertiary.asp?TrackID=andDocumentID=22701

Andersen, K. 2001, 'Welfare State Adjustment in Sweden and the Netherlands', paper presented at the Annual Meeting of the American Political Science Association, San Francisco, August 30-September 2

Andersen, P. 1997, 'Wonderful Denmark?', *CPB Report* 97, 2: 46-47

Andersen, T.M., S.E.H. Jensen and O. Risager 1999, 'Macroeconomic Perspectives on the Danish Economy: Problems. Policies and Prospects', pp. 1-39 in T.M. Andersen, S.E.H. Jensen and O. Risager (eds.), *Macroeconomic Perspectives on the Danish Economy*, London: Macmillan

Appelbaum, E. 2000, 'Employment Development in the US', paper presented at the International Labour Market Conference *Ways and Means of Increasing Employment*, Hannover (Expo 2000), September 5

Applebome, P. 1995, 'Employers Wary of School System', *The New York Times* (February 20): A1, 13

Armingeon, K. 1997, 'Swiss Corporatism in Comparative Perspective', *West European Politics* 20, 4: 164-179

Auer, P. 2000, *Employment Revival in Europe*, Geneva: International Labour Office

AWF (Arbeitsgemeinschaft deutscher wirtschaftswissenschaftlicher Forschungsinstitute) 2002, 'Die Lage der Wieltwirtschaft und der deutschen Wirtschaft im Herbst 2002', *Deutsches Institut für Wirtschaftsforschung – DIW Wochenbericht* 69, 43: 703-712

Ball, L. 1999, 'Aggregate Demand and Unemployment', *Brookings Papers on Economic Activity* 2: 189-236

Bamber, G.J., R.D. Lansbury and N.B. Wailes (eds.) 2003, *International and Comparative Employment Relations*, London: Sage

Bane, M.J. 1997, 'Welfare as We Might Know It', *The American Prospect* 8, 30 (Jan-Feb)

Barrett, A., J. Fitz Gerald and B. Nolan 2000, 'Earnings Inequality, Returns to Education and Low Pay', pp. 127-146 in B. Nolan, P.J. O'Connell and C.T. Whelan (eds.), *Bust to Boom? The Irish Experience of Growth and Inequality*, Dublin: Institute of Public Administration

Barry, F., A. Hannan and E. Strobl 1999, 'The Real Convergence of the Irish Economy and the Sectoral Distribution of Employment Growth', pp. 13-24 in F. Barry (ed.), *Understanding Ireland's Economic Growth*, Basingstoke: Macmillan

BDI (Bundesverband der deutschen Industrie) 1998, *Für ein Attraktives Deutschland in einem Weltoffenen Europa*, Cologne: Bundesverband der deutschen Industrie

Bean, C. 2000, 'The Australian Economic 'Miracle': A View from the North', pp. 73-114 in Reserve Bank of Australia 2000 Conference, *The Australian Economy in the 1990s*, Sydney: RBA

Becker, U. 1999, *Europese Democratieën. Vrijheid, Gelijkheid, Solidariteit en Soevereiniteit in Praktijk*, Amsterdam: Het Spinhuis

Becker, U. 2000, 'Welfare State Development and Employment in the Netherlands in Comparative Perspective', *Journal of European Social Policy* 10, 3: 219-239

Becker, U. 2001a, '"Miracle" by Consensus? Consensualism and Dominance in Dutch Employment Development', *Economic and Industrial Democracy* 11, 4: 453-483

Becker, U. 2001b, 'A "Dutch Model": Employment Growth by Corporatist Consensus and Wage Restraint? A Critical Account of an Idyllic View', *New Political Economy* 6, 1: 19-43

Becker, U. 2001c, 'The U.S., Danish and Dutch Routes to Employment Growth: Examples to Learn From?', paper presented at the Annual Meeting of the American Political Science Association, San Francisco, August 30 – September 2

Becker, U. 2005, 'Competitive Corporatism Below Sea Level? Tides of the Dutch Political Economy 1983 – 2002 in Critical Examination', *European Journal of Public Policy* 4, forthcoming June issue

Bell, S. 1993, *The Australian Manufacturing and the State*, New York: Cambridge University Press

Benner, M. and T. B. P. Vad 2000, 'Sweden and Denmark: Defending the Welfare State', pp. 399-466 in F.W. Scharpf and V.A. Schmidt (eds.), *Welfare and Work in the Open Economy. Vol. II. Diverse Responses to Common Challenges in Twelve Countries*, Oxford: Oxford University Press

Berger, S. and R. Dore (eds.) 1996, *National Diversity and Global Capitalism*, Ithaca: Cornell University Press

Berghäll, E. and J. Kiander 2003, 'The Finnish Model of STI Policy: Experience and Guidelines. Government Institute for Economic Research', Discussion Paper 313, Helsinki: VATT Publishers

Bernasek, A. 1999, 'What the Fed's Worried About', *Fortune* 140, (October 11): 56-60

Bernasek, A. 2002, 'Is Housing the Next Bubble?', *Fortune* 145, (April 1): 77-80

Bernstein, A. 1997, 'Sharing Prosperity', *Business Week* (September 1): 64

BFS 2003, *Ausländische Erwerbstätigkeit: Grosse Unterschiede nach Regionen und Branchen*, Press Announcement, January 31-2003, Neuchâtel: Bundesamt für Statistik.

Bibow, J. 2001, 'The Economic Consequences of German Unification', *Public Policy Brief* 67, Annadale-on-Hudson, N.Y.: The Levy Economics Institute

BIS (Bank for International Settlements) 2002, 72*nd Annual Report*, Basel: BIS

Björklund, A. 2000, 'Going Different Ways. Labour Market Policy in Denmark and Sweden', pp. 148-180 in G. Esping-Andersen and M. Regini (eds.), *Why Deregulate Labour Markets*, Oxford: Oxford University Press

Blanchard, O.J. and P. Portugal 2001, 'What Hides Behind an Unemployment Rate: Comparing Portuguese and U.S. Labor Markets', *American Economic Review* 91, 1: 187-207

Blanchard, O.J. and L. Summers 1986, 'Hysteresis and the European Unemployment Problem', in *NBER Macroeconomics Annual*, Cambridge: MIT Press

Blanchard, O.J. and J. Wolfers 2000, 'The Role of Shocks and Institutions in the Rise of European Unemployment: The Aggregate Evidence', *Economic Journal* 110: C1-C33.

Boeri, T. 2001, 'How far from Lisbon?', in S. Ilmakunnas and E. Koskela (eds.), *Towards Higher Employment. The Role of Labour Market Institutions*, Helsinki: VATT Publishers

Bonner-Tompkins, E. 1994, 'A Changing Workforce and More Job Training Programs', CBCF *Policy Review* 1, 2

Bonoli, G. 1997, 'Social Insurance in Switzerland', in J. Clasen, *Social Insurance in Europe*, Bristol: The Policy Press

Bonoli, G. and A. Mach 2000, 'Switzerland: Adjustment Policies within Institutional Constraints', pp. 131-173 in F.W. Scharpf and V.A. Schmidt (eds.), *Welfare and Work in the Open Economy. Vol. II. Diverse Responses to Common Challenges in Twelve Countries*, Oxford: Oxford University Press

Bonvin, J-M. 1996, 'Les Réponses Suisses aux Phénomènes Migratoires', *L'Année sociologique* 46: 442-473

Bordes, C., D. Currie and H.T. Söderström 1993, *Three Assessments of the Finnish Economic Crisis and Economic Policy*, Helsinki: Bank of Finland

Borner, S., A. Brunetti and T. Straubhaar 1990, *Schweiz AG – Vom Sonderfall zum Sanierungsfall?*, Zürich: Verlag Neue Zürcher Zeitung

Boyer, R. 2000, 'The Embedded Innovative Systems of Germany and Japan: Distinctive Features and Futures', CEPREMAP *Working Paper* 9, Paris: CEPREMAP

Boyle, N. 2004, 'Consensus and Institutional Capacity in Irish Policymaking: The "Irish Model" and Active Labour Market Policy 1987-2004', paper prepared for the 2nd *Pan-European Conference on* EU *Politics*, June 24-26 2004, Bologna, Italy

Bradley, J. 2000, 'The Irish Economy in Comparative Perspective', pp. 4-26 in B. Nolan, P.J. O'Connell and C.T. Whelan (eds.), *Bust to Boom? The Irish experience of growth and inequality*, Dublin: Institute of Public Administration

Breen, R., D.F. Hannan, D.B. Rottman and C.T. Whelan 1990, *Understanding Contemporary Ireland*, Dublin: Gill and Macmillan

Brenner, R. 2001, 'The World Economy at the Turn of the Millennium toward Boom or Crisis?', *Review of International Political Economy* 8, 1: 6-44

Brixy, U. and B. Christensen 2002, 'Flexibilität. Wieviel würden Arbeitslose für einen Arbeitsplatz in Kauf nehmen?', IAB *Kurzbericht* 25, Bundesanstalt für Arbeit

Brown, C., J. Hamilton and J. Medoff 1990, *Employers Large and Small*, Cambridge, MA: Harvard University Press

BSWVT 2000a, *Wirtschaftsstandort Bayern*, Munich: Bayerisches Staatsministerium für Wirtschaft, Verkehr und Technologie

BSWVT 2000b, *Bayerns Stellung im nationalen und internationalen Vergleich. Ausgewaehlte Wirtschaftsdaten*, Munich: Bayerisches Staatsministerium für Wirtschaft, Verkehr und Technologie

Buchanan, J., M. Woodman, S. O'Keefe, and B. Arsovska 1998, 'Wages Policy and Wage Determination in 1997', *Journal of Industrial Relations* 40, 1: 88-118

Bureau of Labor Statistics (United States Department of Commerce) 2002, *Foreign Labor Statistics Homepage*, http://www.bls.gov/fls/home.htm

Burgoon, B. 2001, 'Globalisation and Welfare Compensation', *International Organisation* 55, 3: 509-551

Callan, T. and B. Nolan 2000, 'Taxation and Social Welfare', pp. 179-203 in B. Nolan, P.J. O'Connell and C.T. Whelan (eds.), *Bust to Boom? The Irish Experience of Growth and Inequality*, Dublin: Institute of Public Administration

Cameron, D. 1978, 'The Expansion of the Public Economy: A Comparative Analysis', *American Political Science Review* 72: 1243-61

Capling, M. and B. Galligan 1993, *Beyond the Protective State: Australia's Manufacturing Industry Policy*, Cambridge: Cambridge University Press

CAR (Commonwealth Arbitration Reports) 1970, *Engineering Oil Industry Case, No. 134*, Canberra: Australian Government Printing Service

Carnevale, A. 1991, *America and the New Economy*, San Francisco: Jossey-Bass Publishers

Castells, M. and P. Himanen 2000, *The Information Society and the Welfare State: The Finnish Model*, Oxford: Oxford University Press

Castles, F. 1985, *The Working Class and Welfare*, Sydney: Unwin and Allen

Castles, F. 1988, *Australian Public Policy and Economic Vulnerability*, Sydney: Allen and Unwin

Castles, F. 1993 (ed), *Families of Nations. Patterns of Public Policy in Western Democracies*, Aldershot: Dartmouth

Castles, F. 1994, 'Testing the Limits of the Metaphor: Fordist and Post-Fordist Life Cycles in Australia and New Zealand', *Discussion Paper* 40, Canberra: Australian National University Public Policy Programme

Castles, F.1998a, 'The Really Big Trade-off: Home Ownership and the Welfare State in the New World and the Old', *Acta Politica* 33: 5-19

Castles, F.1998b, *Comparative Public Policies: Patterns of Post-War Transformation*, Cheltenham: Edward Elgar

CBS 1996a, *Tijdreeksen Arbeidsrekeningen 1969-1993*, Voorburg/Heerlen: Centraal Bureau voor de Statistiek

CBS 1996b, *Sociaal-Economische Maandstatistiek 96/11*, Voorburg/Heerlen: Centraal Bureau voor de Statistiek

CBS 1999a, *Sociaal-Economische Maandstatistiek 99/5*, Voorburg/Heerlen: Centraal Bureau voor de Statistiek

CBS 1999b, *Press Release 15 March 1999*, Voorburg/Heerlen: Centraal Bureau voor de Statistiek

CBS 1999c, *Press Release* 25 March 1999, Voorburg/Heerlen: Centraal Bureau voor de Statistiek

CBS 1980ff, *Enquête Beroepsbevolking*, Voorburg/Heerlen: Centraal Bureau voor de Statistiek

CBS n.d., Statline Website, http://statline.cbs.nl

Central Statistics Office 2001, *Household Budget Survey 1999-2000: Preliminary Results*, Dublin: Stationery Office

Cohn, L. 2000, 'From Welfare to Worsefare?', *Business Week* (October 9): 103

Collins, N. 1999, 'Corruption in Ireland: Review of Recent Cases', pp. 64-88 in idem (ed), *Political Issues in Ireland Today*, Manchester: Manchester University Press

Commission of the European Communities 1993, *Growth, Competitiveness, Employment: The Challenges and Ways Forward in the 21st Century*, Supplement 11, 40

Commission on the Skills of the American Workforce 1990, *America's Choice*, Washington, DC: National Center on Education and the Economy

Corsetti, G. and N. Roubini 1996, 'Budget Deficits, Public Sector Solvency and Political Biases of Fiscal Policy: A Case Study of Finland', *Finnish Economic Papers* 9, 1: 18-36

Council on Competitiveness 1987, *America's Competitive Crisis*, Washington, DC: Council on Competitiveness

Cox, R. H. 1997, 'The Consequences of Welfare Retrenchment in Denmark', *Politics and Society* 25, 3: 303-326

Cox, R.H. 2001, 'The Social Construction of an Imperative: Why Welfare Reform Happened in Denmark and the Netherlands But Not in Germany', *World Politics* 53, 3: 463-498

Credit Suisse 2003, *Der schweizer Immobilienmarkt – Fakten and Trends*, Zürich: Credit Suisse

Crotty, W. 1998, 'Democratisation and Political Development in Ireland', pp. 1-26 in W. Crotty and D. Schmitt (eds.), *Ireland and the Politics of Change*, London: Longman

Crouch, C. 1993, *Industrial Relations and European State Traditions*, Oxford: Clarendon Press

Crouch, C. and W. Streeck (eds.) 1997, *Political Economy of Modern Capitalism: Mapping Convergence and Diversity*, London: Sage

Cutcher-Gershenfeld, J. 1991, 'The Impact of Economic Performance of a Transformation in Workplace Relations', *Industrial and Labor Relations Review* 44, 2: 241-260

Daly, M. 2000, 'A Fine Balance: Women's Labor Market Participation in International Comparison', pp. 467-510 in F. Scharpf and V. Schmidt (eds.), *From Vulnerability to Competitiveness: Welfare and Work in the Open Economy*, Volume 2, Oxford: Oxford University Press

Damgaard, B. 2000, *Kommunerne, virksomhederne og den aktive socialpolitik*, Copenhagen: Socialforskningsinstituttet

Dang, T.T., P. Antolin and H. Oxley 2001, 'Fiscal Implications of Ageing: Projections of Age-Related Spending', OECD *Economics Department Working Papers* 305, OECD Economics Department

Danmarks Statistik (various years), *Statistisk Tiårsoversigt*, Copenhagen: Danmarks Statistik

Danthine, J. and J. Lambelet 1987, 'The Swiss Recipe: Conservatives Policies Ain't Enough!', *Economic Policy*, 5:149-179

Danziger, S. (ed) 1999, *Economic Conditions and Welfare Reform*, Kalamazoo, MI: Upjohn Institute for Employment Research

Daveri, F. and O. Silva 2004, 'Not Only Nokia: What Finland Tells Us About New Economy Growth', *Economic Policy* 19, 38: 117-163

Davis, S. and J. Haltiwanger 1991, 'Wage Dispersion Between and Within U.S. Manufacturing Plants, 1963-1986', *Brookings Papers on Economic Activity. Microeconomics 1991*, pp.115-80

Dawkins, P. 2000, 'The Australian Labour Market in the 1990s', pp. 316-352 in Reserve Bank of Australia 2000 Conference, *The Australian Economy in the 1990s*, Sydney: RBA

Delsen, L. 2000, *Exit Poldermodel. Sociaal-Economische Ontwikkelingen in Nederland*, Assen: Van Gorcum

DeMott, J. 1995, 'Welfare Reform: Making It Work', *Nation's Business* (June): 18

Department of Foreign Affairs and Trade 2002, *Composition of Trade. Australia 2001*, Canberra: DFAT

DNB 2001, DNB. *Jaarverslag 2000*, Amsterdam: De Nederlandsche Bank

DNB 2002, 'Vermogensbeheer Nederlandse Gezinnen onder de Loep', *Kwartaalbericht Juni 2002*, Amsterdam: De Nederlandsche Bank

Dore, R. 2000, *Stock Market Capitalism – Welfare Capitalism: Japan and Germany versus the Anglo-Saxons*, Oxford: Oxford University Press

Doremus, P., W. Keller, L. Pauly, and S. Reich 1998, *Myth of the Global Corporation*, Princeton: Princeton University Press

Due, J., J. S. Madsen and C. Strøby Jensen 1993, *Den Danske Model. En Historisk Sociologisk Analyse af det Kollektive Aftalesystem*, Copenhagen: DJØFs Forlag

Due, J., J.S. Madsen, C.S. Jensen, and L.K. Petersen 1994, *The Survival of the Danish Model*, Copenhagen: DJØF Publishing

Dunning, J. 1993, *The Globalisation of Business*, New York: Routledge

ECB 2003, *Structural Factors in the EU Housing Market*, Frankfurt: European Central Bank

Elvander, N. 2002, 'The New Swedish Regime for Collective Bargaining and Conflict Resolution: A Comparative Perspective', *European Journal of Industrial Relations* 8, 2:197-216

Esping-Andersen, G. 1990, *The Three Worlds of Welfare Capitalism*, Harvard: Harvard University Press

Esping-Andersen, G. (ed) 1996, *Welfare States in Transition*, London: Sage

Estevez-Abe, M., T. Iversen and D. Soskice 2001, 'Social Protection and the Formation of Skills: A Reinterpretation of the Welfare State', in P. Hall and D. Soskice (eds.), *Varieties of Capitalism. The Institutional Foundations of Comparative Advantage*, Oxford: Oxford University Press

Evans, P. 1995, *Embedded Autonomy*, Princeton NJ: Princeton University Press

European Commission 1995, *Eurobarometer* 42, Luxemburg: Office for Official Publications of the European Communities

European Commission 1999, *Sixth Periodic Report on the Social and Economic Situation and Development of the Regions of the European Union*, Brussels: Publication Office of the European Commission, http://europa.eu.int/comm/regional_policy/document/radi/radi_en.htm

European Commission 2001, *The Social Situation in the European Union 2001*, Brussels: Publication Office of the European Commission

European Commission 2002, *Statistical Annex of European Economy Spring 2002*, Brussels: Directorate General Economic and Financial Affairs

European Commission 2003, *Third European Report on Science and Technology Indicators*, Brussels: Directorate General for Research

European Comparative Politics 2003, Special Issue on 'Varieties of Capitalism' 1, 2

Eurostat 1996, *A Social Portrait of Europe*, Luxembourg: Office for official publications of the European Union

Eurostat 1999, *Labour Force Survey*, Luxembourg: Office for official publications of the European Union

Eurostat 2001, *The Social Situation in the European Union 2001*, Luxembourg: Office for official publications of the European Union

Eurostat 2002, 'Social Protection in Europe', *Statistics in Focus Population and Social Conditions* 1, Luxembourg: Office for official publications of the European Union

Eurostat 2004, 'Social Protection in Europe', *Statistics in Focus Population and Social Conditions*, 6/2004, Luxembourg: Office for official publications of the European Union

Feder, J. 1999, *The Danish Economy. Medium Term Economic Survey*, Copenhagen; www.fm.dk/udgivelser/publicationer/survey99

Fels, J. and A.Christian 2004, 'Germany: Trade in Transition', *Morgan Stanley. Global Economic Forum*, November 11, New York: www.morganstanley.com/GEFdata/digests/latest-digest.html

Finansministeriet 1998, *Availability Criteria in Selected OECD Countries*, Working Chapter 6, Stockholm: Finansministeriet

Fisher, I. 1932, *Booms and Depressions*, New York: Adelphi

Fitoussi, J.-P., P. Jestaz, E.M. Phelps and G. Zoega 2000, 'Roots of Recent Recoveries: Labor Reforms or Private Sector Forces?', *Brookings Papers on Economic Activity*, 1: 237-311

Fitz Gerald, J. 2000, 'The Story of Ireland's Failure and Belated Success', pp. 27-57 in B. Nolan, P.J. O'Connell and C.T. Whelan (eds.), *Bust to Boom? The Irish Experience of Growth and Inequality*, Dublin: Institute of Public Administration.

Flecker, J. and T. Schulten 1999, 'The End of Institutional Stability: What Future for the 'German Model'?', *Economic and Industrial Democracy* 20, 1: 81-115

Flückiger, Y. 1996, 'Analyse Socio-économique des Différences Cantonales de Chômage', in Forum Helveticum (ed), *Le Chômage en Suisse: Bilan et Perspectives*, Lenzbourg: Forum Helveticum

Flückiger, Y. 1998, 'The Labour Market in Switzerland: The End of a Special Case?', *International Journal of Manpower* 19, 6

Forssen, K. 1998, *Children, Families and the Welfare State. Studies on the Outcomes of the Finnish Family Policy*, STAKES Research Reports 92, Helsinki: National Research and Development Centre for Welfare and Health

Foster Higgins/NAM 1992, 'Employer Cost-Shifting Expenditures', November

Foust, D., M. Arndt and D. Welch 2001, 'Now, Profits Are in Free Fall', *Business Week* (November 5): 44

Freeman, R. 1995a, 'The Large Welfare State as a System', *American Economic Review* 85, 2: 16-21

Freeman, R. 1995b, 'How Labor Fares in Advanced Economies', pp.1-28 in R. Freeman (ed), *Working Under Different Rules*, New York: Russell Sage Foundation

Freeman, R. 1998, 'War of the Models: Which Labour Market Institutions for the 21st Century?', *Labour Economics* 5: 1-24

Freeman, R. 2000a, 'Single Peaked versus Diversified Capitalism: The Relation Between Economic Institutions and Outcomes', *NBER Working Paper* 7556, Cambridge (Mass.): National Bureau of Economic Research

Freeman, R. 2000b, 'Gold or Porzelan? The American Alchemists' Formula for Full Employment', paper presented at the International Labour Market Conference *Ways and Means of Increasing Employment*, Hannover (Expo 2000), September 5

Freeman, R. and J. Rogers 1993, 'Who Speaks for Us?', pp. 13-79 in B. Kaufman and M. Kleiner (eds.), *Employee Representation: Alternatives and Future Directions*, Madison, WI: Industrial Relations Research Association

Fritzell, J. 2001, 'Still Different? Income Distribution in the Nordic Countries in a European Context', pp. 18-41 in M. Kautto, J. Fritzell, B. Hvinden, J. Kvist and H. Uusitalo (eds.), *Nordic Welfare States in a European Context*, London: Routledge

Fuhrer, J. 1996, 'Technology and Growth: An Overview', *New England Economic Review* 21: 3

Furåker, B. 1976, *Stat och Arbetsmarknad: Studier I Svensk Rörlighetspolitik*, Stockholm: Arkiv för Studier i Arbetarrörelsens Historia

Galbraith, J.K. 1967, *The New Industrial State*, Boston: Houghton Mifflin Co.

Galvin, T. 2001, 'Industry 2001 report', *Training* 38, 10: 40-1

Garrett, G. 1998, *Partisan Politics in the Global Economy*, Cambridge: Cambridge University Press

General Accounting Office 2001, *Welfare Reform: Moving Hard-to-Employ Recipients into the Workforce*, Washington, DC: Government Printing Office

Genschel, P. 2001, Globalisation, Tax Competition and the Fiscal Viability of the Welfare State, MPIfG *Working Paper 01/1*, 2001
http://www.mpi-fg-koeln.mpg.de/pu/workpap/wp01-1/wp01-1.html

George, V. 1998, 'Political Ideology, Globalisation and the Welfare Futures in Europe', *Journal of Social Policy* 27, 1: 17-36

Giavazzi, F. and M. Pagano 1995, 'Non-Keynesian Effects of Sharp Fiscal Policy Changes: International Evidence and the Swedish Experience', *Swedish Economic Policy Review* 2

Gilliand, P. (ed) 1990, *Pauvreté et Sécurité Sociale*, Lausanne: Réalités Sociales

Gilliand, P. and S. Rossini 1997, *La Protection Sociale en Suisse*, Lausanne: Réalités Sociales

Goodley, W. and A. Izurieta 2001, 'As the Implosion Begins? Prospects and Policies for the US Economy: A Strategic View', Annandale-on-Hudson, N.Y.: The Levy Economics Institute; www.levy.org/docs/stratan/recess.html

Gough, I. et al. 1997, 'Social Assistance in OECD Countries', *Journal of European Social Policy* 7,1:17-43

Goul Andersen, J. 1995, *Hvorfor vinder regeringen ikke på den økonomiske fremgang?*, MS. Aarhus: Department of Political Science, University of Aarhus

Goul Andersen, J. 2002, 'Denmark: From the Edge of the Abyss to a Sustainable Welfare State. Unemployment and Unemployment Policies in Denmark, 1975-2000', pp. 143-162 in J. Goul Andersen, J. Clasen, W. van Oorschot and K. Halvorsen (eds.), *Unemployment, Welfare Policies and Citizenship*, Bristol: Policy Press

Goul Andersen, J. and J.B. Jensen 2002, 'Different Routes to Improved Employment in Europe', pp. 58-90 in H. Safarti and G. Bonoli (eds.), *Labour Market and Social Protection Reforms in International Perspective*, Aldershote: Asgate

Gourevitch, P., A. Martin and G. Ross (eds.) 1984, *Unions and Economic Crisis: Britain, West Germany, and Sweden*, Boston: Allen and Unwin

Gramlich, E.M. 2002, 'Consumption and the Wealth Effect: the United States and the United Kingdom', Speech in London, February 20

Green-Pedersen, C. 2001, 'Minority Governments and Party Politics: The Political and Institutional Background to the 'Danish Miracle'', *Journal of Public Policy* 21, 1: 63-80

Green-Pedersen, C. 2002, 'Den Danske Velfærdsstat fra afgrundens rand til efterlønsreform. En oversigt', *Politica* 34, 1:69-78

Green-Pedersen, C. 2003, 'Small States with Big Success. Party Politics and Governing the Economy in Denmark and the Netherlands 1973-2000', *Socio-Economic Review* 1, 3: 411-437

Green-Pedersen, C., K. van Kersbergen and A. Hemerijck 2001, 'Neo-Liberalism, the 'Third Way' or What? Recent Social Democratic Welfare Policies in Denmark and the Netherlands', *Journal of European Public Policy* 8, 2: 307-325

Grubb, W. N. 1996, *Learning to Work: The Case for Reintegrating Job Training and Education*, New York: Russell Sage Foundation

Gruen, D. and G. Stevens 2000, 'Australian Macroeconomic Performance and Policies in the 1990s', pp. 32-72 in Reserve Bank of Australia 2000 Conference, *The Australian Economy in the 1990s*, Sydney: RBA

Haataja, A. 1999, 'Unemployment, Employment and Poverty', *European Societies* 1, 2: 169-196

Haffner, M. 1998, 'Woningbelastingen in Europa', *Economisch-Statistische Berichten*, 27: 170-172

Hall, P.A. and D.W. Gingerich 2001, 'Varieties of Capitalism and Institutional Complementarities in the Macroeconomy: An Empirical Analysis', paper prepared for presentation to the Annual Meeting of the American Political Science Association, San Francisco, August 30-September 2, 2001

Hall, P. and D. Soskice (eds.) 2001, *Varieties of Capitalism. The Institutional Foundations of Comparative Advantage*, Oxford: Oxford University Press

Hardiman, N. 1988, *Pay, Politics and Economic Performance in Ireland 1970-87*, Oxford: Clarendon Press

Hardiman, N.1998, 'Inequality and the Representation of Interests', pp. 122-143 in W. Crotty and D. Schmitt (eds.), *Ireland and the Politics of Change*, London: Longman

Hardiman, N. 2000, 'Social Partnership, Wage Bargaining and Growth', pp. 286-

309 in B. Nolan, P.J. O'Connell and C.T. Whelan (eds.), *Bust to Boom? The Irish Experience of Growth and Inequality*, Dublin: Institute of Public Administration

Hardiman, N. 2001, 'Institutional Innovation in Liberal Market Economies: Industrial and Social Development in Ireland', paper presented at the conference *Small States in World Markets: 15 Years On*, Göteborg University, Sweden

Hardiman, N. and C. Whelan 1998, 'Changing values', pp. 66-85 in W. Crotty and D. Schmitt (eds.), *Ireland and the Politics of Change*, London: Longman

Harding, R. 1999, '*Standort* Deutschland in the Globalising Economy: An End to the Economic Miracle?', *German Politics* 8, 1: 66-88

Harris, L. et al. 1986, 'A Survey of the Reaction of the American People and Top Business Executives to the Report on Public Education by the Task Force on Teaching as a Profession of the Carnegie Forum on Education and the Economy', Study No. 864011, Roper Library, "Harris for Carnegie Forum 08/1986" File

Hartog, J. 1999, 'The Netherlands: What's So Special about the Dutch Model?', ILO *Employment and Training Papers* 54, Geneva: ILO

Haskins, R. 2001, 'Giving Is Not Enough', *Brookings Review,* 19: 12-15

Hassel, A. and B. Ebbinghaus 2000, 'From Means to Ends: Linking Wage Moderation and Social Policy Reform', in G. Fajertag and P. Pochet (eds.), *Social Pacts in Europe. New Dynamics*, Brussels: European Trade Union Institute http://www.mpi-fg-koeln.mpg.de/people/hl/downloads/HasseLENOK.pdf.

Hayek, F.A. 1945, 'The Use of Knowledge in Society', *The American Economic Review* 35, 4: 519-530

Hayes, R., S. Wheelwright and K. Clark 1988, *Dynamic Manufacturing*, New York: Free Press

Heise, A., B. Mühlhaupt, C. Schäfer and A. Truger 2000, 'Der Standort Deutschland am Beginn des 21 Jahrhunderts', *WSI-Mitteilungen* 53, 6: 337-354

Hemerijck, A.C. 1995, 'Corporatist Immobility in the Netherlands', pp. 183-226 in C. Crouch and F.Traxler (eds.), *Organized Industrial Relations in Europe: What Future?*, Aldershot: Avebury Ashgate

Hemerijck, A. and K. van Kersbergen 1997, 'Explaining the New Politics of the Welfare State in the Netherlands', *Acta Politica*, 32: 258-281

Hemerijck, A. and M. Schludi 2000, 'Sequences of Policy Failures and Effective Policy Responses', pp. 125-228 in F.W. Scharpf and V.A. Schmidt (eds.), *Welfare and Work in the Open Economy. Vol. 1. From Vulnerability to Competitiveness*, Oxford: Oxford University Press

Héritier, A. and S. Schmidt 2000, 'After Liberalisation: Public Interest Services and Employment in Utilities', pp. 577-578 in F. Scharpf and V. Schmidt (eds.), *Welfare and Work in the Open Economy, Vol. II: Diverse Responses to Common Challenges*, Oxford: Oxford University Press

Hicks, A. and L. Kenworthy 2003, 'Varieties of Welfare Capitalism', *Socio-Economic Review* 1, 1: 27-61

Hilferding, R. 1924, 'Probleme der Zeit', *Die Gesellschaft* 1:1-17

Hjerppe, R. and J. Kiander 2004, *Technology Policy and Knowledge-Based Growth in Small Countries,* Government Institute for Economic Research, Research Report no. 109, Helsinki: VATT Publishers

Hollingsworth, R. and R. Boyer 1997, 'Coordination of Economic Actors and Social Systems of Production', pp. 1-47 in J.R. Hollingsworth and R. Boyer, *Contemporary Capitalism. The Embeddedness of Institutions,* Cambridge: Cambridge University Press

Honkapohja, S. and E. Koskela 1999, 'Finland's Depression: A Tale of Bad Luck and Bad Policies', *Economic Policy,* 29: 399-436

Honohan, P. 2001, 'European and International Constraints on Irish Fiscal Policy', pp. 22-39 in T. Callan and D. McCoy (eds.), *Budget Perspectives,* Dublin: Economic and Social Research Institute

Huber, E. and J.D. Stephens 1998, 'Internationalisation and the Social Democratic Model', *Comparative Political Studies* 31, 3: 353-397

Huber, E. and J.D. Stephens 2001a, 'Welfare State and Production Regimes in the Era of Retrenchment', pp. 107-145 in P. Pierson (ed.), *The New Politics of the Welfare State,* Oxford: Oxford University Press

Huber, E. and J. Stephens 2001b, *Development and Crisis of the Welfare States: Parties and Politics in Global Markets.* Chicago: University of Chicago Press

Humbel, K. (ed) 1987, *Das Friedensabkommen in der schweizerische Maschinen- und Metallindustrie. Dokumente und Vertragspolitik 1899-1987,* Bern.

Hutton, W. 1995, *The State We Are In.* London: Jonathan Cape

ILO 1996, *Globalisation of the Footwear, Textiles and Clothing Industries,* Geneva: ILO

ILO 1999, *Switzerland. Studies on the Social Dimension of Globalisation,* Geneva: ILO

IMD 2003, *The World Competitiveness Yearbook,* Lausanne: International Institute for Management Development

IMD 2004, *The World Competitiveness Yearbook, Press Release,* Lausanne: IMD www02.imd.ch/documents/wcy/content/pressEnglish.pdf

Immergut, E. 1992, *Health Politics. Interests and Institutions in Western Europe,* New York: Cambridge University Press

ITC (International Trade Centre) 2004, *International Trade Statistics. Country Market Analysis Profiles,* New York: International Trade Center (Unctad/WTO) www.intracen.org/menus/countries.htm

ITT 2001, 'The European Innovation Scoreboard 2001', *Innovation and Technol-*

ogy Transfer, special edition (October), Luxemburg
www.cordis.lu/itt/itt-en/o1-5-spec/chapo2.htm

Iversen, T. 1996, 'Power, Flexibility, and the Breakdown of Centralized Bargaining: Denmark and Sweden in Comparative Perspective', *Comparative Politics* 28, 4 (July): 399-436

Iversen, T. 1999, *Contested Economic Institutions. The Politics of Macroeconomics and Wage-Bargaining in Advanced Democracies*, Cambridge: Cambridge University Press

Iversen, T. 2000, 'Decentralisation, Monetarism, and the Social Democratic Welfare State', pp. 205-231 in T. Iversen, J. Pontusson and D. Soskice (eds.), *Unions, Employers and Central Banks*, Cambridge: Cambridge University Press

Iversen, T. 2001, 'The Dynamics of Welfare State Expansion', pp. 45-79 in P. Pierson (ed.) *The New Politics of the Welfare State*, New York: Oxford University Press

Iversen, T. and A. Wren 1998, 'Equality, Employment, and Budgetary Restraint. The Trilemma of the Service Economy', *World Politics* 50, 2: 507-546

Iversen, T., J. Pontusson and D. Soskice (eds.) 2002, *Unions, Employers, and Central Banks*, Cambridge: Cambridge University Press

Jalava, J. 2002, 'The production and use of ICT in Finland (1975-2001)', ETLA Discussion Paper 827, Helsinki: ETLA

Jalava, J. and M. Pohjola 2002, 'Economic Growth in the New Economy: Evidence from Advanced Economies', *Information Economics and Policy* 14, 2: 189-210.

Jasso, G., M. Rosenzweig, and J. Smith 1998, 'The Changing Skills of New Immigrants to the United States', *NBER Working Paper* W6764, Cambridge: National Bureau of Economic Research, October

Jencks, C. 1997, 'The Hidden Paradox of Welfare Reform', *The American Prospect* (May-June): 33

Jonung, L., J. Stymne and H.T. Söderström 1996, 'Depression in the North. Boom and Bust in Sweden and Finland, 1985-1993', *Finnish Economic Papers* 9, 1: 55-71

Jönsson, I. 1999, 'Women and Education in Europe', *International Journal of Contemporary Sociology* 36, 2: 145-162

Junka, T. 2003, *Maailman kilpailukykyisin maa? Tuottavuus ja investoinnit Suomessa 1975-2000*, Government Institute for Economic Research, Research Report 95, Helsinki: VATT

Kalela, J., J. Kiander, U. Kivikuru, H.A. Loikkanen and J. Simpura (eds.) 2001, *Down from the Heavens, Up from the Ashes. The Finnish Economic Crisis of the 1990s in the Light of Economic and Social Research*, Government Institute for Economic Research Publication 27:6, Helsinki: VATT

Kangas, O. and J. Palme 2000, 'Does Social Policy Matter? Poverty Cycles in the OECD Countries', *International Journal of Health Services*, 30: 335-52

Kappel R. and O. Landmann 1997, *La Suisse dans un Monde en Développement*, Fribourg: Presses Universitaires

Kask, C. and E. Sieber 2002, 'Productivity Growth in 'High-Tech' Manufacturing Industries', *Monthly Labor Review* (March): 16-31

Katz, B. and K. Allen 2001, 'Cities Matter', *Brookings Review* 19, (Summer): 30-33

Katzenstein, P. 1984, *Corporatism and Change. Austria, Switzerland, and the Politics of Industry*, Ithaca: Cornell University Press

Katzenstein, P. 1985, *Small States in World Markets. Industrial Policy in Europe*, Ithaca: Cornell University Press

Kautto, M., J. Fritzell, B. Hvinden, J. Kvist and H. Uusitalo (eds.) 2001, *Nordic Welfare States in the European Context*, London: Routledge

Kazis, R. and P. Sabonis 1990, 'Ceta and the Private Sector Imperative', *Social Policy* 10, 4 (January/February): 7

Kiander, J. 2005, 'Growth and Employment in Nordic Welfare States in the 1990s: A Tale of Crisis and Revival', forthcoming in O. Kangas and J. Palme (eds.), *Social Policy in a Development Context: The Nordic Experience*, London: Routledge

Kiander, J. and P. Vartia 1996, 'The Great Depression of the 1990s in Finland', *Finnish Economic Papers* 9, 1: 72-88

King, D. 1995, *Actively Seeking Work. The Politics of Unemployment and Welfare Policy in the United States and Great Britain*, Chicago: The University of Chicago Press

King, M. 1994, 'Debt-Deflation, Theory and Evidence' *European Economic Review* 38, 3-4: 419-445

Kirby, P. 2002, *The Celtic Tiger in Distress Growth with Inequality in Ireland*, Basingstoke: Palgrave

Kitschelt, H., P. Lange, G. Marks and J. Stephens (eds.) 1999, *Continuity and Change in Contemporary Capitalism*, Cambridge: Cambridge University Press

Kleinknecht, A. and C.W.M. Nastepad 2002, 'Schattenseiten des niederländischen Beschäftigungswunders', *WSI Mitteilungen* 6: 319-325

Koch, S., U. Walwei, F. Weissner and G. Zika 2002, 'Wege aus der Arbeitsmarktkrise: Komplexe Probleme Verbieten Einfache Lösungen', *IAB-Kurzbericht* 24/2002, Nürnberg: Bundesanstalt für Arbeit

Kool, C.J.M., A.P. van Veen, C.G. Koedijk and A.van Witteloostuijn 1998, 'Nederland Investeert! Of Toch Niet?', *Economisch-Statistische Berichten* (April 17): 318-320

Koretz, G. 2002, 'Productivity: A Retail Link', *Business Week* (June 10): 30

Korpi, W. and J. Palme 2001, 'New Politics and Class Politics in Welfare State Regress: A Comparative Analysis of Retrenchment in 18 Countries 1975-1995', Paper Presented at the Annual Meeting of the American Political Science Association, August 30 – September 2, 2001, San Francisco

Koski, H., P. Rouvinen and P. Ylä-Anttila 2001, 'ICT Clusters in Europe: The Great Central Banana and the Small Nordic Potato', UNU/WIDER Discussion Paper 2001/6, Helsinki: World Institute for Development Economics Research

Kriesi, H. 1995, Le Système Politique Suisse, Paris: Economica

Krugman, P.R. 1997, 'Good News from Ireland: A Geographical Perspective', pp. 38-53 in A.W. Gray (ed.), International Perspectives on the Irish Economy, Dublin: Indecon

Kuhnle, S. (ed.) 2000, Survival of the European Welfare State, London: Routledge

Kusters, A. and J.Verbruggen 2001, 'Re-Exports and the Dutch Market Position', CPB Report 4: 35-40

Laffan, B. and R. O'Donnell 1998, 'Ireland and the Growth of International Governance', pp. 156-177 in W. Crotty and D. Schmitt (eds.), Ireland and the Politics of Change, London: Longman

LaLonde, R. 1995, 'The Promise of Public Sector-Sponsored Training Programs', Journal of Economic Perspectives 9, 2 (Spring): 149-168

Lane, J.-E. 1999, 'The Public/Private Sector Distinction in Switzerland', Swiss Political Science Review 5, 2 (Summer): 94-104

Lange, P., G. Ross, and M. Vannicelli 1982, Unions, Change, and Crisis: French and Italian Union Strategy and the Political Economy, 1945-1980, New York: Allen and Unwin

Lanouette, W. 1982, 'Chamber's Ponderous Decision Making Leaves It Sitting on the Sidelines', National Journal 14, 30 (July 24): 1298

Larsen, C.A. (forthcoming) 'Employment Miracles and Active Labour Market Policy – A Critical Review of Danish Evaluations', Journal of European Public Policy

Lee, D. and R. McKenzie 1993, Failure and Progress, Washington, DC: Cato Institute

Leitner, S., I. Ostner and M. Schratzenstaller (eds.) 2003, Wohlfahrtsstaat und Geschlechterverhältnis im Umbruch. Was kommt nach dem Ernährermodell?, Opladen: Leske+Budrich

Lesch, H. 2003, 'Der Arbeitskampf als Instrument tarifpolitischer Konfliktbewältigung', Aus Politik und Zeitgeschichte B 47-48: 30-38

Levy, J. 1999, 'Vice into Virtue? Progressive Politics and Welfare Reform in Continental Europe', Politics and Society 27, 2: 239-273

Lindbeck, A. 1997, 'The Swedish experiment', Journal of Economic Literature 35, 3: 1273-1319

Lindbom, A. 2001, 'Dismantling the Social Democratic Welfare Model. Has the Swedish Welfare State lost its defining characteristics?', *Scandinavian Political Studies* 24, 3: 171-193

Lindlar, L. and W. Scheremet 1998, 'Germany's Slump. Explaining the unemployment crisis of the 1990s', *DIW Discussion Paper* 169, Berlin: Deutsches Institut für Wirtschaftsforschung

Ljungqvist, L. and T. Sargent 1998, 'The European Unemployment Dilemma', *Journal of Political Economy* 106, 3: 514-550

Loftager, J. and P.K. Madsen 1997, 'Denmark', pp. 123-145 in H. Compston (ed.), *The New Politics of Unemployment*, London: Routledge

Luxembourg Income Study 2002, http://www.lisproject.org

Lynch, L. 1993, 'Entry-Level Jobs: First Rung on the Employment Ladder or Economic Dead End?', *Journal of Labor Research* 14, 3 (Summer): 251

Lynch, L. 1994, 'Payoffs to Alternative Training Strategies at Work', pp. 63-95 in R. Freeman (ed.), *Working Under Different Rules*, New York: Russell Sage Foundation

Mabbett, D. 1995, *Trade, Employment and Welfare*, Cambridge: Cambridge University Press

Mach A. (ed.) 1999, *Globalisation, Néo-libéralisme et Politiques Publiques dans la Suisse des Années 1990*, Zurich: Seismo

Mach, A., S. Häusermann and Y. Papadopoulos 2003, 'Economic Regulatory Reforms in Switzerland: Adjustment without European Integration, or How Rigidities become Flexible', *Journal of European Public Policy* 10, 2:301-318

Madison, A. 1982, *Phases of Capitalist Development*, Oxford: Oxford University Press

Madsen, J.S., C. Jørgensen and J. Due 2001, *Danmark OK2000*, Forskningsnotat 30, Copenhagen: FAOS

Madsen, P.K. 1999, 'Denmark: Flexibility, Security and Labour Market Success', ILO *Employment and Training Papers* 53, Geneva: ILO www.ilo.org/public/english/employment/strat/publ/etp53.html

Madsen, P.K. 2000, 'The Danish Model of Flexicurity: A Paradise – with Some Snakes', draft for the ISSA/LMSP project *Between labour market shifts and social protection reform*

Maliranta, M. 2001, 'Productivity Growth and Micro-Level Restructuring', ETLA Discussion Paper 757, Helsinki: ETLA

Managing Office Technology Staff 1995, 'Skill Levels Inadequate, Survey Reveals', *Managing Office Technology* 40, 10 (October): 4-45

Mandel, M. 2002a, 'More Productivity, More Profits?', *Business Week* (June 10): 38-40

Mandel, M. 2002b, 'Restating the '90s', *Business Week* (April 1): 50-58

Manow, P. 2001, 'Comparative Institutional Advantages of Welfare State Regimes and New Coalitions in Welfare State Reforms', pp. 146-164 in P. Pierson (ed) *The New Politics of the Welfare State*, New York: Oxford University Press

Manow, P. and E. Seils 2000, 'Adjusting Badly. The German Welfare State, Structural Change and the Open Economy', pp.264-307 in F.W. Scharpf and V. Schmidt (eds.), *Welfare and Work in the Open Economy. Vol. II Diverse Responses to Common Challenges in Twelve Countries*, Oxford: Oxford University Press

March, J. and J. Olsen 1989, *Rediscovering Institutions. The Organisational Basis of Politics*, New York: Free Press

Mares, I. 1997, 'Is Unemployment Insurable?', *Journal of Public Policy* 17, 3: 299-327

Martin, C. J. 2000, *Stuck in Neutral*, Princeton: Princeton University Press

Martin, P. 2002, 'Policies for Admitting Highly Skilled Workers into the United States', pp. 271-289 in OECD (ed), *International Mobility of the Highly Skilled*, Paris: Organisation for Economic Co-operation and Development

Mau, S. 2001, *Patterns of Popular Support for the Welfare State. A Comparison of the United Kingdom and Germany*, Berlin: FS III 01-405, Wissenschaftszentrum Berlin für Sozialforschung

Merrien, F.-X. 2001, 'The Emergence of Active Policy in Switzerland', pp. 213-242 in N. Gilbert and R. van Voorhis (eds.), *Activating the unemployed*, New Brunswick: Transaction Publishers

Merrien, F.-X. 2002, 'Globalisation and Social Adjustment: The Case of the Small Developed Countries: A Comparative View of New Zealand, Sweden and Switzerland', pp. 141-162 in S. Behrendt and R. Sigg (eds.), *Social Security in the Global Village*, New Brunswick: Transaction

Merrien, F.-X. 2005, *L'Etat social. Une perspective internationale*, Paris, Armand Colin

Miller, W. 1996, 'Welfare Reform: Now, the States', *Industry Week* (August 19): 150

Miller, W. 1998, 'Surprise! Welfare Reform is Working', *Industry Week* (March 16):27

Miller, W. 1996, 'Labour Market Policy in Transition', Copenhagen: Ministry of Labour and Ministry of Finance, May

Mosley, L. 2000, 'Room to Move: International Financial Markets and National Welfare States', *International Organisation* 54, 4: 737-773

Murphy, A.E. 2000, 'The 'Celtic Tiger' – An Analysis of Ireland's Economic Growth Performance', *EUI Working paper Series* RSC 2000/16, Florence: EUI

Nannestad, P. and C. Green-Pedersen (forthcoming), 'Keep the Bumblebee Flying:

Economic Policy in the Welfare State of Denmark, 1973-1999' in E. Albæk et al. (eds.), *Managing the Danish Welfare State under Pressure: Towards a Theory of the Dilemmas of the Welfare State*, Aarhus: Aarhus University Press

Nathan, R. and T. Gais 2001, 'Federal and State Roles in Welfare', *Brookings Review* 19, (Summer): 25-29

National Association of Manufacturers 2001, *The Skills Gap 2001*, Washington, DC: National Association of Manufacturers

National Economic and Social Council 2002, *Benchmarking the Programme for Prosperity and Fairness*, Dublin: National Economic and Social Council

Nationmaster 2004, *Nationmaster.Com*, www.nationmaster.com/index.php

Neuteboom, P. 2002, *Een Internationale Vergelijking van de Kosten en Risico's van Hypotheken*, Delft:DGW/Nethur; http://nethur.geog.uu.nl/pages/research/partnership/publicatie%2019.PDF

NFIB 1995, 'NFIB Named 'Most Powerful'', *Capitol Coverage*, Washington, DC: National Federation of Independent Business, December

Nickell, S. 1997, 'Unemployment and Labor Market Rigidities: Europe versus North America', *Journal of Economic Perspectives* 11, 3: 55-74

Nickell, S. 2002, 'A Picture of European Unemployment: Success and Failure', paper presented at the conference *Unemployment in Europe: Reasons and Remedies*, Munich: CESifo and Yrjö Jahnsson Foundation, December

Nickell, S. and J. van Ours 2000, 'The Netherlands and the United Kingdom: A European Unemployment Miracle?', in *Economic Policy*, 30: 137-180

NTMA 2004, *Ireland Information Memorandum, March 2004*, National Treasury Management Agency, Dublin; http://www.ntma.ie/Publications/2004/Irl_Mem_Final020404.pdf

OCDE 1997, *Etudes Economiques – Suisse 1997*, Paris: Organisation de Coopération et de Développement Economiques

OCDE 1999, *Etudes Economiques – Suisse 1999*, Paris: Organisation de Coopération et de Développement Economiques

O'Connell, P.J. 2000, 'The Dynamics of the Irish Labour Market in Comparative Perspective', pp. 58-89 in B. Nolan, P.J. O'Connell and C.T. Whelan (eds.), *Bust to Boom? The Irish Experience of Growth and Inequality*, Dublin: Institute of Public Administration

O'Connell, P.J. and S. O'Riain 2000, 'The Role of the State in Growth and Welfare', pp. 310-39 in B. Nolan, P.J. O'Connell and C.T. Whelan (eds.), *Bust to Boom? The Irish Experience of Growth and Inequality*, Dublin: Institute of Public Administration

O'Connell, P.J. and D. Rottman 1992, 'The Irish Welfare State in Comparative Perspective', pp. 205-240 in J. Goldthorpe and C. Whelan (eds.), *The Develop-*

ment of Industrial Society in Ireland, London: The British Academy and Oxford University Press

O'Donnell, R. 1998, 'Ireland's Economic Transformation: Industrial policy, European Integration and Social Partnership', *Working Paper 2*, University of Pittsburgh: Center for West European Studies, December

OECD 1972, *Economic Surveys – Australia 1972*, Paris: Organisation for Economic Cooperation and Development

OECD 1986, *Flexibility in the Labour Market*, Paris: Organisation for Economic Cooperation and Development

OECD 1989, *Economic Surveys – Australia 1989*, Paris: Organisation for Economic Cooperation and Development

OECD 1994, *Job Study*, Paris: Organisation for Economic Cooperation and Development

OECD 1995a, *Economic Surveys – Ireland 1995*, Paris: Organisation for Economic Cooperation and Development

OECD 1995b, *Employment Outlook 1995*, Paris: Organisation for Economic Cooperation and Development

OECD 1996a, *The OECD Jobs Strategy: Enhancing the Effectiveness of Active Labour Market Policies*, Paris: Organisation for Economic Cooperation and Development

OECD 1996b, *Employment Outlook 1996*, Paris: Organisation for Economic Cooperation and Development

OECD 1997a, *Economic Outlook 1997*, Paris: Organisation for Economic Cooperation and Development.

OECD 1997b, *Employment Outlook 1997*, Paris: Organisation for Economic Cooperation and Development

OECD 1998a, *Economic Surveys 1997-1998 – Netherlands*, Paris: Organisation for Economic Cooperation and Development

OECD 1998b, *Economic Outlook 1998*, Paris: Organisation for Economic Cooperation and Development

OECD 1999a, *Economic Surveys – Denmark 1999*, Paris: Organisation for Economic Cooperation and Development

OECD 1999b, *Revenue Statistics*, Paris: Organisation for Economic Cooperation and Development

OECD 1999c, *Social Expenditure Database*, Paris: Organisation for Economic Cooperation and Development

OECD 1999d, *Economic Surveys – Australia 1999*, Paris: Organisation for Economic Cooperation and Development

OECD 1999e, *Employment Outlook 1999*, Paris: Organisation for Economic Cooperation and Development

OECD 2000a, *Economic Surveys – Denmark 2000*, Paris: Organisation for Economic Cooperation and Development

OECD 2000b, *Economic Surveys – Australia 2000*, Paris: Organisation for Economic Cooperation and Development

OECD 2000c, *Employment Outlook 2000*, Paris: Organisation for Economic Cooperation and Development

OECD 2000d, *Economic Outlook 2000*, Paris: Organisation for Economic Cooperation and Development

OECD 2001a, *Economic Outlook 2001*, Paris: Organisation for Economic Cooperation and Development

OECD 2001b, *Employment Outlook 2001*, Paris: Organisation for Economic Cooperation and Development

OECD 2002a, *The Sources of Economic Growth in the OECD Countries*, Paris: Organisation for Economic Cooperation and Development

OECD 2002b, *Annual National Accounts by Main Aggregates*, Paris: Organisation for Economic Cooperation and Development, www.sourceoecd.org

OECD 2002c, *Economic Surveys – The Netherlands 2001-2002*, Paris: Organisation for Economic Cooperation and Development

OECD 2002d, *Employment Outlook 2002*, Paris: Organisation for Economic Cooperation and Development

OECD 2002e, *Economic Surveys – Denmark 2002*, Paris: Organisation for Economic Cooperation and Development

OECD 2002f, *Economic Outlook 2002*, Paris: Organisation for Economic Cooperation and Development

OECD 2002g, *Public Social Expenditures by Main Category 1980-98*, Paris: Organisation for Economic Cooperation and Development; http://www.oecd.org/dataoecd/43/17/2087017.xls

OECD 2002h, *Social Indicators and Tables*, Paris: Organisation for Economic Cooperation and Development

OECD 2002i, *Social Expenditure Database*, www.sourceoecd.org

OECD 2002j, *Economic Surveys – Germany 2002*, Paris: Organisation for Economic Cooperation and Development

OECD 2003a, *Employment Outlook 2003*, Paris: Organisation for Economic Cooperation and Development

OECD 2003b, OECD *Statistics in International Trade in Trade, 1999-2001*, Paris: Organisation of Economic Cooperation and Development

OECD 2003c, *Annual National Accounts by Main Aggregates*, Paris: Organisation for Economic Cooperation and Development, www.sourceoecd.org

OECD 2003d, *ICT and Economic Growth: Evidence from OECD Countries, Sectors, and Firms*, Paris: Organisation for Economic Cooperation and Development

OECD 2003e, *Economic Outlook 74*, Paris: Organisation for Economic Cooperation and Development

OECD 2004, *Economic Outlook 75*, Paris: Organisation for Economic Cooperation and Development

OECD n.d., *Labour Market Statistics Database*, Paris: Organisation for Economic Cooperation and Development,
http://www1.oecd.org/scripts/cde/viewbase.asp?DBNAME=lfs_data

OECD W.C. 2004, *Labour Productivity – Data: GDP per Hour Worked Index and Percentage*, OECD Washington Center
www.oecdwash.org/DATA/online.htm; Productivity data

Office of Technology Assessment 1990, *Worker Training: Competing in the New International Economy*, Washington, DC: U.S. Government Printing Office

OFS 2002, Annuaire Statistique de la Suisse, Neuchâtel: Office Fédéral de Statistique

O'Grada, C. and O'Rourke, K.H. 2000, 'Living Standards and Growth', in O'Hagan, J. (ed), *The Economy of Ireland*, Dublin: Gill and Macmillan, pp. 178-204

O'Hagan, J. 2000, 'Population, Employment and Unemployment', pp. 150-177 in J. O'Hagan (ed), *The Economy of Ireland*, Dublin: Gill and Macmillan

O'Hearn, D. 1998, *Inside the Celtic Tiger*, London: Pluto

O'Hearn, D. 2000, 'Globalisation, 'New Tigers' and the End of the Developmental State? The Case of the Celtic Tiger', *Politics and Society* 28, 1: 67-92

Olson, M. 1971, *The Logic of Collective Action*, Cambridge, MA: Harvard University Press

Oorschot, W. van and C. Boos 2000, 'The Battle against Numbers: Disability Policies in the Netherlands', in W. van Oorschot and B. Hvinden (eds.), *Disability Policies in European Countries*, special issue of *European Journal of Social Security* 2, 4: 343-362

O'Riain, S. 2000, 'The Flexible Development State: Globalisation, Information Technology and the 'Celtic Tiger'', *Politics and Society* 28, 3: 3-37

O'Riain, S. and P.J. O'Connell 2000, 'The Role of the State in Growth and Welfare', pp. 310-339 in B. Nolan, P.J. O'Connell and C.T. Whelan (eds.), *Bust to Boom? The Irish Experience of Growth and Inequality*, Dublin: Institute of Public Administration

Oschmiansky, F. 2003, 'Faule Arbeitslose? Zur Debatte über Arbeitslosigkeit und Leistungsmissbrauch', *Aus Politik und Zeitgeschichte* B 6-7: 10-16

OSEC 2003, *Swiss Foreign Trade*, Zürich: OSEC, Business Network Switzerland

Osterman, P. 1995, 'Work/Family Programs and the Employment Relationship', *Administrative Science Quarterly* 40: 681-700

Osterman, P. 1999, *Securing Prosperity*, Princeton: Princeton University Press

O'Sullivan, M. 2000, 'Industrial Development: A New Beginning?', pp. 260-285 in J. O'Hagan (ed), *The Economy of Ireland*, Dublin: Gill and Macmillan

Paija, L. 2000, 'The ICT Cluster in Finland: Can We Explain It?', in idem (ed.), *The Finnish ICT Cluster in the Digital Economy*, Helsinki: ETLA

Paija, L. and P. Rouvinen 2003, 'The ICT Cluster in Finland – Can We Explain It?', pp. 47-64 in G. Schienstock (ed.), *Catching Up and Forging Ahead: The Finnish Success Story*, Aldershot: Edward Elgar

Palmberg, C., P. Niininen, H. Toivanen and T. Wahlberg 2000, 'Industrial Innovation in Finland: Results from the Sfinno-Project', VTT Working Paper 47/00, Helsinki: Technical Research Centre of Finland

Papadopoulos, Y. 1997, *Les Processus de Décision Fédéraux en Suisse*, Paris: L'Harmattan

Pauli, R.M. 2002, 'Switzerland: A Brand Name that Sells', *UBS Outlook*, 2nd Quarter 2002, Zürich: UBS

Pierson, P. 1995, 'Fragmented Welfare states: Federal Institutions and the Development of Social Policies', *Governance* 8, 4 (October): 449-478

Plowman, D. 1980, 'National Wage Determination in 1979', *Journal of Industrial Relations*, 22: 79-97

Pochet, P. and G. Fajertag 2000, 'A New Era for Social Pacts in Europe', in P. Pochet and G. Fajertag (eds.), *Social Pacts in Europe. New Dynamics*, Brussels: European Trade Union Institute; www.ose.be/files/socpacintro.pdf

Porter, M. 2003, 'Building the Microeconomic Foundations of Prosperity: Findings from the Business Competitiveness Index', in WEF, *World Competitiveness Report 2003-2004*, Basel: World Economic Forum; www.weforum.org

Porter, M. and S. Stern 2003, 'National Innovative Capacity', in WEF *World Competitiveness Report 2003-2004*, Basel: World Economic Forum www.weforum.org

Priewe, J. 2002, 'Zwischen Abkopplung und Aufholen – das schwache ostdeutsche Wachstumspotenzial', *WSI-Mitteilungen* 12: 706-712

Productivity Commission 1996, *The Changing of Australian Manufacturing*, Canberra: AusInfo

Productivity Commisssion 1999, *Microeconomic Reforms and Australian Productivity: Exploring the Links* (2 vols.), Canberra: AusInfo

Productivity Commission 2002, *Australia's Service Sector: A Study in Diversity*, Canberra: AusInfo

Regini, M. 2000, 'The Dilemma of Labour Market Regulation', pp. 11-29 in G. Esping-Andersen and M. Regini (eds.), *Why Deregulate Labour Markets?*, Oxford: Oxford University Press

Reich, R. 1983, *The Next American Frontier*, New York: Time Books

Reserve Bank of Australia 2002, 'Recent Developments in Housing: Prices, Finance and Investor Attitudes', *Bulletin* (July):1-6

Rhodes, M. 1998, 'Globalisation, Labour Markets and Welfare States: A Future of "Competitive Corporatism"?', pp. 178-203 in M. Rhodes and Y. Mény (eds.), *The Future of European Welfare: A New Social Contract?*, London: Sage

Rhodes, M. 2001, 'The Political Economy of Social Pacts: 'Competitive Corporatism' and European Welfare Reform', pp. 165-194 in P. Pierson (ed.), *The New Politics of the Welfare State*, Oxford: Oxford University Press

Rhodes, M. and B. van Apeldoorn 1997, 'Capitalism versus Capitalism in Western Europe', pp. 171-189 in M. Rhodes, P. Heywood and V. Wright (eds.), *Developments in West European Politics*, Houndmills: Macmillan

Roach, S. 2002, 'Still Blowing Bubbles', *Morgan Stanley Global Economic Forum*, July 18, New York: www.morganstanley.com/GEFdata/digests/latest-digest.html

Roach, S. 2004, 'The Asset Economy', *Morgan Stanley Global Economic Forum*, June 21, New York: www.morganstanley.com/GEFdata/digests/latest-digest.html

Rosen, S. 1996, 'Public Employment and the Welfare State in Sweden', *Journal of Economic Literature* 34, 2: 729-740

Rosholm, M. 2001, *Is Labour Market Training a Curse for the Unemployed? More Evidence from a Social Experiment*, Copenhagen: SFI; www.sfi.dk

Rothstein, B. 1996, *The Social Democratic State. The Swedish Model and the Bureaucratic Problem of Social Reforms*, Pittsburgh: University of Pittsburgh Press

Rouvinen, P. and P. Ylä-Anttila 2003, 'Case study: Little Finland's Transformation to a Wireless Giant', pp. 87-108 in S. Dutta, B. Lanvin and F. Paua (eds.), '*The Global Information Technology Report 2003-2004*', New York: Oxford University Press

Ruysseveldt, J. van and J. Visser 1996, 'Weak Corporatisms Going Different Ways? Industrial Relations in the Netherlands and Belgium', in idem (eds.), *Industrial Relations in Europe*, London: Sage

Sabel, C. 1996, *Ireland: Local Partnerships and Social Innovation*, Paris: Organisation for Economic Cooperation and Development

Sabel, C.F., G.B. Herrigel, R. Deeg and R. Kazis 1987, 'Regional Prosperities Compared: Massachusetts and Baden-Württemberg in the 1980s', *WZB Discussion Paper* IIM/LMP 87-10b, Berlin: Wissenschftszentrum für Sozialforschung

Sala-I-Martin, X. 2003, 'Executive Summary', in *WEF World Competitiveness Report 2003-2004*, Basel: World Economic Forum; www.weforum.org

Salverda, W. 1999, 'Polderblijheid, Polderblindheid', *Economisch-Statistische Berichten*, March 26: 224-229

Salverda, W. 2000, 'De betekenis van de Loonmatiging voor de Ontwikkeling van Arbeidsmarkt and Economie', pp. 11-27 in idem (ed.), *De Houdbaarheid van het Nederlandse 'Model': Verder met Loonmatiging en Deeltijdarbeid?*, Den Haag: Elsevier HR

Salverda, W. 2004a, 'Low Pay and Gender Mainstreaming', in: A. Serrano Pascual, L. Mosesdottir and A. Leitner (eds.), *Overcoming Barriers to Equal Pay in Europe: Monitoring and Gender Mainstreaming*, Brussels: ETUI

Salverda, W. 2004b, 'Youth Unemployment Revisited: Back to the Eighties?', Working Paper, Amsterdam Institute for Advanced Labour Studies

Salverda, W. 2005, 'Does Low Dutch Unemployment Reflect Superior Performance or Labour Market Transformation?' in B. Bluestone et al., *Constructing a New Cross-National Architecture for Labour Market Statistics*, Chicago: University of Chicago Press (forthcoming)

Salverda, W., S. Bazen, and M. Gregory 2001, 'The European-American Employment Gap, Wage Inequality, Earnings Mobility and Skill', European Low-Wage Employment Research Network, June

Sawhill, I. 2001, 'From Welfare to Work', *Brookings Review* 19 (Summer): 4-7

Scharpf, F.W. 1991, *Crisis and Choice in European Social Democracy*, Ithaca: Cornell University Press (originally *Sozialdemokratische Krisenpolitik in Europa*, Frankfurt/M.: Campus 1987)

Scharpf, F.W. 1997a, *Games Real Actors Play*, Boulder: Westview

Scharpf, F.W. 1997b, 'Employment and the Welfare State: A Continental Dilemma', *MPIfG Working Paper* 97/7, Cologne: Max-Planck-Institut fuer Gesellschaftsforschung

Scharpf, F.W. 2000, Economic Changes, Vulnerabilities, and Institutional Capacities', pp. 21-124 in F.W. Scharpf and V.A. Schmidt (eds.), *Welfare and Work in the Open Economy. Vol. 1. From Vulnerability to Competitiveness*, Oxford: Oxford University Press

Schelkle, W. 2000, 'Subsidizing Low Earnings. German Debates and U.S. Experiences', *Vierteljahreshefte zur Wirtschaftsforschung* 69, 1: 1-16

Schettkat, R. 2002, 'Regulation in the Dutch and German Economies at the Root of Unemployment?', *CEPA Working Paper* 2002-05, Center for Economic Policy Analysis. New School University

Schmid, J. and S. Blancke 2001, *Arbeitsmarktpolitik der Bundesländer*, Berlin: Editon Sigma

Schmidt, M. 1985, *Der Schweizerische Weg zur Vollbeschäftigung*, Frankfurt/Main: Campus

Schmidt, V.A. 2002, *The Futures of European Capitalism*, Oxford: Oxford University Press

Schmitter, P.C. 1979, 'Still the Century of Corporatism?', pp. 7-52 in P.C. Schmitter and G. Lehmbruch, *Trends towards Corporatist Intermediation*, London: Sage

Schnabel, M. 1997, 'International Competitiveness: Labor Productivity Leadership and Convergence Among 14 OECD Countries', *Working paper EAS/OPD 97-4*, Economics and Statistics Administration

Schneider, F. 2000, 'The Increase of the Size of the Shadow Economy of 18 OECD Countries. Some Preliminary Explanations', *CESifo Working Paper* no. 306

Schulten, T. 2002, 'A European Solidaristic Wage Policy?', in *European Journal of Industrial Relations* 8, 2: 173-196

Schwartz, H. 1994, 'Small States in Big Trouble: State Reorganisation in Australia, Denmark, New Zealand, and Sweden in the 1980s', *World Politics* (July): 527-55

Schwartz, H. 1998, 'Social Democracy Going Down vs. Social Democracy Down Under? Australian Labor's Strategies for Coping with Internationalized Capital', *Comparative Politics* 30, 3: 253-272

Schwartz, H. 2000, 'Internationalisation and Two Welfare States: Australia and New Zealand', pp. 69-130 in F. Scharpf and V. Schmidt (eds.), *Welfare and Work in the Open Economy, Vol. II: Diverse Responses to Common Challenges*, Oxford: Oxford University Press

Schwartz, H. 2001a, 'Round up the Usual Suspects!', pp. 17-44 in P. Pierson (ed), *The New Politics of the Welfare State*, New York: Oxford University Press

Schwartz, H. 2001b, 'The Danish 'Miracle': Luck, Pluck or Stuck', *Comparative Political Studies* 34, 2: 131-155

Schwartz, H. 2001c, 'Age of Miracles? What to Make of Employment and Export Revival in Australia, Denmark, and the Netherlands', chapter presented at the Annual Meeting of the American Political Science Association, August 30 – September 2, 2001, San Francisco

Sciarini, P. 1994, *Le système politique Suisse face à la Communauté européenne et au GATT: le cas test de la politique agricole*, Genève: Georg

SCP 2000, *Sociaal en Cultureel Rapport 2000*, Rijswijk: Sociaal Cultureel Planbureau

Shiller, R. 2000, *Irrational Exuberance*, Princeton: Princeton University Press

Shonfield, A. 1965, *Modern Capitalism*. Oxford: Oxford University Press

Siaroff, A. 1999, 'Corporatism in 24 Industrial Democracies: Meaning and Measurement', *European Journal of Political Research* 36, 2: 175-205

Siegel, N.A. 2004, 'EMU and German Welfare Capitalism', pp. 103-125 in A. Martin and G. Ross (eds.): *Euros and Europeans. Monetary Integration and the European Model of Society*, Cambridge University Press

Sinn, H.-W. 2000, 'Germany's Economic Unification. An Assessment After Ten Years', *CESifo Working Paper* 247/2000 (also in: *Review of International Economics* 10, 1:113-128, 2000)

Sinn, H.-W. and F. Westermann 2000, 'Two Mezzogiornos', paper presented at the conference on *Politica fiscale, flessibilità dei mercati e crescita* at the University of Pavia, Italy, October 6/7

Slemrod, J. 1998, 'How Costly is a Large, Redistributive Public Sector?', *Swedish Economic Policy Review* 5, 1: 87-105

SNB 1997, *Review of Economic Development 1996*, Bern: Schweizer Nationalbank; http://www.snb.ch/e/download/bericht/e_06-27_ueberb_wirtschaft.pdf

SNB 2002, *94th Annual Report 2001*, Bern: Schweizer Nationalbank; http://www.snb.ch/d/download/bericht01/GB_2001_e.pdf

Soskice, D. 1999, 'Divergent Production Regimes. Coordinated and Uncoordinated Market Economies in the 1980s and 1990s', in H. Kitschelt, P. Lange, G. Marks and J. Stephens (eds.), *Continuity and Change in Contemporary Capitalism*, Cambridge: Cambridge University Press

Standing, G. 1999, *Global Labor Flexibility. Seeking Distributive Justice*, Houndsmill: Macmillan

Stanfield, R. 1992, 'Quest for Quality', *The National Journal* 24, 32 (August 8): 18-32

Starr, A. 2001, 'Is the Safety Net Recession-Ready?', *Business Week* (June 11): 132-134

Stephens, J.D. 1996, 'The Scandinavian Welfare States. Achievements, Crisis and Prospects', pp. 32-65 in G. Esping-Andersen (ed.), *Welfare States in Transition*, London: Sage

Stephens, M. 2003, *Housing Market Instability in Finland Before and After* EMU, Helsinki: Ministry of the Environment
www.yimparisto.fi/download.asp?contentid=11760&lan=en

Steurele, E. 1992, *The Tax Decade*, Washington, DC: The Urban Institute

Stevens, B. 1990, 'Labor Unions, Employee Benefits, and the Privatisation of the American Welfare State', *Journal of Policy History* 2, 3: 233-260

Stevenson, R. 2001, 'Economists Make It Official: U.S. Is in Recession', *New York Times* (November 27): C1

Stodghill, R. 2001, 'Part-Time Recession', *Time* (October 29): 80-81

Streeck, W. 1992, *Social Institutions and Economic Performance*, Newbury Park, CA: Sage Pub

Streeck, W. 1997, 'German Capitalism: Does It exist? Can It Survive?', pp. 33-54 in C. Crouch and W. Streeck (eds.), *Political Economy of Modern Capitalism. Mapping Convergence and Diversity*, London: Sage

Streeck, W. 1999, 'Competitive Solidarity: Rethinking the 'European Social Model'', *Working Paper* 99/8, Cologne: Max Planck Institute for the Study of Societies

Streeck, W. 2001a, 'The Transformation of Corporate Organisation in Europe: An Overview', MPIfG *Working Paper* 01/8, Cologne: MPIfG

Streeck, W. 2001b, 'High Equality, Low Activity: The Contribution of the Social Welfare System to the Stability of the German Collective Bargaining Regime', EUI/RSC Working Papers 2001/06. Florence: The European University Institute

Streeck, W. 2002, 'Notes on Complementarity. How it Comes About and How We Should Analyse it', paper presented at the International Seminar on Institutional Complementarities and Dynamics of Economic Systems. Paris: CEPREMAP, April 5-6
http://pythie.cepremap.ens.fr/~amable/comple/papiers/Complementarities.pdf

Summers, L., J. Gruber and R. Vergara 1993, 'Taxation and the Structure of Labor Markets', Quarterly Journal of Economics 108, 2: 385-411

Sutton, G.D. 2002, 'Explaining Changes in Housing Prices', Bank for International Settlements Quarterly Review (September): 47–55

Swank, D. 2001, 'Political Institutions and Welfare State Restructuring', pp. 197-237 in P. Pierson (ed), The New Politics of the Welfare State, New York: Oxford University Press

Swedish Government 1999/2000, 'Förnyad Arbetsmarknadspolitik för Delaktighet och Tillväxt', Regeringens Proposition 1999/2000: 98

Swedish Government 2000/2001, '2001 års Ekonomiska Vårproposition', Regeringens Proposition 2000/2001:100 appendix 5 (Finans- och penningpolitiskt bokslut för 1990-talet)

Tabin, J.-P. 1998, 'Chômeur Ancien, Chômeur Moderne: Persistance des Représentations?', Revue Suisse de Sociologie 24, 2: 209-236

Tanzi, V. and L. Schuknecht 2000, 'Public Spending in the Twentieth Century: A Global Perspective', Cambridge: Cambridge University Press

Teece, D. 1987, The Competitive Challenge, Cambridge: Ballinger Publishing Co.

Teknologisk Institut 2000, Fleksjob På Fremtidens Arbejdsmarked, Taastrup: Teknologisk Institut (maj.)

Teles, S. and T. Prinz 2001, 'The Politics of Rights Retraction', pp. 215-238 in M. Levin, M. Landy and M. Shapiro (eds.), Seeking the Center, Washington, DC: Georgetown University Press

The Economist 2001, 'America's Greatest Achievement', August 25

The Economist 2002, An Uncertain Giant. A Survey of Germany, December 7

Thelen, K. and J. Kume 1999, 'The Effect of Globalisation on Labor Revisited: Lessons from Germany and Japan', Politics and Society 27, 4: 477-505

Thornthwaite, L. and P. Sheldon 1996, 'The MTIA, Bargaining Structures and the Accord', Journal of Industrial Relations, 38:171-195

Thurow, L. 1992, Head to Head. The Coming Economic Battles Among Japan, Europe and America, New York: William Morrow

Thurow, L. 1996, The Future of Capitalism, New York: W. Morrow

Torfing, J. 1999, 'Workfare with Welfare: Recent Reforms of the Danish Welfare State', *Journal of European Social Policy* 9, 1: 5-28

Towers Perrin produced for the National Association of Manufacturers 1991, 'Today's Dilemma: Tomorrow's Competitive Edge', obtained from Towers Perrin

Training Staff 1994, 'Industry Report', *Training* 31, 10 (October): 37

Tyson, L. 1999, 'Open the Gates Wide to High-Skill Immigrants', *Business Week* (July 5): 16

Ullman, O. 1996, 'Good Politics, Bad Policy', *Business Week* (September 23): 49

UNCTAD 1993, *World Investment Directory 1992: Developed Countries*, New York: United Nations

UNCTC (United Nations Centre on Transnational Corporations) 1988, *Transnational Corporations in World Development*, New York: UNCTC

Van Ark, B. and De Hann, J. 2000, 'The Delta-Model Revisited: Recent Trends in the Structural Performance of the Dutch Economy', *International Review of Applied Economics* 14, 3: 307-321

Van Kersbergen, K. 1995, *Social Capitalism. A study of Christian Democracy and the Welfare State*, London: Routledge

Veen, R. van der and W. Trommel 1999, 'Managed Liberalisation of the Dutch Welfare State', *Governance* 12, 3: 289-310

Victor, K. 1990, 'Helping the Haves', *National Journal* 22, 15 (April 14): 898

Visser, J. and A. Hemerijck 1997, *'A Dutch Miracle:' Job Growth, Welfare Reform, and Corporatism in the Netherlands*, Amsterdam: Amsterdam University Press

Waller, M. 1997, 'Child Carelessness', *The New Democrat* (September-October): 20

Wallerstein, M. and M. Golden 2000, 'Post-war Wage Setting in the Nordic Countries', pp. 107-137 in T. Iversen, J. Pontusson and D. Soskice (eds.), *Unions, Employers and Central Banks*, Cambridge: Cambridge University Press

Weaver, K. 1998, 'Ending Welfare As We Know It', pp. 361- 416 in M. Weir (ed), *Social Divide*, New York/Washington: Russell Sage Foundation Press and Brookings Institution Press

Weber, A. 2001, 'Arbeitslosigkeit in der Schweiz. Was passierte in den Neunzigerjahren?', *Die Volkswirtschaft. Das Magazin für Wirtschaftspolitik* 5:4-9

Weber, A. and B.A. Zürcher 2001, 'Fleissige Schweiz: Über den Zusammenhang von Arbeitsproduktivität und Reichtum', *Die Volkswirtschaft. Das Magazin für Wirtschaftspolitik* 3:28-32

WEF 2003, *Knowledge Navigator*, World Economic Forum; www.weforum.org

Weir, M. 1992, *Politics and Jobs*, Princeton: Princeton University Press

Welfare to Work Partnership 2000, 'Member Survey: Taking the Next Step', *2000 Series 1*

Werner, H. 2002, 'Arbeitsmarkt Schweiz – Ein Noch Wenig Beachtetes Erfolgmodell', *IAB Kurzbericht* 9, May 10

Westergaard-Nielsen, N. 2001, *Danish Labour Market Policy: Is It Worth It?*, Århus: Centre for Labour Market and Social Research, www.cls.dk

Wilkinson, B. 1983, *The Shopfloor Politics of New Technology*, London: Heinemann Educational Books

Wilson, G. 1990, *Business and Politics*, Chatham, NJ: Chatham House Publishers

Wilson, W. J. 1996-7, 'When Work Disappears', *Political Science Quarterly* 11, 4 (Winter): 567-595

WKO 2003, *Statistisches Jahrbuch 2003*, Vienna: Wirtschaftskammern Österreichs

Wood, A. 1994, *North South Trade, Employment and Inequality: Changing Fortunes in a Skill-Driven World*, Oxford: Clarendon Press

Work in America Institute 1984, *Employment Security in a Free Economy*, New York: Pergamon Press: 323-45

WTO 2003, *International Trade Statistics 2003*, Geneva: World Trade Organisation

Xie, A. 2004, 'The Twin Bubbles', *Morgan Stanley Global Economic Forum*, April 6, New York
www.morganstanley.com/GEFdata/digests/latest-digest.html

Yankelovich, Clancy, Schulman 1992, 'Health Care and Health Insurance', prepared for the Nightly Business Report (June 10-19), obtained from the Roper Center, 'Yankelovich for the Nightly Business Report Surveys of Executives 01/93' file.

Zürcher, B.A. 2002, 'Hoher Arbeitseinsatz als Grundlage des Wachstums in der Schweiz', pp. 30-59 in Leistungsbereich "Wirtschaftspolitische Grundlagen" des seco (ed.), *Grundlage der Wirtschaftspolitik Nr. 6, Hintergrundstudien zum Wachstumsbericht des Eidg. Volkswirtschaftsdepartements*, Bern: Staatssekretariat für Wirtschaft

Contributors

Uwe Becker is Associate Professor of Political Science at the University of Amsterdam. He was a visiting scholar at the European University Institute, the Wissenschaftszentrum Berlin and the Center for European Studies at Harvard University. He has published books on class theory (1986; in German), European democracies (1999; in Dutch), edited a number of books and has written articles on theoretical topics, the (Dutch) welfare system and comparative political economy in *Politics and Society, Theory and Society, Journal of Social Policy, Journal of European Social Policy, New Political Economy* and *Politische Vierteljahreschrift*. He is a member of the *Society for the Advancement of Socio-Economics*. Since March 2003 he is the scientific coordinator of an EU-financed international research project (Austria, Denmark, Finland, Netherlands, Sweden, Switzerland) on *The Consensual Political Cultures of the Small West European Countries in Comparative and Historical Perspective*.

Mary Daly is Professor of Sociology at the School of Sociology and Social Policy at Queen's University Belfast. Among the fields on which she has published are poverty, welfare state, gender, family and labour market. Much of her work is comparative, in a European and international context. She is a member of a number of European networks and boards on topics related to the family, welfare state, employment and gender. She is also involved in a number of activities on the future of social policy in an international context for the European Commission, the Council of Europe and the International Labour Office. Among her recent publications are *Gender and the Welfare State* (Polity Press, 2003), *Care Work: The Quest for Security* (ILO, 2001) and *Access to Social Rights in Europe* (Council of Europe, 2002).

Christoffer Green-Pedersen is Associate Professor of Political Science at the University of Aarhus, Denmark. He has published *The Politics of Justification. Party Competition and Welfare-State Retrenchment in Denmark and the Netherlands from 1982 to 1988* (Amsterdam University Press 2002) and articles and book chapters on party politics in comparative perspective and on Scandinavian welfare states in edited volumes and scholarly journals, among others 'New Public Management Reforms of the Danish and Swedish Welfare States: The Role of Different Social Democratic Responses', *Governance* (2002) and 'Small States, Big Success. Party Politics and Governing the Economy in Denmark and the Netherlands from 1973 to 2000', *Socio-Economic Review* (2003).

Jaakko Kiander is Professor and research director at the Government Institute for Economic Research in Helsinki, Finland. He is the author of numerous books and articles, covering labour markets, trade unions, macroeconomics and economic crises, taxation and public finance, and European integration. He was also a programme director of a large multidisciplinary research programme on the Finnish economic crisis of the 1990s in 1998-2001. His recent titles on labour markets and macroeconomics have appeared in *European Journal of Political Economy* (2004), *Scandinavian Review of Economic History* (2003) and *Empirica* (2002). He has co-edited several books, including *Economic growth and social development – Nordic experience* (with Olli Kangas, Routledge 2004), *Down from the heavens, up from the ashes: The Finnish economic crisis of the 1990s* (with J. Kalela, U. Kivikuru, H.A. Loikkanen and J. Simpura, Government Institute for Economic Research 2001) and *Expanding the membership of the European Union* (with Richard Baldwin and Pertti Haaparanta, Cambridge University Press 1995).

Anders Lindbom is Associate Professor of Political Science at Uppsala University, Sweden. He has written government reports on the functioning of Swedish ministries (1997) and the Swedish civil service (2001). He edited a book (2001; in Swedish) on 'The New Housing Policy' and published articles on the welfare state in Swedish and foreign journals, e.g. the review article 'Welfare State Reform' in *Journal of European Public Policy* (2002), 'Dismantling Swedish Housing Policy' in *Governance* (2001), and 'Dismantling the Social Democratic Welfare Model?' in *Scandinavian Political Studies* (2001). Currently, he is involved in a research project on *The Welfare State in Transition*.

Cathie Jo Martin is Professor of Political Science at Boston University. She is the author of *Stuck in Neutral: Business and the Politics of Human Capital Investment Policy* (Princeton University Press 2000), *Shifting the Burden: the Struggle over Growth and Corporate Taxation* (University of Chicago Press 1991), and articles appearing in journals including the *American Political Science Review*, *British Journal of Political Science*, *Comparative Political Studies*, and *Governance*. Professor Martin received her Ph.D. from the Massachusetts Institute of Technology in 1987; she has obtained funding from the Robert Wood Johnson Foundation, the Russell Sage Foundation, the National Science Foundation, the German Marshall Fund, and the Danish Social Science Research Council. She spent 2000-2001 as a visiting professor at the University of Copenhagen.

Francois Xavier Merrien is Professor of the Social Sciences and of Comparative Political Science at the University of Lausanne. His main research interests are in social policy and comparative policy analysis. He is a member of the National Research Committee of the CNRS (France) and a member of the scientific management committee of the European research programme COST A15, *Reforming Social Protection in Europe* (1999-2004). Professor Merrien is the author of *L'Etat-Providence* (Presses Universitaires de France 2000). His latest book is *L'Etat Social: Une Perspective Internationale* (Armand Colin 2005). He has translated Esping-Andersen's famous *Three Worlds of Welfare Capitalism* into French, contributed to a number of edited books, and his articles have appeared in French as well as in English language journals.

Wiemer Salverda is managing director of the Amsterdam Institute for Advanced Labour Studies AIAS at the University of Amsterdam and coordinator of the EU-financed European Low-wage Employment Research Network LoWER and the related research project Demand Patterns and Employment Growth: Consumption and Services in France, Germany, the Netherlands, the UK and the US. Recent publications include *Labour Market Inequalities: Problems and Policies of Low-Wage Employment in International Perspective* (Oxford University Press, 2000) (ed. together with M. Gregory and S. Bazen), an edited special issue (with R. Asplund) of the *International Journal of Manpower* on 'Company Training and Services with a Special Focus on Low Skills' (2004) and articles in international journals on wage flexibility, the Dutch labour market, and low pay and gender.

Herman Schwartz is Professor and Director of Graduate Studies in the Politics Department at the University of Virginia. He is author of *In the Dominions of Debt: Historical Perspectives on Dependent Development* (Cornell University Press 1989) and of *States vs. Markets: Globalisation and the International Economy* (Palgrave 2000) as well as a large number of articles. Recent titles on global macroeconomic imbalances, the Danish political economy, globalisation and domestic politics, and the welfare states in Australia and New Zealand appeared in, respectively, the *Journal of Post-Keynesian Economics* (25:2, 2002-2003), *Comparative Political Studies* (34:2, 2001), Paul Pierson, ed., *New Politics of the Welfare State* (Oxford University Press 2002), and Fritz Scharpf and Vivian Schmidt (eds.), *Welfare and Work in the Open Economy* (Oxford University Press 2000).

Index